LAWYERING

PRACTICE AND PLANNING

By

Roger S. Haydock
Professor of Law
William Mitchell College of Law

Peter B. Knapp
Professor of Law
William Mitchell College of Law

Ann Juergens
Professor of Law
William Mitchell College of Law

David F. Herr
Attorney-at-Law, Minneapolis, Minnesota
Adjunct Professor, William Mitchell College of Law

Jeffrey W. Stempel
Professor of Law
Florida State University College of Law

AMERICAN CASEBOOK SERIES®

WEST GROUP

Bancroft-Whitney • Banks-Baldwin • Clark Boardman Callaghan
Lawyers Cooperative Publishing • WESTLAW® • West Publishing

WEST'S COMMITMENT TO THE ENVIRONMENT

In 1906, West Publishing Company began recycling materials left over from the production of books. This began a tradition of efficient and responsible use of resources. Today, 100% of our legal bound volumes are printed on acid-free, recycled paper consisting of 50% new paper pulp and 50% paper that has undergone a de-inking process. We also use vegetable-based inks to print all of our books. West recycles nearly 27,700,000 pounds of scrap paper annually—the equivalent of 229,300 trees. Since the 1960s, West has devised ways to capture and recycle waste inks, solvents, oils, and vapors created in the printing process. We also recycle plastics of all kinds, wood, glass, corrugated cardboard, and batteries, and have eliminated the use of polystyrene book packaging. We at West are proud of the longevity and the scope of our commitment to the environment.

West pocket parts and advance sheets are printed on recyclable paper and can be collected and recycled with newspapers. Staples do not have to be removed. Bound volumes can be recycled after removing the cover.

American Casebook Series and the West Group logo are used herein under license.

COPYRIGHT © 1996 By WEST PUBLISHING CO.
610 Opperman Drive
P.O. Box 64526
St. Paul, MN 55164–0526
1–800–328–9352

Library of Congress Cataloging-in-Publication Data

Lawyering Skills / by Roger S. Haydock ... [et al.].
    p.   cm. — (American casebook series)
  Includes index.
  ISBN 0-314-06688-8
    1. Practice of law—United States.   2. Attorney and client—United States.   3. Dispute resolution (Law)—United States.   I. Haydock, Roger S.   II. Series
KF300.L299   1995
340'.023'73—dc20

ISBN 0-314-06688-8

TO
ROSALIE E. WAHL
AND
ROBERT MACCRATE

*WHAT WE OWE YOU IS
BEYOND EVALUATION*

*

Acknowledgments

Many persons contributed to the creation, writing, and publication of this book. We each received substantial support and love from our families, friends, and colleagues, especially Julie Antonson, Lucinda Jesson, Jay Weiner, Mary Kay Herr, and Ann McGinley.

We dedicated this book to Robert MacCrate and Justice Rosalie Wahl. Both have contributed significantly to the advancement and growth of lawyering skills training. The MacCrate Report established the fundamental professional skills essential to being a competent lawyer. The Wahl Commission recommended the teaching of these lawyering skills in law school. These efforts served as an impetus and inspiration for this first-of-its-kind book. We also extend a special personal thanks to Rosalie who was our colleague and mentor at William Mitchell.

The staff and students at the William Mitchell College of Law have been especially helpful in the development of this book. Renée Anderson and Jean Krause assisted us in preparing these materials. Sharon Fischlowitz helped review drafts. The students who participated in the original Lawyering course deserve special recognition: Kathleen Berdan, James Brinegar, James Clay, Clara Davis, Andrea Genia, Tiffaney George, Marjorie Griffing, Christina Huson, Elizabeth Lutz, Melissa Otto, Sheryl Palmer, Joel Phillippi, Joanne Piper-Maurer, Cherie Shoquist, Joyce Svoboda, Tibor Tallos, Pamela Thein, and Jessica Warren.

The administrators and faculty at William Mitchell, especially Deans Harry Haynsworth, J. David Prince, Ann Bateson, and C. Paul Jones, provided us with able assistance. Lynnette Shanahan and Patricia Porter at Maslon Edelman Borman & Brand provided valuable assistance. Dean Donald Weidner and the Florida State University College of Law faculty also deserve our thanks.

We gratefully acknowledge our law students, who gave us the opportunity to develop these materials. We further acknowledge all of the clients we have represented, who gave use the experiences illustrated in this book. It has been—and continues to be —a privilege for us to teach and practice.

Preface

This book explains the fundamental lawyering skills, values, and relationships involved in the practice of law. There are three parts to this text: Part One explains how to interview and counsel clients. Part Two describes how to negotiate transactions and resolve disputes. Part Three explains how to prepare for advocacy. This text analyzes the skills, theories, strategies, tactics, norms, and values of client representation.

Chapter One begins with an explanation of professional relationships (they're fun) and the work of the lawyer (it's not all fun). Chapter Two explores the business of practicing law successfully. Chapters Three and Four describe effective client interviewing and counseling. Chapters Five and Six focus on proper planning and preparation for transactional work and dispute resolution. Chapters Seven, Eight, and Nine cover successful negotiations and mediation. Chapter Ten deals with useful information gathering. Chapter Eleven explains how to initiate claims efficiently. Chapter Twelve explains the scope of usable discovery and disclosure. Chapters Thirteen and Fourteen describe depositions and other effective discovery methods. The Epilogue concludes this book with the sometimes necessary transition to advocacy and perhaps more fun.

The analyses contained in these chapters explain the whys and why nots, and the shoulds and should nots of practice. This book presents examples and illustrations of lawyers engaged in the practice of law. These examples reflect the broad range of civil cases and suggest what can be said or done. You, as the attorney, will need to determine the appropriate approach in the context of each client you represent.

This book on professional skills responds to the recommendations of the American Bar Association and the Association of American Law Schools. The ABA MacCrate Report established ten lawyering skills and four critical values essential for the competent representation of clients. The Wahl Commission recommended that law schools provide their students with training in these lawyering relationships. This text covers many of the following skills and values recognized by both the MacCrate Task Force and the Wahl Commission as being essential to the practice of law:

Fundamental Lawyering Skills

Skill 1: *Problem Solving*

In order to develop and evaluate strategies for solving a problem or accomplishing an objective, a lawyer should be familiar with the skills and concepts involved in:

1.1 Identifying and Diagnosing the Problem;

1.2 Generating Alternative Solutions and Strategies;

1.3 Developing a Plan of Action;

1.4 Implementing the Plan;

1.5 Keeping the Planning Process Open to New Information and New Ideas.

Skill 2: *Legal Analysis and Reasoning*

In order to analyze and apply legal rules and principles, a lawyer should be familiar with the skills and concepts involved in:

2.1 Identifying and Formulating Legal Issues;

2.2 Formulating Relevant Legal Theories;

2.3 Elaborating Legal Theory;

2.4 Evaluating Legal Theory;

2.5 Criticizing and Synthesizing Legal Argumentation.

Skill 3: *Legal Research*

In order to identify legal issues and to research them thoroughly and efficiently, a lawyer should have:

3.1 Knowledge of the Nature of Legal Rules and Institutions;

3.2 Knowledge of and Ability to Use the Most Fundamental Tools of Legal Research;

3.3 Understanding of the Process of Devising and Implementing a Coherent and Effective Research Design.

Skill 4: *Factual Investigation*

In order to plan, direct, and (where applicable) participate in factual investigation, a lawyer should be familiar with the skills and concepts involved in:

4.1 Determining the Need for Factual Investigation;

4.2 Planning a Factual Investigation;

4.3   Implementing the Investigative Strategy;

4.4   Memorializing and Organizing Information in an Accessible Form;

4.5   Deciding Whether to Conclude the Process of Fact-Gathering;

4.6   Evaluating the Information That Has Been Gathered.

Skill 5: *Communication*

In order to communicate effectively, whether orally or in writing, a lawyer should be familiar with the skills and concepts involved in:

5.1   Assessing the Perspective of the Recipient of the Communication;

5.2   Using Effective Methods of Communication.

Skill 6: *Counseling*

In order to counsel clients about decisions or courses of action, a lawyer should be familiar with the skills and concepts involved in:

6.1   Establishing a Counseling Relationship That Respects the Nature and Bounds of a Lawyer's Role;

6.2   Gathering Information Relevant to the Decision to Be Made;

6.3   Analyzing the Decision to Be Made;

6.4   Counseling the Client About the Decision to Be Made;

6.5   Ascertaining and Implementing the Client's Decision.

Skill 7: *Negotiation*

In order to negotiate in either a dispute-resolution or transaction context, a lawyer should be familiar with the skills and concepts involved in:

7.1   Preparing for Negotiation;

7.2   Conducting a Negotiation Session;

7.3   Counseling the Client About the Terms Obtained From the Other Side in the Negotiation and Implementing the Client's Decision.

Skill 8: *Litigation and Alternative Dispute-Resolution Procedures*

In order to employ—or to advise a client about—the options of litigation and alternative dispute resolution, a lawyer should understand the potential functions and consequences of these processes and should have a working knowledge of the fundamentals of:

8.1   Litigation at the Trial-Court Level;

8.2   Litigation at the Appellate Level;

8.3   Advocacy in Administrative and Executive Forums;

8.4   Proceedings in Other Dispute-Resolution Forums.

Skill 9: *Organization and Management of Legal Work*

In order to practice effectively, a lawyer should be familiar with the skills and concepts required for efficient management, including:

9.1   Formulating Goals and Principles for Effective Practice Management;

9.2   Developing Systems and Procedures to Ensure that Time, Effort, and Resources Are Allocated Efficiently;

9.3   Developing Systems and Procedures to Ensure that Work is Performed and Completed at the Appropriate Time;

9.4   Developing Systems and Procedures for Effectively Working with Other People;

9.5   Developing Systems and Procedures for Efficiently Administering a Law Office.

Skill 10: *Recognizing and Resolving Ethical Dilemmas*

In order to represent a client consistently with applicable ethical standards, a lawyer should be familiar with:

10.1   The Nature and Sources of Ethical Standards;

10.2   The Means by Which Ethical Standards are Enforced;

10.3   The Processes for Recognizing and Resolving Ethical Dilemmas.

Fundamental Values of the Profession

Value 1: *Provision of Competent Representation*

As a member of a profession dedicated to the service of clients, a lawyer should be committed to the values of:

1.1   Attaining a Level of Competence in One's Own Field of Practice;

1.2   Maintaining a Level of Competence in One's Own Field of Practice;

1.3   Representing Clients in a Competent Manner.

Value 2: *Striving to Promote Justice, Fairness, and Morality*

As a member of a profession that bears special responsibilities for the quality of justice, a lawyer should be committed to the values of:

2.1   Promoting Justice, Fairness, and Morality in One's Own Daily Practice;

2.2   Contributing to the Profession's Fulfillment of its Responsibility to Ensure that Adequate Legal Services Are Provided to Those Who Cannot Afford to Pay for Them.

2.3   Contributing to the Profession's Fulfillment of its Responsibility to Enhance the Capacity of Law and Legal Institutions to Do Justice.

Value 3: *Striving to Improve the Profession*

As a member of a self-governing profession, a lawyer should be committed to the values of:

3.1   Participation in Activities Designed to Improve the Profession;

3.2   Assisting in the Training and Preparation of New Lawyers;

3.3   Striving to Rid the Profession of Bias Based on Race, Religion, Ethnic Origin, Gender, Sexual Orientation, or Disability, and to Rectify the Effects of These Biases.

Value 4: *Professional Self-Development*

As a member of a learned profession, a lawyer should be committed to the values of:

4.1   Seeking Out and Taking Advantage of Opportunities to Increase His or Her Knowledge and Improve His or Her Skills;

4.2   Selecting and Maintaining Employment That will Allow the Lawyer to Develop As a Professional and to Pursue His or Her Professional and Personal Goals.

This book explores and analyzes many of these skills and values so that students of the law can learn to be competent, confident practitioners.

Learning about lawyering requires reading about how lawyers represent clients. We encourage you to read and re-read this text and other books and literature about lawyers, clients, and cases to obtain a broad view of practice. Learning how to be a lawyer also requires observing how attorneys practice. Companion videotapes are available which demonstrate many of the lawyering skills presented in this book. These tapes have been created so that you as the aspiring lawyer can evaluate and critique attorneys performing the skills you will soon be performing yourself.

The conceptual and pragmatic considerations addressed in this book provide an overview of the dynamics of practice. This book is based upon the authors' experiences as practitioners and professors, the contributions of colleagues and commentators, common sense, and the law. We offer a comprehensive view of practice so you can develop your own.

The representation of clients involves a sequence of events that typically occur in a reasonably patterned order. The table of contents of this book outlines that pattern, although this outline is certainly no guarantee that every case will unfold in this order. You should not presume that the real world reflects this precise sequence. It should come as no surprise to you that the facets of practice will be as out of "order" as other facets of your life.

Our occasional attempts at humor that appear throughout the text may, with the right timing, even be funny. We often take ourselves and the practice of law too seriously, and an occasional guffaw, chuckle, or moan may help put things in proper perspective.

We now begin this book with the hope that you will discover the excitement and adventure that accompanies the practice of law. We encourage you to send us comments, suggestions, stories, anecdotes, and examples that we can include in our next edition. We wish you the best at becoming and being a lawyer.

ROGER S. HAYDOCK
PETER B. KNAPP
ANN JUERGENS
DAVID F. HERR
JEFFREY W. STEMPEL

December, 1995

Companion Materials

A series of companion videotapes and transcripts are designed for use with this book:

Lawyering Skills Video Series (with transcripts) by Peter B. Knapp, Ann Juergens, and Roger S. Haydock (West 1996):

Interviewing, Counseling & Negotiation
Demonstrates lawyers effectively interviewing and counseling clients and conducting negotiations.

Mediation & Arbitration
Includes essential stages of a mediation and an arbitration.

Depositions & Trial
Demonstrates lawyers conducting effective depositions, openings, direct and cross-examinations, and summations.

Additional compatible titles include:

Advocacy by Roger S. Haydock and John O. Sonsteng (West 1994). This five book series covers court trials, arbitrations, administrative cases, and jury trials in a highly educational and entertaining way and includes:

Planning to Win: Effective Preparation
Opening and Closing
Examining Witnesses
Evidence, Objections and Exhibits
Jury Trials

Fundamentals of Pretrial Litigation by Roger S. Haydock, David F. Herr, and Jeffrey W. Stempel (West, 3rd ed., 1994) extensively covers pleadings, discovery, motions, and litigation practice.

Trial: Theories, Tactics, Techniques by Roger S. Haydock and John O. Sonsteng (West 1990) contains explanations and examples of effective trial practice and covers the same materials as **Advocacy.**

Trialbook by John Sonsteng and Roger Haydock (West, 1995) is a three ring manual with checklists and forms for the thorough preparation and presentation of a case.

Summary of Contents

Page

ACKNOWLEDGMENTS ————————————————————————— v
PREFACE ———————————————————————————————— vii
COMPANION MATERIALS———————————————————— xiii

Chapter One. Work of the Lawyer ———————————— 1
A. Introduction ————————————————————————— 1
B. Working Relationships ————————————————— 5
C. Representing Clients ————————————————— 14
D. Thinking Like a Practicing Lawyer ————————— 22

PART ONE. LAWYER AND CLIENT RELATIONSHIPS

Chapter Two. The Business of Lawyering———————— 32
A. Introduction ————————————————————————— 32
B. The Organization ————————————————————— 34
C. The Search———————————————————————————— 36
D. The Money———————————————————————————— 38
E. The Protection————————————————————————— 41
F. The Operations————————————————————————— 42

**Chapter Three. Interviewing: What We Need From
Our Clients** ————————————————————————— 46
A. Introduction ————————————————————————— 46
B. Building Trust ———————————————————————— 46
C. Obtaining Information —————————————————— 51
D. Eliciting Direction ———————————————————— 63
E. Forming a Business Agreement ————————————— 68
F. The First Meeting With a Client ————————————— 70
G. Structuring the Meeting————————————————— 72

**Chapter Four: Counseling: What Clients Need From
Us** ————————————————————————————————— 74
A. Working as a Lawyer: A Range of Perspectives ———— 74
B. Assessment ————————————————————————— 75
C. Options——————————————————————————————— 79
D. Predictions————————————————————————————— 82
E. Making Decisions ————————————————————— 86
F. Preparing for the Meeting ————————————————— 90
G. Structuring the Meeting————————————————— 93

PART TWO.   PLANNING AND NEGOTIATIONS

Page

Chapter Five. Planning the Transaction: The Other Side of Practice _____ 96
A.   Introduction _____ 96
B.   Differences Among Distinctions _____ 100
C.   Transactional Goals _____ 103
D.   The Role of the Client _____ 105

Chapter Six.   Planning for Dispute Resolution: What Are We to Do? _____ 109
A.   Introduction _____ 109
B.   Assessing the Dispute _____ 109
C.   Determining Remedies _____ 111
D.   Seeking Relief _____ 113
E.   Selecting a Dispute Resolution Method _____ 115
F.   Dispute Resolution Goals _____ 121

Chapter Seven.   Planning for Negotiation: What Is It Your Client Wants? _____ 124
A.   Introduction _____ 124
B.   Establishing Goals _____ 125
C.   Selecting a Negotiation Approach _____ 130
D.   Evaluating the Negotiation _____ 138
E.   Assessing Ethical Concerns _____ 151

Chapter Eight.   Negotiations: Getting What Your Client Wants _____ 157
A.   Planning Information Exchange _____ 157
B.   Engaging in the Negotiation _____ 161
C.   Ending the Negotiation _____ 181
D.   Reviewing the Negotiation Process _____ 188

Chapter Nine. Mediation: Help! _____ 190
A.   Introduction _____ 190
B.   Why Mediate, or Why Not _____ 191
C.   How to Mediate _____ 194
D.   Mediation Approaches _____ 200

PART THREE.   DISPUTE RESOLUTION PREPARATION

Chapter Ten.   Investigations: Obtaining Information From Those in the Know _____ 208
A.   Introduction _____ 208

Chapter Ten. Investigations: Obtaining Information From Those in the Know—Continued

Page

B. The Human Touch 209

C. The Stuff 213

D. The How.. 215

Chapter Eleven. Asserting Claims and Defenses: The Right Way 224

A. Introduction.. 224

B. Selecting the Right Forum for the Right Reason 227

C. Complaining the Right Way 228

D. Drafting the Right Papers 233

E. Responding With the Right Defenses and Motions........ 234

Chapter Twelve. Disclosure and Discovery: What Do You Know?... 241

A. Introduction.. 241

B. Scope of Disclosure and Discovery............................... 246

C. Planning.. 253

Chapter Thirteen. Depositions: Getting to Know You 258

A. The Why.. 258

B. The How.. 259

C. The Planning.. 264

D. The Taking 266

E. The Deponent.. 281

F. The End 285

G. The Future... 288

Chapter Fourteen. Discovery Methods: Is That All There Is?.. 289

A. Introduction.. 289

B. Getting Documents 289

C. Getting Information 297

D. Getting Admissions 305

E. Getting an Examination.. 308

Epilogue.. 310

Index... 313

*

Table of Contents

		Page
ACKNOWLEDGMENTS		v
PREFACE		vii
COMPANION MATERIALS		xiii

CHAPTER ONE. WORK OF THE LAWYER 1

A. INTRODUCTION 1
- 1.1 Welcome to the Practice of Law 1
- 1.2 The Tapestry of Law Practice 3
  - 1.2.1 The Tapestry Pattern 4
  - 1.2.2 The Tapestry 5

B. WORKING RELATIONSHIPS 5
- 1.3 Lawyer Relationships 5
  - 1.3.1 Working With Clients 6
  - 1.3.2 Dealing With Other Attorneys and Parties 7
  - 1.3.3 Seeking Help or Information From Others 7
  - 1.3.4 Dealing With Decision Makers 8
  - 1.3.5 Working Within the Legal Profession 9
  - 1.3.6 Working as a Practitioner 10
  - 1.3.7 Working With Colleagues 11
  - 1.3.8 Working With Yourself 12
- 1.4 The Balanced Life 13

C. REPRESENTING CLIENTS 14
- 1.5 The Hallmark of Lawyering 14
  - 1.5.1 The Attorney-Client Privilege 15
  - 1.5.2 Professional Responsibility Rules 16
  - 1.5.3 The Law of Malpractice 16
- 1.6 The Role(s) of a Practicing Lawyer 17
  - 1.6.1 The Lawyer as Technician 17
  - 1.6.2 The Lawyer as Wise Counselor 18
  - 1.6.3 The Lawyer as Creator or Problem Solver 19
- 1.7 Client Views of Our Roles 20
- 1.8 The Extent of Client Relationships 21

D. THINKING LIKE A PRACTICING LAWYER 22
- 1.9 Sources of Laws 22
- 1.10 The Role of the Thinking Lawyer 25
  - 1.10.1 Thinking Creatively 25
  - 1.10.2 Thinking Productively 27

D. THINKING LIKE A PRACTICING LAWYER— Continued

Page

1.11 Smart Preparation 28
1.12 Your Goal as a Lawyer 30

PART ONE. LAWYER AND CLIENT RELATIONSHIPS

CHAPTER TWO. THE BUSINESS OF LAWYERING .. 32
A. INTRODUCTION 32
2.1 Working as a Businessperson 32
2.2 The Lost, or Found, Profession 33

B. THE ORGANIZATION 34
2.3 Organizing the Practice Entity 34
2.4 Law Firm Shapes and Sizes 34

C. THE SEARCH 36
2.5 Attracting and Retaining Clients 36
  2.5.1 Referrals 37
  2.5.2 Advertising 37

D. THE MONEY 38
2.6 Charging Fees 38
  2.6.1 Hourly Billing 38
  2.6.2 Contingent Fees 39
  2.6.3 Flat Fees 39
  2.6.4 Hybrid Fees 39
  2.6.5 Costs 39
  2.6.6 Retainers 40
  2.6.7 Billing Mechanics 40
  2.6.8 Written Business Agreements 40

E. THE PROTECTION 41
2.7 Insuring Against Malpractice 41
  2.7.1 Risk Management 41
  2.7.2 Insurance 42

F. THE OPERATIONS 42
2.8 Operating a Law Practice 42
2.9 Employing and Managing Staff 44
2.10 Paying Taxes 45

CHAPTER THREE. INTERVIEWING: WHAT WE NEED FROM OUR CLIENTS 46
A. INTRODUCTION 46
3.1 Four Elements 46

Page

B. BUILDING TRUST.. 46
   3.2 What Does Trust Mean?.. 46
       3.2.1 Why Is Trust Important? 48
       3.2.2 Why Is Trust Elusive? 48
   3.3 Competent Communication 48
       3.3.1 Good Listening..................................... 49
       3.3.2 Appropriate Comfort 49
       3.3.3 Faithful Silence 51

C. OBTAINING INFORMATION 51
   3.4 What Information Do We Need From Clients?...... 51
       3.4.1 Data.. 51
       3.4.2 Background Information.......................... 52
       3.4.3 Context 52
       3.4.4 Why Is Information Important? 52
   3.5 Techniques for Obtaining Information 53
   3.6 Building a Narrative.. 54
       3.6.1 The Opening Snapshot 54
       3.6.2 The Videotape 54
       3.6.3 Neutral Prompts.................................. 55
       3.6.4 Directive Prompts 56
       3.6.5 Time Posting....................................... 56
       3.6.6 Recapping.. 57
   3.7 Probing for Additional Information 57
       3.7.1 Flashback 57
       3.7.2 Slow-Motion....................................... 58
   3.8 Difficulties in Obtaining Information 59
       3.8.1 Setting the Scene 60
       3.8.2 The Triggering Detail........................... 61
       3.8.3 Help From Other Sources 61
       3.8.4 Sensitive Subjects 61
       3.8.5 Agenda Differences 62
       3.8.6 Snap Judgments 63

D. ELICITING DIRECTION 63
   3.9 Why Is Direction Important? 63
   3.10 What Is Direction? 64
       3.10.1 Immediate Goals................................ 64
       3.10.2 Overarching Goals 65
       3.10.3 Process Preferences........................... 65
   3.11 How Should a Lawyer Elicit Direction From a
       Client? 66
       3.11.1 Techniques for Eliciting Direction 66

D. ELICITING DIRECTION—Continued

Page

3.11.2 Limits on Client Direction _____ 67

E. FORMING A BUSINESS AGREEMENT _____ 68

3.12 Responsibility Issues _____ 68

3.13 Why Is a Business Agreement With a Client Important? _____ 68

    3.13.1 How Should a Lawyer Discuss Business With a Client? _____ 69

    3.13.2 Talking About Fees and Costs_____ 69

    3.13.3 Express Agreement and Authorization _____ 70

    3.13.4 Written Representation Agreement _____ 70

F. THE FIRST MEETING WITH A CLIENT _____ 70

3.14 Preparing for the Meeting _____ 70

3.15 Chairs and Desks; Pencils and Paper _____ 71

G. STRUCTURING THE MEETING _____ 72

3.16 A Suggestion for Structure _____ 72

CHAPTER FOUR. COUNSELING: WHAT CLIENTS NEED FROM US _____ 74

A. WORKING AS A LAWYER: A RANGE OF PERSPECTIVES _____ 74

4.1 What Is Legal Advice?_____ 74

B. ASSESSMENT _____ 75

4.2 What Is Assessment? _____ 75

    4.2.1 Why Is Assessment Important? _____ 76

    4.2.2 How Should a Lawyer Assess a Client's Legal Concerns? _____ 77

4.3 Listening to the Client_____ 77

4.4 Talking to the Client _____ 78

C. OPTIONS _____ 79

4.5 Clients Need Choices _____ 79

4.6 Presenting Options to the Client _____ 79

    4.6.1 Describe the Process_____ 79

    4.6.2 Explain How the Option Fits the Goals ____ 81

    4.6.3 Talk Openly About the Downside _____ 81

    4.6.4 How Much Will it Cost? How Long Will It Take? _____ 81

D. PREDICTIONS _____ 82

4.7 Predicting Success _____ 82

    4.7.1 Describing Success _____ 83

D. PREDICTIONS—Continued

Page

4.8 Developing a Language of Prediction _____ 84
    4.8.1 Establish the Necessity of Flexibility _____ 85
    4.8.2 Give the Client Reasonably Definite Information _____ 85

E. MAKING DECISIONS _____ 86
4.9 The Lawyer's Role in Decision Making _____ 86
4.10 Client Decisions, Lawyer Decisions _____ 87
4.11 Helping the Client Reach a Conclusion _____ 88
    4.11.1 Match Goals and Options _____ 88
    4.11.2 Winnow the List _____ 89
    4.11.3 Reframe the Choice _____ 89
4.12 Choose Two. Change Your Mind _____ 90

F. PREPARING FOR THE MEETING _____ 90
4.13 What a Lawyer Needs From the Client _____ 91
4.14 Thinking and Planning _____ 91
    4.14.1 Legal Investigation _____ 91
    4.14.2 Fact Investigation _____ 92
4.15 Checking Your Work _____ 92
4.16 Agendas and Lists _____ 92

G. STRUCTURING THE MEETING _____ 93
4.17 A Suggested Structure _____ 93

PART TWO. PLANNING AND NEGOTIATION

CHAPTER FIVE. PLANNING THE TRANSACTION: THE OTHER SIDE OF PRACTICE _____ 96
A. INTRODUCTION _____ 96
5.1 The Practice Without a Name _____ 96
5.2 The Nature of the Work: Translation, Definition, and Transaction _____ 97
    5.2.1 Translation: Bringing the Law to Clients 97
    5.2.2 Creation and Definition: Making the Law Work for Clients _____ 98
    5.2.3 Transaction: Using the Law to Work With Others _____ 99

B. DIFFERENCES AMONG DISTINCTIONS _____ 100
5.3 Differences and Distinctions _____ 100
5.4 I Got Here as Soon as I Could, and I'm Not Planning on Leaving Any Time Soon _____ 100

B. DIFFERENCES AMONG DISTINCTIONS—Continued

Page

5.5 Excuse Me, Could You Direct Me to the Federal Rules of Transactional Procedure? 101

5.6 I Don't Have to if I Don't Want to 103

C. TRANSACTIONAL GOALS 103

5.7 Doing Transactional Work: Taking Goals Seriously 103

5.7.1 Immediate Goals: Clarify and Condense ... 104

5.7.2 Overarching Goals: Learn and Serve 105

D. THE ROLE OF THE CLIENT 105

5.8 Process Preferences: Passenger, Driver, or Map-Maker 105

5.9 The Other Side: All the Same Issues Squared 107

5.10 Why Don't My Clients Smile When I Walk in the Room? 107

CHAPTER SIX. PLANNING FOR DISPUTE RESOLUTION: WHAT ARE WE TO DO? 109

A. INTRODUCTION 109

6.1 Planning What to Do 109

B. ASSESSING THE DISPUTE 109

6.2 Dispute Resolution Planning 109

6.3 Can a Claim Be Made? 110

6.3.1 Should the Claim Be Brought? 111

6.3.2 What Type of Claim Can Be Brought? 111

C. DETERMINING REMEDIES 111

6.4 What Remedies Can Be Sought? 111

6.4.1 Money, That's What We Want 111

6.4.2 Stop, in the Name of the Law 112

6.4.3 Just Decide 112

6.4.4 Pay My Lawyer, Too 112

6.5 What Are the Legal and Practical Limits on Seeking Relief? 113

D. SEEKING RELIEF 113

6.6 Who Can Seek Relief? 113

6.7 Whom Can You Seek Relief From? 114

E. SELECTING A DISPUTE RESOLUTION METHOD 115

6.8 Negotiating Your Own Accord 115

E. SELECTING A DISPUTE RESOLUTION METH-OD—Continued

Page

6.9 Available Dispute Resolution Forums 115
  6.9.1 Enforceability 115
  6.9.2 Litigation 116
  6.9.3 Arbitration 117
  6.9.4 Administrative Hearings 118
6.10 Mediation 119
6.11 Case Evaluations and Opinions 120
  6.11.1 Minitrial 120
  6.11.2 Summary Jury Trial 120
  6.11.3 Early Neutral Evaluation 120
6.12 Creating Your Own Dispute Resolution Process.... 121
6.13 Fortune Teller 121

F. DISPUTE RESOLUTION GOALS 121
6.14 Goals of Dispute Resolution Method 121
6.15 Mandated Alternative Dispute Resolution 123

CHAPTER SEVEN. PLANNING FOR NEGOTIATION: WHAT IS IT YOUR CLIENT WANTS? 124
A. INTRODUCTION 124
7.1 The Stages of Negotiation Planning 124

B. ESTABLISHING GOALS 125
7.2 Negotiation Goals 125
  7.2.1 Goals of the Client 125
  7.2.2 Goals of the Other Side 126
  7.2.3 Understanding Different Perceptions........ 126
  7.2.4 Why Not Reach an Agreement? 128
7.3 Authority to Negotiate an Accord 129

C. SELECTING A NEGOTIATION APPROACH 130
7.4 Negotiation Approaches 130
7.5 Traditional and Modern Bargaining Models 131
7.6 Assessing Negotiation Influences 134
  7.6.1 Power, Power, Power 134
  7.6.2 It's Always Been a Matter of Trust 135
  7.6.3 The Experience of a Lifetime 136

D. EVALUATING THE NEGOTIATION 138
7.7 A Checklist 138
7.8 General Evaluation of a Transaction 139
7.9 General Evaluation of a Lawsuit 140

D. EVALUATING THE NEGOTIATION—Continued

Page

7.10 Evaluating Your Interests and Values 141

    7.10.1 What Are Your Interests and Needs? 141

    7.10.2 What Are Your Values? 142

    7.10.3 Will You Listen to Yourself? 142

7.11 Evaluating and Understanding the Other Side 142

7.12 Preparing a Theory of the Deal or Case 143

7.13 Preparing for the Negotiation 144

    7.13.1 Preparing a Negotiation Notebook 144

    7.13.2 Preparing an Agenda 145

7.14 I Want to Contact Them. How? 145

    7.14.1 I Want to Write Them. Why? 145

    7.14.2 I Want to Call Them. Why? 146

    7.14.3 I Want to See Them. Why? 146

7.15 I Want to Negotiate Here. No, Here 146

7.16 I Want to Negotiate Too. What About Me? 147

7.17 I Want to Negotiate Now, Not Later 148

7.18 How Much Time Do We Have? 149

E. ASSESSING ETHICAL CONCERNS 151

7.19 Ethical Rules 151

    7.19.1 Ethical Norms 152

7.20 The Truth? 152

    7.20.1 Facts, Data, and Evidence 153

    7.20.2 Law, Precedent, Cases 154

    7.20.3 Opinions, Tactics, and Positions 154

7.21 Remaining an Ethical Character 156

CHAPTER EIGHT. NEGOTIATIONS: GETTING WHAT YOUR CLIENT WANTS 157

A. PLANNING INFORMATION EXCHANGE 157

8.1 Information You Want the Other Side to Have 157

8.2 Legal Effects of Disclosures 158

8.3 Protecting Information From Disclosure 158

    8.3.1 Using Non-Disclosure Techniques 158

    8.3.2 Obtaining Information From the Other Side 159

    8.3.3 Maintaining Accountability 160

    8.3.4 Assessing Responses 160

8.4 Informing and Updating the Client 160

B. ENGAGING IN THE NEGOTIATION 161

8.5 Making a Wish 161

    8.5.1 How Should a Negotiation Begin? 161

B. ENGAGING IN THE NEGOTIATION—Continued

Page

    8.5.2 What Are the Advantages and Disadvantages in Making or Receiving the First Proposal? 162

    8.5.3 How Should Positions Be Expressed? 163

    8.5.4 How Should Component Issues Be Discussed? 164

    8.5.5 What Responses Can Be Made? 164

    8.5.6 How Should Positions Be Adjusted? 165

  8.6 Making a Persuasive Statement 165

    8.6.1 Focus on Complementary Interests............ 166

    8.6.2 Focus on the Real Interests of the Party ... 167

    8.6.3 Exchange Valuable Concessions 167

    8.6.4 Propose Alternative Positions 167

    8.6.5 Say What You Mean 168

    8.6.6 Use Objective Explanations and Reasons .. 168

    8.6.7 Assess the Effect of Tax Considerations..... 172

    8.6.8 Consider a Structured Settlement in Litigation Negotiations.............................. 173

  8.7 Making a Threat... 174

    8.7.1 How to Respond to Threats 174

    8.7.2 How to Resolve Problems 175

    8.7.3 How to Gain the Cooperation of the Other Negotiator 175

    8.7.4 How to Respond to Gambits 176

    8.7.5 How to Unlock a Deadlock 176

    8.7.6 Whether to Use the Take-It-Or-Leave-It-Approach 177

    8.7.7 Whether to Walk Out 177

  8.8 Employing Creative Approaches............................ 178

    8.8.1 The Consumer Camper Case...................... 178

    8.8.2 The Surviving Spouse Case........................ 179

    8.8.3 The Ski Accident...................................... 180

    8.8.4 The Seven Percent Solution...................... 180

    8.8.5 Selling the Farm 181

C. ENDING THE NEGOTIATION 181

  8.9 Concluding a Negotiation 181

    8.9.1 When Is a Final Position a Final Position? 182

    8.9.2 How Can a Negotiation Be Reconvened After a "Final Position"? 183

    8.9.3 Has the Accord Been Reduced to Writing? 184

C. ENDING THE NEGOTIATION—Continued

Page

8.9.4 How Should the Attorney Draft the Accord? _____ 185

8.9.5 What Type of Settlement Document Should be Used? _____ 185

8.9.6 Did I Succeed? _____ 187

D. REVIEWING THE NEGOTIATION PROCESS _____ 188

8.10 An Overview _____ 188

CHAPTER NINE. MEDIATION: HELP! _____ 190

A. INTRODUCTION _____ 190

9.1 Help! _____ 190

9.2 Participants in the Mediation Process _____ 190

B. WHY MEDIATE, OR WHY NOT _____ 191

9.3 Reasons to Mediate _____ 191

9.4 Reasons Not to Mediate _____ 193

C. HOW TO MEDIATE _____ 194

9.5 Preparing for the Mediation _____ 194

9.5.1 Assessing Factors _____ 195

9.5.2 Preparation by Mediator _____ 197

9.6 The Mediation Session _____ 197

9.6.1 Disclosing Mediation Information _____ 198

9.6.2 Communicating With the Other Side _____ 199

D. MEDIATION APPROACHES _____ 200

9.7 Mediation Tactics and Techniques _____ 200

9.7.1 Assess the Case _____ 200

9.7.2 Communicate With the Parties _____ 200

9.7.3 Propose Alternative Resolutions _____ 201

9.7.4 Continue or Conclude the Mediation _____ 203

9.7.5 Employ Advanced Mediation Approaches __ 203

9.8 Termination of Mediation _____ 205

9.8.1 Settlement Agreement _____ 205

PART THREE. DISPUTE RESOLUTION PREPARATION

CHAPTER TEN. INVESTIGATIONS: OBTAINING INFORMATION FROM THOSE IN THE KNOW _____ 208

A. INTRODUCTION _____ 208

10.1 Scope of Information _____ 208

Page

B. **THE HUMAN TOUCH** ---------------------------------- 209
  10.2 People -- 209
      10.2.1 Friendly Witnesses --------------------- 209
      10.2.2 Neutral Witnesses ---------------------- 209
      10.2.3 Adverse Witnesses --------------------- 210
      10.2.4 Experts ---------------------------------- 210
  10.3 Witness Cooperation --------------------------- 211
  10.4 Difficult Witnesses ---------------------------- 212
  10.5 Witness Payments ------------------------------ 213

C. **THE STUFF** -- 213
  10.6 Documents -------------------------------------- 213
      10.6.1 Types ------------------------------------- 214
      10.6.2 Sources ---------------------------------- 214
      10.6.3 Format ----------------------------------- 215
  10.7 Things --- 215

D. **THE HOW** -- 215
  10.8 Ask. Look. Demand ---------------------------- 215
      10.8.1 Asking ----------------------------------- 215
      10.8.2 Looking ---------------------------------- 216
      10.8.3 Demanding ------------------------------- 216
  10.9 The How, The When, The Where, The Who -------- 217
      10.9.1 The How --------------------------------- 217
      10.9.2 The When -------------------------------- 217
      10.9.3 The Where ------------------------------- 217
      10.9.4 The Who ---------------------------------- 218
  10.10 Interview Approaches ------------------------- 219
      10.10.1 Interview Techniques ------------------- 219
      10.10.2 Advising Witnesses --------------------- 220
  10.11 Recording the Interview --------------------- 221
      10.11.1 File Memo -------------------------------- 221
      10.11.2 Witness Statements -------------------- 221
  10.12 Recording the Statement -------------------- 222
  10.13 Writing a Screenplay ------------------------- 223

CHAPTER ELEVEN. ASSERTING CLAIMS AND DEFENSES: THE RIGHT WAY ------------------- 224
A. **INTRODUCTION** -------------------------------------- 224
  11.1 Asserting the Right Jurisdiction ------------- 225
      11.1.1 Personal Jurisdiction ------------------ 225
      11.1.2 Subject Matter Jurisdiction ----------- 226

Page

B. **SELECTING THE RIGHT FORUM FOR THE RIGHT REASON** _____ 227
    11.2   How to Select a Jurisdiction _____ 227
    11.3   Where Can Relief Be Obtained? _____ 227

C. **COMPLAINING THE RIGHT WAY** _____ 228
    11.4   How to Bring a Litigation Claim _____ 228
    11.5   What Are the Components of a Complaint?_____ 229
          11.5.1   Caption _____ 229
          11.5.2   Contents_____ 229
          11.5.3   Request for Relief _____ 232
          11.5.4   Signature _____ 232
    11.6   How to Bring an Arbitration Claim _____ 232
    11.7   How to Initiate an Administrative Case _____ 233
    11.8   Is That All There Is? _____ 233

D. **DRAFTING THE RIGHT PAPERS** _____ 233
    11.9   How to Draft_____ 233

E. **RESPONDING WITH THE RIGHT DEFENSES AND MOTIONS** _____ 234
    11.10 How to Respond _____ 234
          11.10.1 Admissions and Denials _____ 235
          11.10.2 Affirmative Defenses _____ 235
          11.10.3 Counterclaims_____ 235
          11.10.4 Defensive Motions _____ 235
          11.10.5 Other Claims and Defense_____ 236
    11.11 Asserting the Right Motions_____ 237
          11.11.1 Motion to Dismiss _____ 237
          11.11.2 Motion for Summary Judgment ____ 238
          11.11.3 Other Motions_____ 238
          11.11.4 Reasons Not to Bring a Motion _____ 239
          11.11.5 Motion Documents_____ 240
          11.11.6 More on Motion Practice_____ 240

CHAPTER TWELVE. DISCLOSURE AND DISCOVERY: WHAT DO YOU KNOW? _____ 241
A. **INTRODUCTION** _____ 241
    12.1   Purposes of Disclosure and Discovery _____ 241
          12.1.1   Early Disclosure _____ 242
          12.1.2   Disclosure During a Proceeding ____ 243
    12.2   Methods of Discovery _____ 244
          12.2.1   Availability of Discovery Methods_____ 245

Page

B. **SCOPE OF DISCLOSURE AND DISCOVERY** 246

12.3 Relevant Information and Documents............. 246

    12.3.1 Litigation 247

    12.3.2 Arbitration Proceedings........................ 248

    12.3.3 Administrative Proceedings.................. 248

12.4 Discovery Restrictions 248

    12.4.1 Privileges... 248

    12.4.2 Work Product (Trial and Case Preparation Materials) 249

    12.4.3 Attorney Mental Processes 251

12.5 Disclosure and Discovery of Expert Information 251

    12.5.1 Trial and Hearing Experts 252

    12.5.2 Retained or Employee Experts.............. 252

    12.5.3 Informally Consulted Experts.............. 252

    12.5.4 Inexpensive Experts 252

12.6 Supplemental Disclosure and Discovery 253

C. **PLANNING**.. 253

12.7 Disclosure and Discovery Planning..................... 253

12.8 Disclosure and Discovery by Agreement 254

12.9 Discovery Plan and Order 254

12.10 Disclosure/Discovery Orders............................. 255

    12.10.1 Protective Orders................................ 255

    12.10.2 Enforcement Orders........................... 256

CHAPTER THIRTEEN. DEPOSITIONS: GETTING TO KNOW YOU.. 258

A. **THE WHY** 258

13.1 Why Should I Take a Deposition? 258

B. **THE HOW** 259

13.2 Whom Should I Depose? 259

13.3 When Can or Should I Depose? 259

13.4 How Often Can I Depose? 260

13.5 Where Should I Depose? 260

13.6 How Long Can I Depose? 260

13.7 How Do I Notice a Deposition?........................... 261

13.8 When Should I Schedule the Deposition?............ 262

13.9 Who Is Present at a Deposition?......................... 262

13.10 Do I Have to Attend?....................................... 263

13.11 How Is the Deposition Recorded? 263

13.12 When Is a Transcript Needed? 264

13.13 How Much Do Depositions Cost?....................... 264

Page

C.   **THE PLANNING** _____ 264
   13.14 Deposition Preparation _____ 264

D.   **THE TAKING** _____ 266
   13.15 How Is the Deposition Room Arranged? _____ 266
   13.16 How Does the Deposition Begin? _____ 266
   13.17 How Do I Begin the Deposition? _____ 266
   13.18 What Should My Demeanor Be? _____ 269
   13.19 What Should I Ask? _____ 269
   13.20 How Do I Effectively Ask Questions? _____ 270
   13.21 How Do I Effectively Probe? _____ 270
   13.22 How Should I Ask Questions? _____ 271
   13.23 What Do I Do About Documents? _____ 272
   13.24 How Can I Handle Exhibits Effectively? _____ 274
   13.25 What Do I Do With the Exhibit? _____ 275
   13.26 What About Confidential Information? _____ 275
   13.27 How Do I Depose an Expert? _____ 276
   13.28 What Shouldn't I Say or Do During the Deposition? _____ 277
   13.29 How Should I React to Objections? _____ 278
   13.30 How Do I Control Interference During a Deposition? _____ 279
   13.31 How Do I Conclude the Deposition? _____ 280

E.   **THE DEPONENT** _____ 281
   13.32 Defending the Deponent _____ 281
      13.32.1 Preparing the Deponent _____ 281
      13.32.2 Making Objections During the Deposition _____ 282
      13.32.3 Protecting the Deponent _____ 283
   13.33 Questioning the Deponent _____ 285

F.   **THE END** _____ 285
   13.34 Concluding the Deposition _____ 285
      13.34.1 Review of the Deposition by the Deponent _____ 286
      13.34.2 Signing the Deposition _____ 287
      13.34.3 Filing the Deposition _____ 287
      13.34.4 Stipulations _____ 287

G.   **THE FUTURE** _____ 288
   13.35 Use of the Deposition _____ 288

Page

CHAPTER FOURTEEN. DISCOVERY METHODS: IS THAT ALL THERE IS? 289

A. INTRODUCTION 289

14.1 More Discovery Methods 289

B. GETTING DOCUMENTS 289

14.2 How Do I Obtain Documents? 289

    14.2.1 Whom Can I Ask? 290

    14.2.2 What Can I Demand From Parties? 290

14.3 When Can I Make a Demand? 290

14.4 How Do I Make a Demand? 291

    14.4.1 How Do the Documents Need to Be Described? 291

    14.4.2 How Do I Draft These Descriptions? 291

14.5 How and When Can I Obtain the Documents? 293

14.6 How May the Other Side Respond? 293

14.7 How Do I Know I Got Everything? 294

14.8 How Do I Test an Item? 294

14.9 How Do I Obtain Computerized Information? 295

14.10 What Are Available Objections to Production Demands? 295

14.11 How Do I Obtain Documents From Non-parties? 296

14.12 How Do I Obtain Documents From the Government? 296

C. GETTING INFORMATION 297

14.13 What Are Interrogatories? 297

    14.13.1 When Can I Submit Them? 297

    14.13.2 What Information Can I Seek? 297

14.14 How Do I Draft Interrogatories? 298

    14.14.1 Instructions 299

    14.14.2 Definitions 299

    14.14.3 Questions 300

14.15. How Do I Effectively Draft Questions? 300

14.16 How Many Questions Can I Ask? 301

14.17 How Are Interrogatories Responded to? 302

    14.17.1 How Are Questions Answered? 302

    14.17.2 What Is an Appropriate Answer? 302

14.18 What Objections May Be Made to Interrogatories? 304

14.19 What Can I Do If I Don't Get What I Want? 305

D. GETTING ADMISSIONS 305

14.20 What Are Requests for Admissions? 305

Page

D. GETTING ADMISSIONS—Continued

14.21 How Do I Draft Requests for Admissions? 305
14.22 What Are Responses to Requests? 306
14.23 Can I Challenge a Response? 307
14.24 Can a Response Be Changed? 307
14.25 What Is the Effect of an Admission? 307

E. GETTING AN EXAMINATION 308

14.26 Why Would I Want to Request an Examination? 308
    14.26.1 What Is a "Controversy?" 308
    14.26.2 What Examination Documents are
           Needed? 308
14.27 What Happens at the Examination? 309
14.28 What Happens After the Examination? 309

EPILOGUE 310

Index 313

LAWYERING

PRACTICE AND PLANNING

*

Chapter One
WORK OF THE LAWYER

I'm looking forward to being a lawyer because I can ... what is it that I can do?

I can do a lot of things. I can counsel clients with my wisdom and expertise. I can draft documents and create transactions out of whole cloth. I can create relationships for clients and dissolve their relationships. I can help them resolve their disputes.

No stage of life is beyond my expertise. No client is beyond my ability. From adoptions to wills I can take care of their needs. I can champion individual, constitutional, and consumer rights. I can represent businesses, executives, laborers, farmers, the rich and the poor, the common and the uncommon.

I can be and do all. I can negotiate anything and do any deal. I can appear before judges, jurors, arbitrators, administrative judges, from small claims court to the world court in the Hague. I can argue anything, anyplace, anytime.

Well, within reason. I do want to balance my professional life with family, friends, and fun. I need a vacation in order to be an effective lawyer. Where did I put those travel brochures?

A. INTRODUCTION
1.1 WELCOME TO THE PRACTICE OF LAW

This book explains and explores fundamental professional skills involved in practicing law. You will learn how to interview and counsel a client, negotiate with other attorneys, plan for transactions and dispute resolutions, initiate and defend claims, and gather and discover information. You will learn what to do, when to do it, where to do it, and why to do it.

These materials focus primarily on the civil practice of law, although much will apply to whatever you do in your professional life after law school. The materials analyze and present

1

approaches used by successful lawyers. Each chapter describes alternative strategies, tactics, and techniques.

Companion videotapes supplement this book. You can and will learn much by observing and critiquing lawyers practice law. The videotapes present client interviews, counseling sessions, negotiation conferences, mediation sessions, and depositions. Observing what these lawyers do and don't do, evaluating their efforts, and suggesting alternative approaches will help you further understand how to think, be, feel, and act like a lawyer.

The decisions lawyers make—from the initial client interview to the conclusion of a case—are based on analytical legal reasoning and incisive judgments. Both the theory and practice of why and how lawyers think and reason are analyzed. You will learn how to make well-reasoned professional decisions.

In the beginning there may have been no lawyers, but there were the makings of the need for lawyers. The first people formed relationships and transactions and became involved in disputes. The relationships evolved into various types of commercial and personal transactions requiring the services of wise counselors at law. The disputes created the need for wise attorneys and decision makers.

The legal profession is a helping profession. We have as lawyers the privilege and responsibility to help clients. This humanistic view of lawyering shapes and influences our work. The situations presented in this book and demonstrated in the companion videotapes involve and affect the lives of clients, lawyers, and other people. You need to bring to life what you read and what you see so you can experience this human dimension of practice.

Ethical issues permeate the practice of law. A major premise of this book is that lawyers must hold themselves to high ethical standards. An understanding of your responsibilities and duties as explained in this text will help you identify and resolve ethical concerns.

There is no one way to "practice" law. Those of you still searching to find the ultimate source of the law should reconsider your vocation and avocation. The bulk of lawyering involves judgment about which road to take: to the right or to the left or on the road less traveled. Yes, there are some established rules and there are some commonly accepted approaches, but much in the practice requires you to exercise professional discretion. The choices may be many or few, but the choices will be up to you and your client.

Lawyers make mistakes, and problems commonly occur. One of the keys to being an effective lawyer is not to let the mistakes and problems overwhelm you. Thorough preparation and an understanding of available solutions explained in these materials will help you anticipate and avoid mistakes and problems.

Civil practice resembles most life experiences. There will be times of success (yes!), failure (oh no), happiness (joy!), frustration (sigh), excitement (wow!), anxiety (ugh), and satisfaction (ahh!). These psychological and emotional dimensions involved in practice are also described throughout this book.

The ultimate goal of this book is to help you become a professional, competent, and confident lawyer. We learn from how things have been done in the past, from each other, and from thinking about how things should be in the future. As you read and digest these materials you will become knowledgeable, informed, surprised, curious, and shocked. Not everything in the practical and theoretical world of lawyering will conform to your experience, your expectations, and your notions of what it means to be a lawyer. We present both the way things are and the way things could or should be. Your task, in part, is to make all these things coalesce.

1.2　THE TAPESTRY OF LAW PRACTICE

A lawyer has to weave threads together when representing clients. These threads include:

- Gathering information
- Counseling clients
- Negotiating with opposing counsel and parties
- Planning transactions
- Preparing to resolve disputes
- Creating agreements

- Resolving problems
- Investigating cases
- Bringing and defending claims
- Selecting dispute resolution forums
- Discovering information from opposing parties
- Planning cases before dispute resolution forums
- Leading a balanced life and enjoying it all

These are the threads you will need to weave together with the other threads you learn in law school and life to create a pattern of effective practice.

1.2.1   The Tapestry Pattern

A number of basic elements compose this tapestry practice pattern:

Facts. The gathering and selection of facts occurs throughout client representation. For example, a lawyer drafting a will needs (at a minimum) to know the testator's identity, family relations, financial life, and desired disposition of wealth. Only then can a lawyer draft a will that both fulfills the client's objectives and complies with legal requirements. For another example, a lawyer representing a client in a dispute must (at a minimum) know the client's story, the other side's story, the issues that need to be resolved, and the applicable law. It is critical for lawyers in all types of cases to gain a mastery of all relevant facts connected with the transaction, project, or dispute before moving forward to draft a contract, propose a solution, or file a complaint. Obviously, the fact finding lawyer is bound by some degree of common sense in the world of limited client resources. The client will be unlikely to spend $10,000 on fact gathering for a $2,000 transaction. Neither will the client pay to have the lawyer fly by Concorde to Paris to resolve a small dispute (unless the dispute has a chance of becoming huge and the Louvre is open).

Law. You are learning and will continue to learn substantive and procedural law in your other law school courses. You will also learn in this book some of the substantive law of practice and the procedural laws, rules, and regulations involved in civil practice.

Application of law to facts. All the most brilliant legal learning and sophisticated fact gathering will come to naught if the lawyer cannot weave the law and facts into the right tapestry. This is the art of being an effective lawyer. Legal analysis and fact application are both critically important to client representation.

Theory and skills. If you know what to do but not how to do it, you will create a mess. If you know how to do it but do not know what to do, you will be a menace. Effective lawyering requires you to blend together the theories and professional skills of lawyering into a whole tapestry.

1.2.2 The Tapestry

The threads of lawyering that create patterns comprise a whole tapestry of representation. Sections of this book describe the threads, and the chapters reflect the patterns. The elements discussed throughout this text reflect elements of human behavior. People tend to act in certain ways, whether they are a client, an opposing lawyer, or a decision maker. While we have divided the lawyer's work into discrete segments, there are similar approaches to lawyering whether an attorney is working with the client, an opposing attorney, or a decision maker. Approaches that make a good client interview, also make an effective witness interview, also make good deposition questions, and may later make for a good direct examination. Factors that influence clients may also persuade other attorneys during negotiations, or later persuade decision makers. These common threads and patterns of lawyering apply across the whole height and width of the tapestry of client representation. You will need to study each thread separately, step back and view the pattern, step further back to see the entire design, and then step forward to touch and feel the tapestry.

B. WORKING RELATIONSHIPS

1.3 LAWYER RELATIONSHIPS

The practice of law involves an appreciation and understanding of a number of relationships. Lawyers spend their time:

- Working with clients
- Dealing with other attorneys and parties
- Seeking information or help from others
- Dealing with decision makers
- Working within the legal system
- Working as a practitioner
- Working with colleagues
- Working with yourself

1.3.1 Working With Clients

How does one become a practicing lawyer? Get a client. What our clients minimally expect from us is this: they expect that during our representation of them nothing in our professional life is more important. They expect the full measure of our energy and efforts to fulfill their needs. They expect our best commitment whether it takes five minutes or five years of representation.

This is not easy to do. We have other clients (hopefully). We have other responsibilities in our professional and personal lives. We have our own needs. As a professional, however, we have a real obligation to meet our clients' minimal expectations. They would not retain an attorney—would you?—who would say to them: "I'll devote less than my full attention to your case. I'll make half-hearted attempts to get what you want. I'll make mediocre efforts to represent you." They have a right to expect our best. If we cannot provide that, we should not be representing them.

A dichotomy of practice is that we help people who are in trouble, make stupid mistakes, experience pain and suffering, and want something at the expense of others. Lawyers need to understand these human dimensions. You will need continually to view your clients as *people with problems* and not as problems who cause you more problems. A major dissatisfaction with practice can result from focusing on solving problems instead of on helping people solve their problems. As a lawyer, you need to welcome the challenge of difficult cases, feel the excitement of helping others, and enjoy resolving seemingly unresolvable situations.

1.3.2 Dealing With Other Attorneys and Parties

Dealing effectively with other attorneys and parties is primarily a matter of how we treat them. We know we ought to be professional and civil. What is professional or civil? Many judges, professors, and lawyers have attempted to write and speak about "professional civility" in journal articles, at bar association lunches, and at CLE conferences. We can complicate our own analysis by behaving with different levels of civility towards different attorneys and clients, sort of like situational ethics. We can simplify our approach with the right attitude and behavior: we should treat other lawyers and parties the way *we* would expect and want to be treated if *we* were them. This approach helps eliminate or reduce the debate about whether we can or should be disrespectful, engage in personal attacks, dishonestly withhold information, or be mean. Another simple way of analyzing the appropriateness of our treatment of other lawyers and parties is to imagine yourself being videotaped dealing with them. Would you or others reviewing what you said or did believe it to be a professional and civil way to treat others? If so, do it. If not, become a mud wrestler. You can be effective and successful while being civil, decent, and yourself. You don't have to wrestle in the mud, unless you want to.

1.3.3 Seeking Help or Information From Others

In addition to relationships with clients and other attorneys and parties, lawyers frequently contact individuals for information or assistance. An attorney may contact someone for assistance, or an expert for advice. How should a lawyer treat these individuals? Reasonably and respectfully, of course. These approaches are not only the right thing to do, they usually will get you what you want quickly and affordably. Some situations will require you to be persistent, firm, and even aggressive. But no situation justifies you being unprofessional and uncivil. This approach is not only a poor tactic but is also a slur on you and our profession.

1.3.4 Dealing With Decision Makers

Much of lawyering involves lawyers in decision making processes. Clients make choices, opposing lawyers take positions, and decision makers decide cases. The person or persons who will decide your client's fate need to be treated in a way that will increase the chance of your client winning. You want to be perceived by the decision maker as being honest, well prepared, and right. You do not want to be perceived as acting inappropriately. What is appropriate may be a matter of perception and disagreement. Lawyers may believe they need to be liked by the decision maker to be influential. The risk of wanting to be liked is that you may become too reverential toward the decision maker and consequently ineffective. The risk of not being liked is that you may be perceived as being unprofessional and ineffective.

The initial critical question to ask of your dealings with decision makers is: how will this decision maker decide this case? Judges, juries, and arbitrators are expected to decide based upon the facts and law. But they will also be influenced by other factors. You need to understand these factors to determine which of them may influence whether your client wins or loses.

Beyond the law and facts, common factors that influence all people who have to make a choice, take a position, or decide are:

Values. Values reflect a person's beliefs, morals, norms, or goals. Values may be based on a sense of individual needs (me), the collective good (family, friends, society), or spirituality (an ultimate source). It is more likely that people will say or do something that reflects their values than agree to something that contradicts their values.

Needs and Interests. Everyone has some needs or interests that they will be inclined to promote or enhance when they say or do something. These personal and professional needs and interests may be as varied as individuals. Common needs are security, love, self-esteem, and a sense of belonging.

Financial Considerations. Much of what a lawyer does affects personal and professional financial matters. It may involve the completion of a financial transaction or seeking or defending claims for money damages. Economics will sharply affect what clients decide to do, or not to do, and how wealth should be distributed may affect decision makers.

Feeling good. Psychological and emotional demands and expectations influence people's statements and actions. Healthy people prefer to say or do things that make them feel good. Feeling good may be based upon a spectrum of sources from their own narrow interest—getting what they want—to altruism.

It will always be helpful to consider the following four questions in dealing with clients, parties, attorneys, and decision makers:

What values does this person consider important?

What are the needs and interests of this person?

What economic considerations affect this person?

What will make this person feel good?

1.3.5 Working Within the Legal Profession

Take a moment to consider why you chose the law as your career. Time's up. Whether it is clear or unclear to you why you selected the legal profession, you have. Your decision (along with passing the bar exam) will permit you to practice law. Your attitude towards practice will help make you an effective or ineffective lawyer.

The legal profession allows you to practice in various areas which match your interests and values. You can work with and for others, or you can work for yourself. You can represent individuals who seek to recover for wrongs done to them. You can represent businesses which create new transactions or need their actions defended. You can be a legal services lawyer, or devote a significant part of your private practice to pro bono work. You can represent the government and pursue public policies.

What you end up doing should be based on your preference and on the market. You should accept a job that matches your interests and values and provides you with the standard of living you want. You should select an area of practice that will satisfy you philosophically, economically, psychologically, and emotionally.

The responsibilities of being a lawyer create conflicts. What is best for your client may not be best for you. Resolving a dispute quickly may meet your client's needs but deny you an opportunity to gain experience or deprive you of a significant source of income. What is best for your client may not be best for the community. Your client may benefit tremendously from a deal, but the transaction may have some adverse effects on your community. What is best for the client and community may not be good for your family. The time it takes to help your client and others takes away precious time from the ones you love.

It is necessary for you to reflect on your role as an attorney and your goals as a person. How much of your time are you willing to devote to your being a lawyer? What are you willing to do to maintain this role? Accept fewer clients? Reduce your income? What are your goals as a person? How do you want to live your life? You decide.

1.3.6 Working as a Practitioner

Working as a practitioner involves an understanding of types of lawyers, their various roles, and client expectations. There are two broad categories of lawyer types: lawyers who represent clients, and all other lawyers doing whatever they do. The focus of this book is the representation of clients. These clients include individuals, corporations, organizations, government agencies, fee paying clients, indigent clients, and any other person or entity represented by an attorney. This book focuses on practicing law as a private practitioner or as a public lawyer and explains professional skills covering this type of lawyering work. These skills also parallel much of the work law graduates do who do not practice law.

What is it that all other lawyers do? They can be:

Business executives. There are many business people with law degrees who are not involved in traditional law practice. They may do many things lawyers do, but they do not hold themselves out nor consider themselves to be acting as lawyers.

For example, a corporate executive who holds a law degree but who does not work for the legal department of the corporation may act as both a lawyer and an executive for the company.

Lobbyists. Lawyers may be retained by clients (individuals, associations, businesses) to work on legislative matters. Many lobbyists are lawyers, and many are not. This type of specific work is beyond the scope of this book.

Public employees. Government work finds many lawyers working as legislators, administrators, staff members, politicians, regulators, and in other myriad positions. This work is also beyond the ken of this book. For more information, move to Washington or your local seat of government, depending upon your preference.

Public service workers. Lawyers may work in a variety of positions for non-profit organizations. Their work may involve some of the skills discussed in this book as well as work similar to what occurs in the business and governmental world. Many practitioners contribute substantial amounts of time to these organizations on a pro bono basis.

1.3.7 Working With Colleagues

Colleagues include all employees, partners, associates, attorneys, paralegals, secretaries, law clerks, and other co-workers. Working effectively with all of them is usually a reflection of how well you treat them. All these individuals deserve the same treatment, and it is what we previously described with your other relationships. You should treat them the way you would want to be treated—with respect, understanding, and caring. You may decide to treat them this way because it is pragmatic and you realize without them you can not be an effective practitioner. Or you may decide to treat them this way because it is the right way. Whatever your reason, your success depends upon their success.

Your success also depends upon how good a businessperson you are. You need to understand how to succeed in business and you also need to know how to manage your law practice efficiently and economically. Many of you will actively manage your law firm, including small, large, and government firms. Knowing how to work with your colleagues and administer your firm will be essential to your being an effective lawyer.

1.3.8 Working With Yourself

You will spend a lot of time with yourself as a practitioner. You spend a lot of time with yourself now. You will be most effective if you like yourself, your life, your work, and your profession. How to like yourself and others is well beyond the scope of this book. You need to assess that on your own and with others you know. How to like your work and your profession is both within and without the scope of this book. We can describe how the practice of law can be enjoyable, rewarding, and fulfilling. We can tell you that this reflects our experience with practice. We can also suggest that we believe lawyers who like their work and profession are more effective—and happier— lawyers. We cannot tell you how you can best enjoy your work and profession. But you can and will need to do that.

The law can be a wonderful profession. As we will describe throughout this book, the law is a helping profession in which you can do great good. You can achieve success, a sense of purpose, and financial security. But the practice of law can also be dissatisfying, boring, mundane, frustrating, and difficult (a little like law school?).

You had a life before law school and you bring it to your life as a lawyer. You come to law school with experience about the skills discussed in this book. Some of you have a lot of experience, some of you have less experience. All of you in your life have asked questions, obtained information from others, provided advice, negotiated, and tried to convince a variety of decision makers they should give you what you want. Some of you have experienced these skills in other areas, such as employment, business, volunteer work, and just being around.

As you read our analysis of lawyering, you need to analyze yourself to understand your level of experience and how you presently understand and do some of the things lawyers do. How you do them now will affect how you will do them in the future for your clients. After analyzing yourself, you want to continue to use those skills that are effective and discontinue those that are ineffective. As you develop as a lawyer, you want to continually analyze what you do, how you do it, why you do it, and how you can improve. Or you can call us or others for individual counseling.

1.4 THE BALANCED LIFE

You have a life inside law school. Such as it is. What you learn in other courses during law school will help you be a better lawyer. But some of what you learn in law school may hinder your development as a practicing lawyer. Law school encourages and rewards students to reach decisions quickly, conform the facts and law to their positions, use legal jargon, and state opinions without hesitation. These approaches can be useful in practice, or can interfere with being an effective lawyer. Novice lawyers need to adapt approaches they developed in law school to the requirements of the real world.

You also have a life outside of law school. You need to nurture and develop a balanced life that will continue during practice. A lawyer's personality and temperament are often as important as knowledge and intellectual ability. Lawyers (and law students) are more effective if they balance their practice (and their studies) with a reasonably healthy dose of other adventures of life. These experiences will make you a more relaxed and effective attorney. You will also be better able to understand the forces that drive client's interests and needs, better able to appreciate the pressures felt and reacted to by opposing counsel, and better able to handle losses and celebrate wins.

You need to lead a life balanced with family, friends, hobbies, leisure time, and vacations. This balance is critical to your being a well rounded lawyer. Admit it, wouldn't you rather be painting an oil canvas, shooting hoops, singing in harmony, working out, reading the books you were supposed to during college, visiting the Inns of Court in London, touring Glacier Park, sitting in your easy chair, tending your garden, motorcycling the Alps, or _____ (fill it in). Do it now, and do it while you are a lawyer.

There will also be a life for you after law school. There is hope. This life can be a rich life, with many opportunities to help others and to help yourself. Lawyers help people in ways no other professionals can. Clients may seldom host a celebratory thank you party after you represent them, but you will be blessed with gifts of internal satisfaction and accomplishment.

Not everyone will think you are great. Our legal profession is not viewed as the most cherished profession by many in our society and the world. The perception of many is that lawyers are nit-picking deal killers, or combative gladiators, or greedy money-grabbers, or all three. You will need to understand this perception, and you will need to be as good a lawyer as you can be to reduce this perception. For almost every person who thinks there are too many lawyers doing useless work, there is a client waiting to retain *you* to help them.

C.   REPRESENTING CLIENTS
1.5   THE HALLMARK OF LAWYERING

Representation of clients is the hallmark of lawyering. A lawyer in private practice may serve many; a government lawyer or in-house counsel may serve only one. The lawyer's primary duty, regardless of the number of clients, is responsible and effective representation.

The link between the lawyer and the client can be simple or complex, distant or close. A lawyer working on behalf of a client may become involved in much more than legal representation. Working on transactions or resolving disputes may have as much to do with personal issues, economic interests, psychological matters, family conflicts, business difficulties, or moral dilemmas as with legal issues. Through it all, the client's needs and interests remain the primary goal.

Every person, business, and government agency needs legal advice at some point. (See, you chose the right profession.) These different clients have vastly different kinds of legal needs and vastly different levels of experience dealing with the legal system. There are, however, two common rules relating to clients: first, the client isn't necessarily that person sitting on the other side of the desk; second, no two clients are alike.

With regard to the first point, lawyers have as clients corporations, partnerships, associations, and a host of other legal entities represented by individuals. The lawyer owes a professional allegiance to the corporation or agency, and not the individual representing the entity. A corollary to this rule is that the client isn't necessarily the person paying the bill. For example, insurance companies frequently hire and pay lawyers to represent policy holders. The insurance company may sign the check, the lawyer may report regularly to the claims supervisor, but the policy holder is usually still the lawyer's client and entitled to have the lawyer place the client's interests above those of the insurance company.

Second, no two clients are alike. It is easy to make assumptions about clients based on jobs, income, or status, but these assumptions are often inaccurate. The corporate executive who has virtually no experience in litigation may need a lengthy explanation of an upcoming deposition instead of only a cursory description. The AFDC recipient who understands administrative procedures does not need a detailed and condescending explanation of the law. Categorizing clients is difficult as well as dangerous. What each client needs should be based upon their individual identity, experience, knowledge, and background.

For the most part, the relationship between lawyer and client is not defined by rules or laws. There are, however, three important areas of regulation: the attorney-client privilege, professional responsibility rules, and legal malpractice.

1.5.1 The Attorney–Client Privilege

The attorney-client privilege provides communications between a lawyer and a client with a unique sort of protection. While the law differs somewhat among jurisdictions, in general the attorney-client privilege protects communications:

- Between a lawyer and that lawyer's client
- Meant to be kept confidential
- Concerning the work the lawyer does for the client.

The attorney-client privilege can be powerful because it prevents the attorney or the client from being compelled to testify about protected communications. It can also be fragile because its protections can be easily lost. If confidential client communications are disclosed to a party outside the attorney-client relationship, then the privilege may be waived to the extent of the subject matter of the disclosure. For example, a client may tell friends or co-workers about what the lawyer said. Or, a lawyer could destroy the privilege through the accidental disclosure of client communications, such as the inadvertent production of a privileged document during discovery. It is the lawyer's responsibility to safeguard the privilege, and because it is a privilege that can be lost, it is a responsibility that must be exercised vigilantly.

1.5.2 Professional Responsibility Rules

In all jurisdictions, rules or codes of professional responsibility govern lawyers' ethical behavior and conduct. Many states have adopted some form of the "Rules of Professional Conduct." These rules require a lawyer to be competent, diligent, and communicative while representing clients, and also forbid a lawyer from divulging client confidences (except in limited situations) and from representing clients with conflicting interests (except in certain situations). The professional rules are a mix of aspirations, common sense, and taboos. They guide us to be good lawyers; they remind us about what we already know; and they tell us what we cannot do. You will or have learned more about these rules in another course entitled Professional Responsibility.

1.5.3 The Law of Malpractice

Each jurisdiction has its own law about what constitutes attorney malpractice. Knowledge of this law is important, and lawyers need to be aware of the relevant case law defining legal malpractice in their jurisdiction. But reading these cases to learn how to practice law is a little like watching car wrecks to learn how to drive. You really don't need to be told *not* to drive drunk or recklessly. Likewise, you don't need to be told *not* to lie, cheat, or steal. Malpractice starts with you. Stop it by not starting it. It's so easy for us to give good advice. Once you're a lawyer, you will also have opportunities to give good advice.

1.6 THE ROLE(S) OF A PRACTICING LAWYER

The literature of the law is filled with attempts to define our profession and to explain just what it is that makes us different or special. Some of this writing is self-absorbed and jargon-laden, but much is the product of honest attempts to survey the occupational, ethical, and moral boundaries of the practice of law. The writings on these issues are sufficiently complex and voluminous to defy either easy summary or even easy characterization. The subject is important, though, because the literature is really just the theoretical tip of a practical iceberg of different views of what it means to be a lawyer—views that are played out and applied every day by thousands of practicing lawyers representing clients.

Boiled down to its essence, most of the discussion of what it means to be a practicing lawyer consists of two questions:

What amount of responsibility do we have **for** our clients?

What amount of responsibility do we have **to** our clients?

The answers to these questions are scattered across a wide spectrum of views of what it means to be a lawyer.

1.6.1 The Lawyer as Technician

Near one end of the spectrum is the vision of the lawyer as technician. Some lawyers see themselves as professionals who do little more than find the law for clients and then help clients reach immediate goals as efficiently as possible. These lawyers conceive of the profession as a craft, and believe that the good lawyer is the lawyer who effectively plies this craft. These lawyers see their responsibility **to** a client as a limited one: once the lawyer has finished with the promised legal work, the responsibility to the client ends. In the same way, these lawyers also view themselves as having limited responsibility **for** a client: the lawyer is only responsible for completing legal tasks competently, the client (and perhaps the justice system) are responsible for the results. Under this view, the lawyer is accountable for the means and the client is accountable for the ends.

This view of the profession is sometimes condemned as a "hired gun" perspective, but this is somewhat unfair. Much of any lawyer's work does involve the capable performance of particular legal tasks, and some lawyers find that competence is the surest touchstone of professional satisfaction. Many lawyers, however, rebel at the notion that their responsibility to and for clients is limited to the competent performance of legal tasks.

1.6.2 The Lawyer as Wise Counselor

Near the other end of the spectrum is the view that the lawyer serves the client best when the lawyer takes on the role of wise and trusted counselor. Lawyers who see themselves in this role believe that they have a responsibility to clients that extends far beyond competent performance of particular legal tasks. In a sense, these lawyers view themselves as "legal healers" charged with the duty of treating all their clients holistically. Not surprisingly, these lawyers also see themselves as having a much greater responsibility **for** their clients. Wise counselors are, in some sense, responsible for both the ends and means of their clients. Lawyers acting as wise counselors should be accountable for what they help clients do and should not, it is contended, be permitted to excuse themselves or their clients with the explanation that they were simply doing what the law allowed.

Critics complain that this view of lawyering is too hard on lawyers and too hard on clients. It is too hard on lawyers because no practicing lawyer ought to be expected to solve all of a client's problems, nor should any practicing lawyer be held morally accountable for what a client chooses to do. It makes little sense, for example, to say that a lawyer who properly advises a client regarding environmental laws is somehow personally responsible for later environmental damage intentionally committed by the client. Critics also charge that this view of the profession is too hard on clients. Clients should be permitted to make their own decisions and should be expected to bear the legal, social, and moral consequences of those decisions. Anything less suggests that clients are somehow less human than lawyers. A wise counselor is, these critics charge, little more than an unwelcome meddler for many clients—a meddler trying to foist an unwanted moral agenda on an unsuspecting client.

Even in the face of these complaints, the vision of the lawyer as wise counselor still has much to recommend it. It is important, for example, to see clients as something more than customers at a "legal pharmacy," prescriptions in hand ready to be filled. Lawyers should be attuned to clients' immediate goals, but should also be aware of the clients' long-term goals (overarching goals) and the clients' preferences about how to do things (process preferences). It is also important for a lawyer to feel a responsibility to society that is independent of the lawyer's responsibility to a client. There is something unpersuasive and morally chilling about a lawyer who says: "I helped my client do something evil but that's not a problem for me because it's not my fault that my client is evil."

1.6.3 The Lawyer as Creator or Problem Solver

Somewhere in the middle of the spectrum is the view of the lawyer as a creator or problem solver. According to this view, the lawyer is responsible for more than the competent performance of particular legal tasks. The lawyer is responsible for learning about concerns and problems that motivate the client to seek legal advice, and is then responsible for offering the client potential solutions. According to this view, the lawyer also bears a greater responsibility **for** clients. Lawyers should advise clients of the legal—and perhaps ethical—risks of seeking unjust ends. In extreme cases, if the lawyer feels strongly that the client is seeking something that is truly unjust, then the lawyer should refuse to represent the client. Of course, lawyers should also recognize that they are asked to solve client problems within the context of a legal system that is basically good, though sometimes flawed. For proponents, the view of lawyer as a creator and problem solver makes our legal system primarily accountable for the unjust ends that lawyers sometimes achieve.

Like any moderate position, there is much appeal to the vision of lawyers as creators or problem solvers. Like any moderate position, however, this view also suffers from some significant "So What?/Now What?" problems. For instance, if this view says nothing more than lawyers should make sure that the legal tasks they undertake might actually help the client now or solve the client's immediate problem, then "So What?" That is not a particularly deep or helpful insight. On the other hand, perhaps the view means to go further and advise a lawyer to make sure that the legal tasks will serve the client's interests but also prevent problems from recurring. If that is the case, then where are we to draw the line between this moderate view and the view of lawyers as wise counselors—in short, "Now What?"

We mean to offer no neat theoretical solutions to these quandaries. Our point is not to advocate a single vision of the lawyer's role in society. Indeed, most lawyers find that there are times that they are called upon to act as wise counselors, as well as times they are called upon to act as technicians. Rather than proclaiming one of these views as correct, we invite you to use all three of these visions of lawyering as tools to help understand some of the problems involved in day-to-day practice.

1.7 CLIENT VIEWS OF OUR ROLES

Though clients do not usually write about their own views of the lawyers' roles (at least not at the length lawyers, judges, and professors do), clients certainly do have views and expectations about what it is their lawyers should do. These views and expectations can, of course, vary enormously from client to client. Some clients come to lawyers looking for wise counselors; some come looking for legal technicians. Some clients come to lawyers looking for little more than competent performance of a specific legal task. For example, a defendant in a fraud case may want nothing more from a lawyer than victory; a corporate client may only want a lawyer to negotiate and draft documents implementing a particular transaction. On the other hand, the defendant may want the lawyer to help restore his reputation in the community; the corporate client may need the lawyer to offer guidance about alternative means of accomplishing the overarching goals of the transaction.

Do the client's choices about what they want or need from a lawyer make a difference? Certainly, a client may have very definite expectations about what the lawyer is paid to do, and these expectations will shape the business agreement between the lawyer and the client. Well then, does a lawyer's choice about the proper role make any difference? Absolutely, but lawyers need to be aware that their own expectations about their role may, at times, be dramatically out of sync with their clients' expectations. If expectations do differ, these differences need to be sorted out near the beginning of the relationship with the client. A client who wants a legal technician may have a great deal of difficulty working with a lawyer who means to serve as a wise counselor. A client who is looking for a wise counselor may feel ill-served by a lawyer who intends to be only a legal technician.

Lawyers who feel that clients routinely have different role expectations are receiving an important signal that they may be working in the wrong law job. The legal technician who is frequently called upon to serve as a wise counselor will feel incompetent and risks not only client dissatisfaction, but malpractice. The wise counselor who is asked to be a technician will chafe at this constraint, risking both professional and moral dissatisfaction. Both lawyers should think seriously about working with different clients.

1.8 THE EXTENT OF CLIENT RELATIONSHIPS

My client is a young woman who doesn't have much money and has come to me to prevent her from being evicted. I can defend the eviction. Should I also advise her to look for a less expensive apartment or to look for a better job? Should I lend the client some money to buy groceries? Should I offer to take her apartment-hunting?

My client is a corporation that makes popcorn. The client has come to me and asked for trademark advice about a package design. There is no trademark problem with the design, but should I tell my client that the design is similar to packaging for an old brand of cat food? Should I advise the client to diversify their product line? Should I tell the client that I think their popcorn tastes bad?

At some point in practice, every lawyer—even those who see themselves as a wise counselor—faces the question of where to draw the line between legal advice and unwanted meddling. Clients come to lawyers with a wide variety of problems, and those problems have dimensions that raise issues well beyond the substance of our professional training. The line is not always easy to draw, but there are times when it must be drawn.

When it is time to draw the line, it is helpful to remember that there is a difference between a lawyer and a friend. Our friends usually have more freedom than our clients. We can decide to risk the friendship and say to a friend, "You need to change your life," or even, "What a stupid decision!" If they don't like us, our friends can choose new companions. Our clients do not always have this choice. Clients come to the lawyer having made business or life choices that may seem to have been unwise or worse. As lawyers, we need to be reasonably accepting and non-judgmental about those past choices. We also need to remember that even clients seeking wise counselors come to a lawyer's office looking for **legal** advice.

D. THINKING LIKE A PRACTICING LAWYER

1.9 SOURCES OF LAWS

Working within our legal system requires an understanding of the law itself, the sources of law, and factors that influence the development of law. Our society has developed and relies on the law for a variety of purposes. Our law regulates relationships and transactions, adjudicates disputes, articulates public values and behavioral norms, acts as a mechanism for organizing society, and establishes the parameters of rights or responsibilities for society. Our law is both autonomous and derivative, as are its sources.

The obvious sources are the common law, statutes, regulations, rules, constitutional provisions, and customs. Another primary source is you. Your clients come to you for legal advice and results. What you tell them and what you do for them will be the law that determines what they do and do not do. Your knowledge, understanding, and interpretation of the law form the basis of your legal advice.

More law is developed in the law offices of attorneys than in all the cases, statutes, and other legal sources you study during law school. Whether they are right or wrong, these lawyers shape and influence the law for their clients. This law is as significant to these parties as the issuance of judicial opinions and the enactment of statutes. If you are going to be a primary source of law, you want to be as right as you can be. This is certainly an incentive to study more and stay current on legal developments, isn't it?

The law today is a broad and demanding enterprise. Law has assumed, for better or worse, a much greater role in our society today than it has in prior generations or in other societies. Modern law is a multi-disciplinary enterprise, requiring lawyers to have a broad-based understanding of the many facets of law and other areas of learning. There are many factors that touch and influence the status and development of the law.

Economics. Macroeconomics views how law distributes wealth and affects income; microeconomics views how individual clients affect and are influenced by the law. The economics of practice also shape the law. Attorneys, as good business people, may only do or promote certain things they are compensated to do. Issues may be pursued and disputes resolved because economic forces encourage or allow resolution. Other important matters may be left untouched because of the lack of economic resources.

Sociological trends. Our society tends to view the law as a panacea for many issues and problems. Our citizens rely on lawyers for all sorts of assistance, while other cultures and societies look to other professions for this help. The number of lawyers in our society, and their individual and collective power, reflect society's reliance on your profession-to-be.

Psychological influences. We are, it seems, for better or worse, a society of individuals with varying psychological perspectives. We may not want to hold ourselves individually accountable, but want to insist that others are accountable to us. We may not want to take responsibility for events that happened to us, and prefer to blame others for problems that touch our lives. We may want to solve our own problems, while increasingly relying on attorneys and other professionals to help us. We may complain there are too many lawyers while retaining these lawyers to represent us in increasing numbers. We may complain about our civil justice system while continuing to pursue new and innovative legal theories and remedies. For whatever reasons our society does these things, we lawyers provide this service.

Political trends. Partisan politics affects the kinds and numbers of laws enacted and the judicial philosophy which predominates our federal and state benches. Less partisan political trends such as attitudes toward the government, views about government intervention, ethical norms, feelings about individual freedom, and confidence in private economic markets, also significantly affect the law. Political attitudes have in the past spawned growth industries in the law. Lawyers as legislators, the growth of administrative agencies and regulation, the passage of numerous statutes, and the increasing reliance on lawyers as advocates reflect political beliefs.

Public policy. Whatever it is, however it is defined, whoever conceives it, public policy shapes the law. The grounding of this public policy reflects views of the American government. Should the federal government retain or expand its power and control, or share more of it? Should state and local government reclaim areas ceded to the federal government over the past few decades? Should there be greater or lesser legislative, administrative, and judicial interference with our public and private lives? Your view, your clients' view, and societal views of these public policy issues affect the law.

Jurisprudential thinking. The legal academy contains a chorus of different multi-disciplinary and theoretical voices. Legal realism, the law and society movement, critical legal studies, feminist jurisprudence, critical race theory, and other schools of thought affect the development of law in court rooms and offices. Although much of this debate may seem irrelevant to whether a Minnesota county court should grant a defense motion for summary judgment, much is not. The trend of jurisprudential thinking about the nature of law and adjudication can be harnessed by attorneys to better advise a client and advocate a client's case. Positions taken by a client or arguments advanced by an advocate can be clothed by some positive law such as precedent or legislation and can also be made persuasive when the defined issues include fairness, efficiency, due process or the enhancement of other widely accepted values.

Outstanding lawyers are both generalists and specialists. Your goal should be to become a well-rounded student of the law, both because of the epistemological reasons described in this section and because well-rounded persons are usually more effective attorneys. They better understand the role of the multi-disciplinary factors, they possess a better sense of appropriate and inappropriate behavior, and they are able to be more creative and adaptable.

Knowing everything can be very tiring. Keeping current can be exhausting. You need to rely upon others to help you understand the major influences on the law. Experts, colleagues, authors, friends, family, scholars, directors, artists, and poets can tell us much about the law. It should now be apparent to you that you can learn a lot about the law from sources outside of law school. But you should still attend your classes.

We suggest as part of the course requirements for this course and other law school classes that you learn as much as you can about the various factors that comprise the multi-disciplinary facets of the law. Books, newspapers, magazines, television, movies, theater, software, CD–ROM, and Internet provide sources of the law that will make you a better lawyer. But finish reading this book first and viewing the companion videotapes.

1.10 THE ROLE OF THE THINKING LAWYER

What is it to think like a lawyer? Lawyers think similarly and differently than other professionals. Law school initially, and some may say primarily, teaches you legal reasoning and critical analysis, along with how to read even (and odd-numbered) footnotes with understanding and how to write clearly or ambiguously. This book broadens this scope of thinking to include the professional skills appearing in the table of contents.

When professors tell you to "think like a lawyer," they are usually advising you to be analytical, to reason with "rigor." Critical analysis is an important skill for a lawyer, but you will need more than analytical thinking to succeed in practice. You will also need to think *creatively* and *productively*

1.10.1 Thinking Creatively

Telling someone "Be creative!" is a lot like telling someone "Be smart!" or "Be really persuasive!" No one can disagree with the advice because, after all, no one would tell a lawyer:

"Be really dull and unimaginative." The advice isn't very helpful, however, because it simply points to a destination when what is really needed is a pathway to that destination. It is not easy to explain how to be creative, but there are some steps that will help develop creative thinking:

- Move beyond the first thought
- Move beyond the traditional
- Move beyond "lawyer" approaches

Move Beyond the First Thought. When a client brings a legal problem or concern to a lawyer and asks for advice, one approach to dealing with the problem will usually occur to the lawyer fairly quickly. This "first thought" approach may be obvious or it may be subtle. It may be the standard approach; it may be the approach the lawyer has used before; it may be the least costly approach; it may be the easiest approach. Whatever its merits, this "first thought" approach has one significant drawback. This first thought may stifle any second thought or third thought. Rather than attempting to think of alternatives, the lawyer may focus efforts on perfecting and implementing the first thought.

Novice lawyers in particular need to resist this impulse. The first thought may possibly be the best, but there is no way of knowing that unless the lawyer has second and third thoughts as well. One of the best ways to move beyond the first thought approach is to imagine that it is not an alternative for this client: "If this approach weren't available, what would the alternatives be?" Finding the answer to that question—through research, investigation, or cogitation—is the first step to thinking creatively. The assumption that the first thought approach isn't available is important, because it forces the lawyer to think seriously about other alternatives. Without the assumption, it is too easy to dismiss alternative approaches as inferior to the first thought.

Move Beyond the Traditional. The second step toward creative thinking is moving beyond traditional legal approaches to a problem. Moving beyond the traditional means thinking imaginatively about the range of legal remedies available to the client, and considering new or different ways of solving familiar problems. Is there a new statute or new case that creates an alternative remedy? Is there a different way of structuring the transaction? Different and new certainly do not mean better—in fact, approaches to problems often become the "traditional" way of doing things because they work well. But a willingness to at least **consider** the different or new is another step toward creative thinking.

Move Beyond "Lawyer" Approaches. An important part of creative thinking is **not** thinking like a lawyer. Solutions involving the justice system, lawyers, litigation, and paperwork are all well and good—but they tend to be expensive and time-consuming. Not all client concerns and problems will bear this time and expense. Sometimes solutions involving quick telephone calls, client-conducted negotiations or other lawful forms of self-help better meet clients' overarching and immediate goals. The lawyer who fails to consider these solutions is failing the client and failing to think creatively.

1.10.2   Thinking Productively

The realities of practice make productive thinking as important as creative thinking. Imaginative lawyers also need to be practical lawyers. The options and choices lawyers present to clients need to be workable, plausible solutions. Lawyers are well-attuned to the practical limitations they deal with on a daily basis, and lawyers tend to take these limitations into account when presenting options to clients. Most lawyers would recognize, for example, that time spent crafting a legally implausible option for a client is time spent unproductively (unless they are trying to emulate bad lawyering).

Productive thinking requires more than attention to the limitations of the law and legal process. It also requires lawyers to be attuned to the practical limitations their clients face. Too often, lawyers (and law professors) create options that work in the law office or courtroom, but not in the "real world." The best remedy for this problem is a thorough understanding of a client's immediate and overarching goals and of a client's process preferences. For example, a lawyer who loses sight of these goals may suggest a "scorched earth" litigation strategy to resolve a dispute with one of the client's long-time customers. Taking the time to understand the client's goals will help prevent this. Taking the time to match legal strategies with client goals will insure that thinking is productive, as well as creative.

1.11 SMART PREPARATION

Some things in life go better if spontaneous and unplanned, such as improvisation. Good lawyering is not an extemporaneous comedy routine, although it may seem that way on a particularly hectic day. Lawyering activities generally work best for all concerned when they occur within a matrix of planning. This is a maxim for all lawyering including transaction work and dispute resolution.

In all phases of practice, the concept of planned lawyering starts well before the lawyer's specific preparation for a particular client in a specific situation or case. Most lawyers today are specialists. They do not attempt to represent every client in every situation. Good lawyers recognize that they may lack adequate competence in an area, or that it is not cost effective for the client to subsidize the lawyer's obtaining adequate competence. Part of good preparation is knowing what you can and should do and what others can and should do.

Once a lawyer has a defined practice, planning usually means assessing the client's situation and organizing the strategy for achieving the client's objectives. The objective sought may be positive, affirmative, and even grandiose ("acquire the Omega corporation" or "file a class action lawsuit against the federal government") or may consist largely of damage control (protect the business or consumer client from bankruptcy). The client's needs and interests require an attorney to develop a strategy (a general policy for dealing with the situation) and tactics (particular steps for implementing the strategy). Subsequent chapters will discuss what clients need from us and how we can effectively plan for specific situations and cases. Part of that process involves initial planning and preparation such as:

Exploring applicable law. The lawyer needs to both review the current law and consider proposing new law. The substantive law of the jurisdiction determines what law applies. Other courses you take in law school help prepare you for this planning. The lawyer may also need to create a legal theory or remedy by developing a good faith argument expanding existing law. Usually this process occurs in small increments in an evolutionary way. Occasionally, it occurs in a revolutionary way with a big bang.

Finding facts. The lawyer must also gather and create facts. Fact gathering includes learning about all sorts of information about a client's situation or case. The lawyer may also need to "create" information by shaping and molding the information that is gathered.

Selecting the right approach. Whether it is transactional or dispute resolution work, the lawyer must select the most effective approach to satisfy the client's needs and interests. There are almost always alternative approaches to situations and cases lawyers need to assess. Selecting the right one can be difficult, but so is law school. It can be done.

Developing a plan. The lawyer needs to develop details of the plan. Sports lawyers call them game plans; religious lawyers call them God's plan. This plan consists of strategies, tactics, and techniques to get what the client wants.

Predicting the future. Various aspects of planning require the lawyer to predict the future. Effective planning means anticipating problems and setbacks. Dealing with other lawyers and decision makers requires the attorney to predict how they may react and what they might do. It helps to be naturally clairvoyant but extra sensory legal abilities can be developed through experience.

Helping the Client. The lawyer throughout planning needs to continually review how the client is doing. Circumstances of a situation determine the scope of this concern. Two important areas of concern are cost and time. An attorney needs to develop and implement a plan that is cost effective and time efficient. Other areas of concern may include business and personal matters. Does the plan advance or hinder the business of the client? How may the plan affect the psychological and emotional state of a client? A lawyer needs to remember that real people are involved and affected, most directly the client.

Implementing the plan. Just do it. And don't unnecessarily run over anyone, or get stepped on doing it. The remainder of this book focuses on implementing the plan.

Modifying the plan. The attorney will likely need to adjust elements of the plan as it is implemented. Change, as Euclid suggested, is constant.

Getting sufficient rest. And you thought planning would be the easy part of practice.

1.12　YOUR GOAL AS A LAWYER

Your goal is to be a good a lawyer as you can be. What is it that makes good lawyers? What is it that some lawyers have that make them better, sometimes much better, than other lawyers?

We know what it is not. It is not just law school class rank (although, you should still try to do your best). Nor is it pure knowledge of the law, nor is it an understanding of the skills it takes to be an excellent lawyer.

Several things combine to make a good lawyer. One is a yearning to be good. It could happen accidentally, but usually it takes a desire. Another is preparation. There is no substitute for concentrated work, most of the time. And another—and perhaps the most significant—is judgment.

Judgment is as judgment appears. It is difficult to define and categorize. When it happens, everyone knows it. When it happens occasionally, it may only be serendipity. When it happens more often, it is good lawyering. When it happens a lot, it is wisdom.

Your goal of being a good lawyer is to develop good judgment. It is the one elemental thing law schools attempt to develop. It is the primary thing law firms look for in new lawyers. It is why clients retain us again and again.

Now, where are all those clients who want you?

Part One
LAWYER AND CLIENT RELATIONSHIPS

Chapter Two
THE BUSINESS OF LAWYERING

I've been in this business for fifteen years, and most of that time I've spent doing accounting work for lawyers. When I started working with lawyers, I was amazed how little most of them knew about running a business. It doesn't surprise me anymore.

Oh, don't get me wrong. The lawyers I work with are very intelligent, very capable, very competent people. It's just that many don't know very much about what it takes to manage a business.

Maybe they're too confident, and they don't think they need to ask any questions. Maybe they're just embarrassed to admit there are questions they don't know how to answer. Or, maybe they just don't see themselves as business people. They are, though.

You would think that law school would teach lawyers how to practice the business side of law as well, but I guess not.

What do they teach these people in law school anyway?

A. INTRODUCTION
2.1 WORKING AS A BUSINESSPERSON

Are we professionals or businesspersons? Most of us enter the practice of law with at least some devotion to the lofty ideal of being "a professional." Yet we need to earn a living and pay back all those loans from law school as well. Are we entering a business or a profession? Well, of course, the practice of law is both. Weren't you told this when you began first year?

The original "professions" were law, medicine and theology. The term profession traditionally was associated with advanced study, service to humanity, and a special set of ethical standards. This was distinguished from being "in trade," where goods or technical skills were exchanged in kind or for money and that exchange was an end in itself. When society was divided explicitly into classes, professionals became elevated to a higher class status than those engaged in trade. The "Inns of Court" in London fostered a multi-tiered status, even among lawyers, as English barristers tried cases and solicitors represented clients and collected and distributed fees in part to the barristers.

2.2 THE LOST, OR FOUND, PROFESSION

Lawyers have always sought to earn a living at their calling, and there has always been a business aspect to the practice of law. Several factors over the last decades have caused lawyers and their clients to pay more attention to the business side of law practice. These factors have resulted in some lamentation about lost "professionalism" and some dissatisfaction with practice.

First, the supply of lawyers has increased dramatically in recent years. According to Economics 101, that means that lawyers' prices should go down. It also means that competitive pressure among lawyers will increase dramatically.

Second, the bar is no longer the homogeneous men's club it was before World War II. The GI Bill made it possible for many men—particularly children of immigrants—who earlier would not have had the opportunity—to go to college and professional school. The Civil Rights movement and the women's movement also changed the demographics of law school and the profession. The close relationships among the members of the bar—to the extent they existed as remembered—have been disrupted by the newcomers: some assumptions are no longer shared, some trust has been shaken or replaced with wariness.

Third, lawyers' expectations for their earnings have increased as has the cost of a law degree. Logically, the number of billable hours required to achieve that degree and those earnings has gone up as well. Much longer working hours and the result—more one-dimensional lives—have increased dissatisfaction within the profession and led to criticism of its seeming obsession with marketing and billing to the detriment of public service and personal satisfaction.

At their worst, these changes have combined to make lawyers feel their value as a lawyer is measured in "billable hours."

Every minute of their days must be accounted for and charged to some client, so that the teaching of new associates, informal (i.e., nonbillable) interchange with clients and with colleagues, and family and community life are either made impossible or rendered invisible to the firm.

On the other hand, the marketplace law of supply and demand has seen a renewed emphasis on client service as clients ask for more in a buyers' market. Law firms are learning that clients do not want to be treated primarily as profit centers. Client demand is causing the pendulum to swing back to an emphasis on good communication and efficient service. Law firm practices, such as charging the client for every cup of coffee during meetings, are receding as clients ask that those costs be included in basic hourly charges.

New lawyers should not take any law office business norms for granted, because those norms change—are changing—in response to the market. Rather, law practice business norms should be examined, understood, and adopted or revised in accord with lawyer and client needs. You as a lawyer can set high client satisfaction expectations, more humane work norms, or more modest material expectations. You will have this choice to make before and during the practice you choose, or the practice that chooses you.

The following sections highlight some of the various business aspects of practice.

B. THE ORGANIZATION
2.3 ORGANIZING THE PRACTICE ENTITY

All practicing lawyers practice in some form of business entity. Some (notably in-house counsel) are true employees of another entity, most are either employees (as associates) or owners or co-owners of what may loosely be called a "law firm." Government lawyers are invariably employees of some public entity. The key is to select the best organizational entity for your firm.

2.4 LAW FIRM SHAPES AND SIZES

Law firms come in all sizes and shapes, though a few forms predominate.

Sole Proprietorships. This conventional form of small business is termed in lawyers' parlance the "solo practice." It is sought after by many because it is a remarkably simple organization, with a noted shortage of "bosses." The ability to "be on one's own" is one of the attractions of this form. It is essentially the alter ego of the proprietor, and often has a business name that is the proprietor's name following the phrase "Law Office of." Sole practitioners may also adopt some form of professional corporation, but there may be no good reason to do so.

Partnerships. The partnership is the traditional form for all law practices involving more than one lawyer. Partnerships are easy to establish (a written agreement isn't even legally required, but usually recommended) and a large body of partnership law defines the rights and obligations of partners. Many partnerships have been created informally between two lawyers who decided to join forces to practice together.

Professional corporations. In the 1960's and 70's most states allowed professionals, including doctors, accountants and other professions as well as lawyers, to incorporate as "professional corporations." Though similar to business corporations, professional corporations are generally covered by a different statute, and the nature of the limitations on liability are somewhat different. The statutes generally require the entity to include "P.C.," "S.C.," "Ltd.," or "Chartered" in the firm name to give notice of the limited liability.

Limited Liability Companies. Limited Liability Companies ("L.L.C.'s") became available in the 1980's in many states. The L.L.C. allows a business to have some attributes of a corporation and some of the advantages, particularly tax treatment, of individual ownership. Some states have a variation of the L.L.C. for professionals, called a Professional Limited Liability Company ("P.L.L.C.") This form is probably superior to the older professional corporation, though it is not as well-established.

Limited Liability Partnerships. This form, and its specialized sibling for professional entities, the professional limited liability partnership ("P.L.L.P."), has most recently been established by statutes in an expanding number of states. This form allows the firm to retain most of the characteristics of partnership, but to add to the partnership the limited liability features of L.L.C.'s or business corporations. A P.L.L.P. allows its partners to be partners, rather than shareholders. If all this doesn't make sense, you may want to seek H.E.L.P. to decide what you should do.

In addition to those owning a private practice, many lawyers practice law as employees of public entities or private corporations. Some individuals even employ a lawyer for their own affairs. And with the ever expanding number of lawyers in this country, eventually every American family can have it's own live-in lawyer.

C. THE SEARCH

2.5 ATTRACTING AND RETAINING CLIENTS

By some means, every practitioner needs to develop and cultivate clients, and the more the merrier (within reason), although quality (i.e. financial resources) may be more vital than quantity. As the practice of law has become more bottom-line oriented, this truth is becoming more recognized. In larger firms a lawyer may not need to cultivate clients immediately upon embarking on practice, but eventually all practitioners want or need to develop clients of their own.

Marketing 101 students learn that an important part of marketing is developing a product (or service) to sell that customers (or "clients" as we prefer to call them) want or need. Developing legal ability and even excellence is a great way to start developing a practice. This ability may be in a narrow area of law or in a number of broad areas. Eventually lawyers are rewarded for handling cases competently and professionally. Clients call with a new matter to handle, and former adversaries may call to hire you or refer a matter to you. They can call you whenever they want.

In addition to having the ability or expertise to handle legal matters, somehow that ability has to be known to clients. In some cases, you will have developed that expertise on behalf of a client with repeat legal business, and the client will call again. More often, legal business comes from getting the word out to other prospective clients and referral sources. In practice, many lawyers get a majority of their work from other lawyers. Being nice—and very good—does pay.

2.5.1 Referrals

A significant portion of most lawyers' new business comes from referrals—from clients, other lawyers, even from former opposing parties. Referrals can be encouraged by letting referral sources know of your availability and interest in handling additional matters. Lawyers also encourage referrals by letting the potential referral sources know they will competently handle matters and will bill fairly. A referring lawyer should want, more than anything, to know that the client will be happy with the referral recommendation. Some referring lawyers want to know that by referring a single matter to the new lawyer, especially where the referral is prompted by a conflict of interest relating to the single referred matter, the new lawyer will not take all the client's business. Some lawyers want to be assured that if they make a referral it will be reciprocated. Such an understanding, though not uncommon, raises ethical issues relating to the motivation for and independence of the referral advice. An agreement to pay a referral fee may be unethical, especially if the referring attorney performs no work.

Referrals come for all sorts of reasons. Actual expertise and personal experience with the lawyer may prompt a referral. In many cases, the referring lawyer will make a referral based on reputation, knowing of a lawyer's writings, CLE speeches, the handling of a well-known case, or any number of other factors. A lawyer setting up a private practice probably wants to maximize all these potential reasons for referrals. Unfortunately, perfect law school attendance is not a significant reason.

2.5.2 Advertising

There was a time when lawyers simply didn't advertise, or at least when they only advertised in "dignified" ways. Simple yellow-page listings of name and phone number were allowed, as were "tombstone" announcements in the newspaper of new firms. These forms of advertising continue to be all many large firms with established practices want. Federal and state court decisions and professional rules, however, now permit expanded advertising. Many lawyers use a wide variety of more extensive (and more expensive) advertising, including print ads, radio and television spots, direct mailings, and subliminal ads in books (but not this one . . . you don't feel an urge to call one of us, do you?)

The nature of a lawyer's practice may determine the wisdom of advertising and the type of advertising, if any, likely to bear fruit or clients. Blanketing the airwaves with half-hourly TV ads is an expensive way to troll for prospective clients. If a lawyer entering practice plans to advertise for clients, the advertising program should probably be targeted to a specific type of client and type of legal matter. And, if you decide to do it, be sure to wear the right make-up.

D. THE MONEY

2.6 CHARGING FEES

The essence of private—as opposed to public interest or government—practice of law is the hiring of the lawyer by a client. Payment for services rendered is a fundamental part of the relationship. Some lawyers even enjoy sending bills. More enjoy getting paid, however.

The overall fee must be reasonable regardless of how it is calculated. Fees may be charged in a variety of ways, or a hybrid of the following ways.

2.6.1 Hourly Billing

Many lawyers charge clients an hourly fee for the time the lawyer spends working on the client's matter. This method of billing is particularly common when the lawyer is defending the client in civil litigation or counseling the client on a business matter. Most lawyers billing by the hour charge clients their normal hourly rate for all their time spent working for the client, including time for legal research, fact investigation, and discussions with the client. Some lawyers charge less than their hourly rate for travel time or other "non-productive" time; some lawyers do not charge their clients at all for this time; others charge their full hourly rate. Lawyers billing by the hour should charge their clients on the basis of the number of minutes worked, including all preparation, thinking, and event work.

Some lawyers record their time on the basis of tenths or quarter hours for the time charged.

2.6.2   Contingent Fees

Lawyers representing plaintiffs in civil litigation frequently charge their clients "contingent fees." Typically, this means that the client will pay the lawyer a portion of the total recovery as a fee. If the lawyer fails to recover on behalf of the client, then the lawyer will receive no fee. The percentage of recovery lawyers request as a contingent fee varies according to the lawyer's experience and reputation, as well as the type of the case. A typical contingent fee in a plaintiff's personal injury action would be thirty-three percent. Most jurisdictions forbid a lawyer from charging contingent fees when representing divorce clients or criminal defendants.

2.6.3   Flat Fees

A third common fee structure is the flat fee or base fee. A lawyer charging this fee will agree to handle the client's legal matter for a fixed sum. The client pays this sum regardless of the outcome of the matter, or the client pays the fixed sum plus some additional flat amount if, for example, an appeal is filed.

2.6.4   Hybrid Fees

A variation or combination of these three fee structures may comprise value billing. A portion of the fee may be figured on an hourly or flat fee rate, and another portion may be based on a contingency fee. Other factors that affect the amount of a fee are the case's complexity, novelty, and value to the client.

2.6.5   Costs

Most lawyers also require their clients to reimburse them for costs associated with handling their legal matters. Indeed, the Rules of Professional Responsibility usually require clients to pay litigation costs, though lawyers may advance clients these costs until the completion of litigation. Lawyers charge clients for filing fees and process serving, and many also charge for the costs of services such as photocopying, printing, or telephone calls. In addition, lawyers also require clients to reimburse costs associated with taking depositions, hiring expert witnesses, and travel related to the client's matter. During the last decade, some lawyers have charged clients amounts for services such as photocopying that exceed the lawyer's direct or actual costs for those services. A lawyer charging for "costs" in this fashion should discuss this practice with clients at the outset of the attorney-client relationship, and have a really good explanation.

2.6.6 Retainers

Quite often, a lawyer will require a client to make an initial, up-front payment before beginning work. This payment is usually called a retainer. If the lawyer is billing the client on an hourly basis, the lawyer's time may be charged against the retainer. The lawyer may also draw on the retainer to pay costs and expenses associated with work on behalf of the client. Typically, lawyers are required to return, at the end of their work for particular clients, any advance payment of unearned fees.

2.6.7 Billing Mechanics

For many years, most lawyers sent clients bills that contained precious little information other than the total amount the client owed the lawyer. Quite often, lawyers would not bill a client until completion of work. Times have changed. Now it is a common practice for lawyers to send clients bills that contain a detailed day-by-day description of the different tasks done for the client and an indication of how long each individual task took. Many lawyers now bill clients on a regular quarterly or monthly basis. Contingent fees are an exception to this practice, of course. Contingent fees are collected at the time the settlement or judgment is paid.

2.6.8 Written Business Agreements

The applicable ethical or disciplinary rules may require a fee agreement to be in writing, especially if it is a contingent fee agreement. Regardless of whether this is required by the rules, however, prudent lawyers put all fee agreements in writing. This practice avoids disputes later in the relationship, and may preserve the attorney-client relationship. Furthermore, the written business agreement provides the lawyer with an excellent framework and checklist for the discussions with the client. At some point prior to beginning work for the client, the lawyer can walk the client through the business agreement step-by-step. This will provide the client ample opportunity to ask questions about billing and about the work the lawyer will do. The fee agreement need not be cumbersome or arcane. An engagement letter can simply welcome the opportunity to assist the client, confirm the terms of the representation, the fee to be charged, the basis for reimbursement of expenses, the right to withdraw, and any other matters that warrant preservation.

E. THE PROTECTION
2.7 INSURING AGAINST MALPRACTICE

Malpractice insurance is an important consideration for any lawyer in private practice. The premium is one of the more significant expenses the lawyer incurs. Insurance is only part of what lawyers think of more broadly as "risk management." Of course, if you know for certain no one will ever perceive you made even an itsy-bitsy error, then you won't need insurance.

2.7.1 Risk Management

Risk management in a law firm includes a number of important components. The most important part of the program ought to be prevention of malpractice. This is essentially "quality control," and is intended to assure that the legal work performed by the lawyer or the firm is of the quality the firm expects and of the quality the client expects. Another important part of risk management is the prevention of claims. Many malpractice claims occur not because the lawyer has deviated in any way from the standard of care for lawyers. Rather, lawyers get sued because clients are dissatisfied with the services rendered, without particular regard to the quality of the legal work. One good example of how lawyers doing good work still get sued is failure to communicate. A client whose calls and inquiries go unanswered, or even the patient client who doesn't inquire but also doesn't hear anything, builds up a dangerous dissatisfaction with the lawyer. This is true regardless of whether the lawyer has won discovery battles increasing the value of the client's case, has done brilliant research to clinch a deal, or has done other wonderful things. Clients have a right to know promptly what you are doing and why, and how you are spending their money.

2.7.2 Insurance

Insurance against professional liabilities (e.g., malpractice) is the last defense. Although not required in most states, it offers important protection to the lawyer against a wide variety of potential liabilities. Buying the insurance includes protection against any liability that may be found (the indemnity provision of the policy) as well as the defense of any claims that are made (the defense provision).

This protection can be very comforting, and especially satisfying if it unfortunately has to be used. In professional liability matters, the defense obligation may be more valuable since a large number of claims are ultimately dismissed without any indemnity payment. Although the quality of defense offered may vary considerably from insurer to insurer, there is value to most lawyers in being able to turn the claim over to the insurer and letting assigned defense counsel take care of it. After all, you don't want to have to represent yourself, and run the risk of having a fool for a client.

Professional liability insurance is usually available from a number of different insurance carriers. Many state bar associations have "captive" insurers for this coverage; more have arrangements with an "endorsed" insurer that offers a standard policy on standard terms. Other domestic carriers operate in most states, and larger captive insurers may be available, such as for large law firms or for members of some national bar association group. These insurers offer policies either tailored to the particular type of firm or law practice. Larger firms or firms needing either tailor-made coverage or special considerations in insurance may find custom insurance written through large carriers, or battleships.

F. THE OPERATIONS
2.8 OPERATING A LAW PRACTICE

Set up a firm, hang out the shingle, win a few cases, send some bills, retire to Bali Hai. What could be easier?

In practice, running a law practice is an arduous and time-consuming task which causes many lawyers stress and distress. The ability to practice law without the concerns of running a practice is one thing that draws many lawyers to large firms or law departments. Operating a law practice involves a plethora of minute details. Arrangements for an office, access to a conference room, provision of computer and telecommunications support, all require attention. Colleagues and other staff require ongoing management time and attention.

Despite the challenges, it is possible to run a law practice for fun and profit. Equipment to assist in the practice is widely available. Copiers, fax machines, telephones, voice mail, filing systems, and similar office equipment and systems permit an efficient practice. Staff and personnel are also readily available. Office sharing arrangements, trained paralegals, and employee leasing arrangements provide experienced support staff. A law office can be set up with a minimum of effort (and at much lower cost than years ago).

It is impossible now to think of practicing law without access to computers in various forms. Sometimes thought to be the province of large firms, in fact the computer has become a significant tool of the small firm. It has also become an important tool to permit a small office to be essentially "self-contained." A solo practitioner in a small community may, by access to Westlaw or a CD–ROM disk, have the equivalent of a large firm library immediately at hand. Similarly, word processing systems and moderately-priced computers allow lawyers to create the highest quality legal documents efficiently regardless of the size of the firm. Law management computer systems also offer the small firm or solo practitioners sophisticated accounting and billing capabilities.

A variety of essential tasks can be accomplished through computer communications. Access to legal research databases, predominantly Westlaw and Lexis, and to more general databases such as Dialog, is now viewed as an indispensable part of legal research. Communication over networks, including the Internet, CompuServe, ABA–Net and numerous others is also very important and helpful to lawyers. Many courts, and more all the time, provide access to court records electronically.

Communications software also allows transfer of documents electronically. This obviates the delay caused by mail, the expense of overnight courier and of facsimile transmission. Even lengthy documents can be transmitted to clients or other lawyers for review. The process may take only a few seconds to place a document on the desk of a colleague two time zones away. Fax boards and software allow transmissions of documents that never exist in tangible form on paper.

Computer systems also manage and retrieve the masses of documents created or used in discovery and in litigation, arbitration, or other disputes. Once exclusively the province of high stakes litigation involving large number of documents, advocacy support software is now available and useful in small cases. Many firms automate all but the smallest cases.

We hesitate to say much more about law office equipment and systems, for fear that anything we say will be obsolete before this book becomes a best seller. You can choose to have an actual or a virtual office, equipment that will allow you to work at home or (oh, no) at the cabin, and network systems that permit you to communicate with anyone, any place, any time. Move over Bill Gates.

2.9 EMPLOYING AND MANAGING STAFF

Most lawyers in private practice quickly become employers, or at least supervisors, of others shortly after they begin practice. And even if you work by yourself, you still have to tell yourself what needs to be done. Supervising others is not a skill everyone has, and certainly is not one deeply cultivated in law school. Nonetheless, lawyers generally find themselves employing, either directly or indirectly, receptionists, messengers, file clerks, legal assistants, law clerks, paralegals, and other personnel. In addition to hiring these people, the lawyer must supervise them. This is an express ethical responsibility under the Model Rules of Professional Conduct. It is also common sense.

The lawyer's role as employer also carries with it the duty to comply with broad and increasingly complex employment law requirements. These may include enforcing discrimination laws, providing a safe workplace, accommodating workers' disabilities, and complying with wage and hour laws. Whether you want to or not, you or someone else in your firm will need to know all about employment laws and obligations.

2.10 PAYING TAXES

Another important detail of practicing law is paying taxes. Lawyers obviously have to pay their own income taxes, at least if they generate income (which is the good news). Failure to do so may subject the lawyer to professional discipline (as if the tax law penalties were insufficient). Lawyers also may be required to collect and pay a sales or service tax on the services they render, though most states have avoided imposing this particularly burdensome form of misery tax. As employers, lawyers or law firms must withhold and pay various taxes on behalf of their employees. Yes, the practice of law can be taxing, but now the real fun begins when the client seeks help from you.

Chapter Three
INTERVIEWING: WHAT WE NEED FROM OUR CLIENTS

My first client. I wonder what to expect.

This is a wonderful profession. Someone is about to share with me a part of their life, and I will have the privilege of helping them. Maybe it will be a major crisis in their life they need me to help them resolve. Maybe it will be about their hopes and their dreams. Or maybe they will want me to create something for them. I'm ready for it all.

Am I? I think I know what it means to be a lawyer. Well, I don't know everything about the law, but I do know where to look and whom to call. Or I'll find out.

I remember sitting in law school and wondering when this day would come. It's here. Am I going to like this as much as I hoped? Being a lawyer is going to be a challenge. Being a lawyer had better be fun and rewarding as well.

I think everything is in place. I like the office, although I do wish I could have gotten a better view. I hope I meet my client's expectations of what a lawyer should be.

The client is here now. The moment has come. . . . That's my client?

A. INTRODUCTION
3.1 FOUR ELEMENTS

In a nutshell, when a lawyer in private practice is working with a client, that lawyer needs four things: trust, information, direction, and a business agreement. This chapter offers some guidance about all four, as well as some suggestions about preparing for and conducting the first meeting with a client.

B. BUILDING TRUST
3.2 WHAT DOES TRUST MEAN?

When a client trusts a lawyer, that client has:

- Faith in the lawyer's fidelity
- A belief in the lawyer's competence
- Some degree of comfort when dealing with the lawyer

Faith in a lawyer's fidelity means that the client understands that the lawyer will keep confidences, will put the client's interests ahead of the lawyer's own, and will continue to work on the client's behalf despite unforeseen problems and unexpected inconveniences. To be sure, a client cannot reasonably expect a lawyer's undying devotion. If a client believes that the lawyer will abandon the case when the going gets rough, however, that client will never trust the lawyer.

Likewise, a client need not believe that a lawyer can perform miracles in order to trust the lawyer, but trust cannot grow without client confidence in a lawyer's ability. Clients hire lawyers because they need help accomplishing tasks they cannot undertake themselves. Clients realize that they must rely on the special skills that lawyers have. If a client does not believe the lawyer is—at a minimum—competent, then that client will not trust the lawyer.

For many clients, dealing with lawyers is not a particularly pleasant experience. People typically visit lawyers either because they have a problem or because they are afraid they may have a problem sometime soon. Consequently, almost by definition, a client is a person under stress. So it is undoubtedly asking too much to hope that any client will ever say "Oh goody! Today is the day I get to talk with my lawyer." Nonetheless, it is not too much to hope that a client be able to tell a lawyer sensitive or even damaging information. To do this, a client must feel some measure of comfort when dealing with the lawyer.

Faith in the lawyer's fidelity, belief in the lawyer's competence, and comfort when dealing with the lawyer all are part of the client's trust in the lawyer. These three elements work together to foster trust, each reinforcing the other two. For example, a client who has faith in the lawyer's fidelity will feel more comfortable telling the lawyer damaging information because the client will be less worried that the lawyer will sever the relationship due to the damaging information.

3.2.1 Why Is Trust Important?

Clients who trust their lawyers are clients who are willing to provide the lawyer with needed information and appropriate direction. Lawyers do not want clients who hide sensitive information or insist on watching over the lawyers' every step. In addition, clients who trust their lawyers are clients who bring their business back. Without trust, a client will neither talk nor listen to the lawyer.

3.2.2 Why Is Trust Elusive?

Trust between a lawyer and client may be elusive. Many people are somewhat distrustful of all lawyers. A client may be initially distrustful of a lawyer, and may not feel any real trust for the lawyer until time and experience prove the lawyer trustworthy. There may be nothing that the lawyer can immediately do to dispel suspicion, but along the way, there are steps that the lawyer can take to build a client's trust.

3.3 COMPETENT COMMUNICATION

The first step in building a client's trust is competent communication. There is no substitute for regular communication with a client, and nothing can do more to prevent client dissatisfaction with the lawyer. A lawyer can build trust and goodwill simply by making regular progress reports to the client. The client who has to call the lawyer in order to find out what is going on is the client who begins to suspect that the lawyer is hiding something.

Competent communication is clear and comprehensible. Law school teaches us wonderful words that delight our professors and baffle our friends. These are the words to lay aside when talking with clients, however. A lawyer may hope to use technical legal terms to impress a client, but the actual effect is likely to be the opposite. A client is apt to distrust a lawyer who rattles off legalese, believing that the lawyer has resorted to this foreign language in order to hide the truth.

Competent communication must also be open and accurate. No one enjoys receiving bad news, but sooner or later every lawyer must give a client bad news. If the lawyer is straightforward with the client, the client is much more likely to develop respect and trust for the lawyer. Clients do not like bad news, but they will accept it more willingly if it does not come as a complete surprise. If a lawyer's communication with a client has been clear and regular, no bad news should come as a complete surprise.

3.3.1   Good Listening

Listening is as important to building trust as talking. Good listening is more than simply keeping quiet while a client talks. Good listening begins with the ability to listen to a client while keeping an open mind. No client is well-served by a lawyer who is impatient and overly judgmental. A lawyer needs to be able to listen to a client and suspend judgment until all the facts are in. Snap decisions and quick judgments close the mind and interfere with good listening. The good listener learns to wait patiently— not for the client to finish talking, but for the story to unfold completely.

Good listening helps build trust only so long as the client believes that the lawyer is indeed hearing what is being said. Good eye contact and encouraging nods of the head may help persuade the client that the lawyer is listening, but thoughtful and perceptive responses will work even better. The lawyer who can suspend judgment to listen both sympathetically and critical- ly will find it much easier to respond to the client with percep- tion, emotion, and honesty.

3.3.2   Appropriate Comfort

Client trust depends in part on client comfort while working with the lawyer. The lawyer can do much to foster client comfort by sending signals to the client that will put the client at ease. Three types of signals are particularly reassuring to clients: signals of competence, signals of empathy, and signals of safety.

Signals of Competence. A lawyer sends a signal of compe- tence to reassure a client that the lawyer is a trained profession- al capable of dealing with the client's concern. A lawyer can signal competence in a variety of ways, such as explaining the relevant law, talking about past experience with the kind of problem that concerns the client, or suggesting creative solutions to the problem.

Example: Ms. Cullen, I think we may be able to work out a solution to this problem. This is an area of law I'm familiar with, and I think you have more options than you may realize. . . .

Signals of competence may also feel reassuring to the lawyer, and there is a temptation to signal competence more often than needed. A little goes a long way. The danger of self-professed competence is that the reassurance begins to ring hollow fairly soon. The client who listens to repeated signals of competence will first feel that the lawyer is boasting and then feel that the lawyer is insecure.

Signals of Empathy. A signal of empathy is meant to reassure clients that the lawyer understands and cares about the concerns the client has expressed. Signals of empathy are powerful tools, particularly when dealing with a client who has strong emotions about a legal problem. The lawyer can signal empathy by expressly recognizing the client's emotion and then explaining why that emotion seems appropriate.

Example: Mr. Lamar, you seem very upset about what has happened to you, and I can understand that. You have been a good tenant for many years, and now the landlord is refusing to make these repairs. That must seem very unfair.

Signals of Safety. At times, a lawyer can best foster trust by sending the client a signal of safety. The signal of safety is meant to reassure the client that the lawyer will remain loyal to the client. The signal of safety is particularly useful when the client is concerned about revealing sensitive or damaging information.

Example: Mr. Lamar, you seem worried about your discussion with the landlord. It sounds like you got pretty angry during that discussion. I want you to feel free to tell me everything you can remember about that conversation. I promise you, I won't be shocked by what you say. I've worked with a lot of clients that got mad at their landlords.

3.3.3 Faithful Silence

Careless talk about confidential matters is a breach of professional ethics and a threat to the attorney-client privilege. Careless talk about client confidences is also devastating to client trust. Clients have interesting problems and tell lawyers interesting things. It is natural for a lawyer to want to talk about these things—especially with other lawyers. New lawyers need to be particularly wary of this temptation. Legal communities are much smaller than they at first seem to be, and it is surprising how quickly stories spread.

C. OBTAINING INFORMATION

3.4 WHAT INFORMATION DO WE NEED FROM CLIENTS?

What information is relevant to a lawyer? At the beginning of practice, most new lawyers answer this question too narrowly. This is hardly surprising. Almost everything about our professional training schools us to answer every question we are asked as narrowly as possible. In the classroom, we are challenged to state the precise holding in the appellate court decision and then articulate the few critical facts on which that holding rests. We break down torts and crimes into a small handful of elements and then recite the key facts that prove those elements. Outside the classroom in the world of practice, work with clients is refreshingly wide open. What is relevant is not defined by narrow rules or simple formulas. Instead of narrowing our questions, the work we do with clients asks that we open our minds and broaden the scope of our inquiry.

When we are working with clients, the information that is relevant can be loosely grouped into three different categories: data, background, and context. A lawyer needs a client to provide information in all three categories.

3.4.1 Data

The category "data" is meant to suggest cold, hard facts—the kind of information that seems the most immediately relevant to the description of any legal issue. This category includes two kinds of information: "legal data" and "narrative data."

"Legal data" is the information immediately relevant to a client's cause of action or legal problem. It is the easiest information for a lawyer to ask about because everything in our training has taught us to care about this kind of information. Appellate decisions are filled with the information we describe as "legal data." When a client comes to a lawyer with a contract problem, chances are the lawyer's mind fills with questions about offer, acceptance, and consideration. For the most part, the information that answers these questions is legal data.

"Narrative data" is information about the events that gave rise to the client's legal problem or cause of action. In a contract action, narrative data is information about the negotiations leading to the agreement, the drafting and signing of the contract, and the breach of the contract. Simply put, narrative data is the step-by-step account of the events that brought the client to see the lawyer.

3.4.2 Background Information

"Background information" is the explanation of the circumstances that encompass the events of the client's legal problem or cause of action. It is the kind of information that gives greater depth and texture to the flat narrative data that describes the client's legal concerns. For example, if a client is concerned that a customer has breached a contract, the lawyer may seek information about the client's business, whether there is an industry custom about the formation of contracts, or whether the client had dealt with that customer before.

3.4.3 Context

"Context" is information about a client's insights, motives, preferences, and concerns. In our breach of contract situation, the client may have suspicions about why the customer breached the contract, reasons for wanting to negotiate a settlement with the customer, and insight about whether or not the customer is trustworthy. This is information about the client context.

3.4.4 Why Is Information Important?

The importance of legal and narrative data is self-apparent. If a lawyer is going to represent a client, the lawyer needs an account of the events that gave rise to the need for representation. In most circumstances, the client is going to be one of the most important sources for this information.

The question that is more perplexing for new attorneys is why any information **other than data** is important. The fact of the matter is that information about background and context may be just as critical for the lawyer's understanding of the legal issues bedeviling the client. Cold, hard data may help the lawyer understand **what** events have occurred, but background and context information may be more important to the lawyer for understanding **why** these events occurred.

Information—data, background, and context—helps the lawyer assess the client's legal concerns and give effective advice. This same information serves a second purpose, moreover. At some point quite early in the work with a client, a lawyer needs to make a decision about whether to accept representation of the client. There is no question that legal and narrative data will help a lawyer make this decision. Listening to the client's explanation of background and context information may be just as important in assessing whether or not the lawyer can represent the client.

3.5 TECHNIQUES FOR OBTAINING INFORMATION

Lawyers obtain information from many different sources. The lawyer's own client is one of the most important sources of information. In fact, the client may be the only available source for some of this information. This section discusses how a lawyer can obtain information from a client. Other sections (e.g., Chapter 10) discuss information gathering from others.

Typically, much of the initial interview between the lawyer and client is devoted to obtaining information. Your goal is to achieve completion, clarity, and closure. The process of obtaining information does not end with that first interview, however. Across the course of representation, things change. The client's life or business may alter in a way that has a direct impact on the work the lawyer is doing. The client may develop greater trust in the attorney and reveal information not previously discussed.

3.6 BUILDING A NARRATIVE

A nearly complete narrative can be developed with a client with the use of a few helpful approaches.

3.6.1 The Opening Snapshot

One of the first principles of traveling is if you don't know where you're going, it's hard to get there. This same principle applies to work with clients. It is difficult to conduct a detailed interview of any client until you have some sense of what the interview is all about. Usually an attorney will have information, at a minimum, about the general type of problem that has caused the client to seek out a lawyer. Often, however, a lawyer may know little more than the client has had a problem with a landlord or needs advice about a domestic dispute.

For this reason, it is often very helpful to ask clients for an initial broad-based description of their legal problems. In a sense, this description is a quick "snapshot" of the client's legal concern. With this picture in hand, the lawyer will have a better understanding of the client's later explanation of events and be able to ask more intelligent and cogent questions.

Care should be taken, however, not to make snap decisions on the basis of this snapshot. A client's one-minute description of a complicated series of events is inherently subjective and necessarily limited. At times, a client will give a quick picture of events that differs radically from the more detailed description.

3.6.2 The Videotape

After obtaining a quick picture of the legal problem to serve as a guide, it is often productive to ask a client to give a more detailed narrative of the events leading up to that problem. Since most people tell stories chronologically, it usually makes sense to ask clients to give an account of what happened from start to finish. Essentially, the client is narrating a "video" of the events that led up to the client's decision to seek legal advice. A chronological account of events is often the best choice, but it is certainly not the only choice. If it makes more sense, a lawyer could ask a client to recount facts topic-by-topic or begin with critical events and move on to less important events.

One of the best ways to begin a client's narrative is to fix the time of the first event and simply ask a client to describe what happened next:

Example: Ms. Cullen, you've told me that you're here because you've had problems with your tenant. When did you lease the store?.... What was the first problem?.... What happened next?

Some clients can give a surprisingly detailed narrative description of events if the lawyer simply invites them to do so. Some, of course, are going to need more help. Generally speaking, however, it is worthwhile to permit a client to attempt a description of events with a minimum of prompting or assistance from the lawyer. This may require patient listening but it will be patience well-rewarded. Letting the client tell the story may help put the client at ease and help the lawyer develop a sense of the client's credibility and persuasiveness.

3.6.3   Neutral Prompts

Even the most articulate clients will occasionally need assistance when giving a narrative account of events. One of the most effective ways of assisting a client is offering a "neutral prompt." A neutral prompt is a question or comment that moves the video forward without suggesting the content of the next scene. Neutral prompts are useful when the client has lost the thread of the narrative and needs help to move forward.

The Top Five Neutral Prompts—Verbal Division

- Please go on.
- What happened next?
- Can you tell me more about that?
- What did you say then?
- You just mentioned [Event X]. What happened after that?

These verbal neutral prompts can be very effective in moving a narrative forward and they can also be very effective in reassuring a client that the lawyer is listening to the client and following the narrative. Sometimes a non-verbal prompt may be even more helpful. For purposes of reassuring a client, almost nothing beats a sympathetic nod of the head, good eye contact, and patient silence.

3.6.4 Directive Prompts

Directive prompts are comments or questions that move a narrative forward and **do** contain a suggestion about the content of the next event described. When a lawyer asks a client for information about a specific event or subject then that lawyer is using a directive prompt.

> **Example:** Ms. Cullen, did you have a conversation with your tenant about water problems in the store?

Directive prompts are particularly useful to focus the client's attention on a particular issue of concern to the lawyer. They are also useful in moving the narrative to a new event.

The risk associated with directive prompts is that they do re-focus the client. When the lawyer uses a directive prompt to suggest a discussion of a new topic, the client may be upset at being interrupted or also may lose track of the narrative and forget to tell the lawyer something important. There is also a chance that a directive prompt may cause a client to feel pressured to provide details about the topic the lawyer has suggested, even though the client cannot remember those details. Lawyers should not phrase directive prompts in a way that encourages clients to make up details:

> **Example:** Mr. Lamar, I'm sure your landlord must have assured you the store had no water problems. Could you tell me about those conversations?

During the client's narration of events, it is usually wise to use directive prompts sparingly. If the client is narrating events in a reasonably concise and cogent fashion, allow the client to complete the narrative with a minimum of interruptions.

3.6.5 Time Posting

As the client moves through a narrative description of events, it is extremely helpful to keep track of the date or time of critical events. Often, the client will supply these during the course of the narrative. If the client does not, the lawyer may simply ask a question such as, "When did that happen?" At the

end of the client's narrative, the lawyer will have a rough
chronology of the critical events. This will assist the lawyer in
structuring the remainder of the interview and it will also flag
any significant chronological gaps in the client's narrative.

3.6.6 Recapping

"Recapping" is one of the most powerful tools for building a
complete narrative. When a client has finished the narrative,
the lawyer may briefly recap or summarize what the client has
said. There are two advantages to doing this. First, it gives the
client and the lawyer the opportunity to clear up any misunderstanding before the interview continues. Second, recapping is an
opportunity for the lawyer to signal competent listening and
empathetic understanding of the client's situation.

If the client's initial narrative description is fairly brief, then
it may make sense for the lawyer to recap the entire narrative
once the client has finished. Sometimes, a client will need to
describe a more complex set of events or want to give a more
detailed narrative description. In these situations, it may make
more sense for the lawyer to recap each topic as the client
finishes.

3.7 PROBING FOR ADDITIONAL INFORMATION

Once the lawyer has a reasonably complete narrative and
chronology, the lawyer can begin to probe for more detailed
information. Two particularly useful probing techniques are
"flashback" and "slow-motion."

3.7.1 Flashback

Flashback is an extremely simple technique used to probe
for background or context information. Quite often, clients will
focus on data during their narrative description of events and
omit background or context information. A lawyer can use
flashback to fill in these gaps. After hearing the narrative, the
lawyer can decide what background and context information
would be helpful. The lawyer can then identify a specific incident or party and directly ask for background or context information.

Examples:

Mr. Lamar, you mentioned that plaster fell from the ceiling in the store in May. Can you tell me about the first time you noticed any problems with the roof or ceiling?

Ms. Parker, you said that your customer, Madison Brickwork, failed to pay you for the October shipment. Tell me more about Madison. When did your company first begin doing business with them?

Captain Ahab, you say that this whale was following the *Pequod*. Why do you think the whale would do that? Had you had dealings with this whale before?

A flashback gives the client the opportunity to provide this kind of background and context information. It is information that can do much to explain the events in the narrative.

3.7.2 Slow–Motion

One of the most common techniques used to probe for additional information is "slow-motion." A lawyer using this technique identifies a particular event from the narrative and then asks the client to recount that event in step-by-step manner. The lawyer and the client can explore the event in greater detail, with the lawyer asking progressively more specific, directed questions.

If the client has given only a brief sketch of the event during the narrative, the lawyer may want to begin probing with an open-ended inquiry:

Example: Ms. Cullen, you said you had a conversation with your property manager about repairs he made at the store. I'd like you to tell me everything you can about that conversation.

Once the client has given a reasonably detailed narrative description of the event, the lawyer can make some decisions about what further information would be useful. This is the time for the lawyer to use knowledge of legal doctrine and intelligent curiosity to guide further questioning. It is also the time for the lawyer to use more directive prompts and closed-ended questions.

For filling in details about narrative data, background, and context information, the lawyer needs to use who, what, where, when, how, and why questions.

Examples: Ms. Cullen, I have some more questions about the conversation you had with your property manager.

Where did the conversation take place?

Who else was present?

When did the conversation take place?

How long did the conversation last?

What did the property manager say about the roof?

Why did you ask the property manager to make these repairs?

Information about legal data may require more directed questions. Quite often, a lawyer will want information about a key legal point that a client will talk about only in passing or, perhaps, not at all. The lawyer may need to ask about these issues directly:

Example: Mr. Lamar, when did you first notify your landlord about the problems?

One of the most common mistakes new lawyers make is relying too heavily on these kind of questions. Most clients feel some discomfort about talking to lawyers. Directed, closed-ended questions about legal data can increase that discomfort and make the client feel as if the lawyer is conducting a cross-examination. A little patience can do much to help this problem. Direct questioning of this sort should be put on hold until the client has had a fair opportunity to explain events.

3.8 DIFFICULTIES IN OBTAINING INFORMATION

Clients are often the first and best source of information for lawyers. They are only human, however, so they are not perfect sources of information. At times, a client may at first be reluctant or unable to give the lawyer important information. This section discusses techniques that a lawyer can use when faced with some of the more common difficulties in obtaining information. Care should be taken, however, particularly at the initial meeting, not to press a client too hard.

Loss of memory is another common obstacle a lawyer faces while obtaining information. A lawyer may want information about an event that took place years before. Details that may seem critically important in the law office may have seemed trivial at the time they transpired. Whatever the reason, clients often have difficulty remembering all the information a lawyer might desire.

There are a number of ways to help a client revive a dim recollection. One of the best places to begin is to remember that while lawyers are intently focused on the written and spoken word, many other people are not. Rather than attempting to prompt clients to remember words, it is frequently more useful to help clients remember situations and events.

Three common techniques for refreshing memory are described below: setting the scene, the triggering detail, and other sources. A lawyer should keep in mind, however, that clients are human, and like all of us subject to all the vagaries of memory. Even the most skillful lawyer will find some recollections that simply cannot be refreshed. Pushing a client too hard can only cause a lapse of trust or a lapse of integrity. Neither is desirable.

3.8.1 Setting the Scene

Frequently, a client may initially recall little more about a meeting than the fact that the meeting occurred. The lawyer may be most interested in learning what was said at the meeting, but pressing the client for details of the conversation will probably be futile. Visual images can often be a springboard to better memory. Consequently, the lawyer can ask the client to recall as much as possible about the setting of the meeting:

Example: M. Proust, you say you don't remember much about the meeting. When was the meeting? ... What time of day? ... Who was present? ... Where were you all sitting? ... Did you have lunch during the meeting? ... What did you have to eat?

By encouraging the client to recall details about the physical setting of the meeting, the lawyer may foster recollection of the conversations during the meeting.

3.8.2 The Triggering Detail

Sometimes memory can be triggered by a single unusual detail. Whether the client remembers the detail that sparks the memory may depend on the lawyer. Any lawyer can ask the client, "Do you remember anything at all about that day? Anything unusual?" The question will not yield a lot of information unless the lawyer has the patience to wait for the client to answer, and the client feels sufficiently at ease. If the lawyer is patient and the client at ease, however, it is surprising how often this simple question can yield worthwhile information.

3.8.3 Help From Other Sources

A great deal of information—particularly where business or government is concerned—is set down in writing. A lawyer may also have information from witnesses other than the client. Often, information from these other sources can be used to refresh a client's memory. Sometimes the simplest way to restore a client's memory is to tell the client about the information available and see if the client can add anything. It is often best to use other methods of refreshing a client's memory first, however, since many people are reluctant to admit to a recollection at odds with a written record. Lawyers should also remember that in most jurisdictions, writings used to refresh witness' recollections are subject to discovery production.

3.8.4 Sensitive Subjects

Sometimes lawyers want information that clients are reluctant to divulge. This may be information that concerns a sensitive or personal topic or this may be information that the client believes jeopardizes a position. Either way, the client may not have enough trust in the lawyer to reveal the information. Often the best solution for the lawyer is to wait until the client feels more trust. If the lawyer does a good job fostering trust, the client may feel it is safe or appropriate to reveal the information. Sometimes postponing discussion of sensitive issues until later in the same interview will be enough to give the client confidence to speak freely. If not, the lawyer may want to wait to revisit these topics until a later meeting with the client.

This approach may not always be possible. If a client is reluctant to talk about sensitive issues, there are things a lawyer can do to put that client at ease. First, the lawyer may want to build trust by reassuring the client of the lawyer's fidelity.

> **Example:** Ms. Cullen, I understand your reluctance to talk about this issue, but I want you to know that I have a duty to keep confidential everything you tell me.

Alternatively, it may help for the lawyer to explain why it is important for the client to reveal the information:

> **Example:** Mr. Lamar, I know this isn't easy to talk about, but I need this information in order to do a good job preparing your case. When I sit down to talk with the other side, it's important I know as much as possible about this situation. I don't want to be surprised.

By building trust and explaining the need for the information, it is often possible to encourage clients to talk about sensitive issues.

3.8.5   Agenda Differences

A client may feel a particular event or issue is extremely important and want to devote a great deal of time talking about that event or issue. This may create problems, particularly if the attorney feels that other issues or events merit more attention. An attempt to steer the client toward another subject may worsen the difficulty. The client may feel that the lawyer has underestimated the importance of the event and resist any attempt to change the subject.

A lawyer faced with this kind of difficulty should offer reassurance that the client's concerns are taken seriously and also offer appropriate empathy. Quite often, a client will insist on continuing discussion of an emotional issue because the lawyer has not signaled any understanding of the client's distress. Once the lawyer has reassured the client, the client may feel more comfortable moving onto other issues. This technique can be coupled with an explanation about the importance of discussing additional issues and events.

> **Example:** Mr. Bingham, I understand you are very upset about the way your supervisor treated you. I know how difficult it can be to work for a boss that treats you that way. I'm glad you've told me about this problem, and I know it's something we'll talk about more. I also need to spend some time today hearing about other things that happened to you. During the half-hour we have left, can you tell me about. . . .

3.8.6 Snap Judgments

Law school teaches us to make a decision quickly and then conform the facts at hand to that decision. This may be a good habit in the classroom, but it can be disastrous in the office. A quick decision can interfere with listening; it is hard to hear when your mind is already made up. The lawyer who keeps an open mind is the lawyer who listens best, and the lawyer who listens best is invariably the lawyer who is the most successful in obtaining information from a client.

Sometimes, a lawyer may be unable to agree with or perhaps even understand a decision that a client has made. When a client tells a lawyer about an action that seems foolish or wrong, the temptation to respond judgmentally should be resisted. The more appropriate response is to seek additional context information. This may both foster greater understanding of the client and greater trust between the lawyer and client.

D.   ELICITING DIRECTION

One of the most important things a lawyer needs from a client is direction. From the first meeting with a client through the termination of the lawyer-client relationship, a lawyer needs to build and update an understanding of what it is that the client wants.

3.9 WHY IS DIRECTION IMPORTANT?

An understanding of a client's goals will help the lawyer in two ways. First, provided that the client's goal is lawful and ethical, that goal should serve as the lawyer's lodestar. The client's goal should guide the lawyer's actions during the course of representation. Second, it is worthwhile for the client to articulate goals and for the lawyer and client to reach an express understanding of those goals. This will help the lawyer make later decisions about appropriate legal advice and may also help prevent the client from forming unrealistic expectations about what the lawyer can achieve.

All this may seem self-evident, but it is surprising how often a new lawyer may neglect to promptly elicit this sort of direction from a client. For example, a client meets with a novice lawyer to talk about an eviction notice. The attorney begins by asking the client many questions to obtain information needed to defend against the eviction. The client grows increasingly frustrated and finally interrupts the lawyer to explain that she no longer wants to live in the apartment. Oops. The client has asked for legal advice about eviction. The assumption that the client wants to avoid eviction is a natural one, but it is inappropriate. It is the lawyer's responsibility to elicit direction from the client, and the first step in eliciting that direction is explicitly asking what the client wants.

3.10   WHAT IS DIRECTION?

As discussed in the previous section, the direction that a lawyer needs from a client has a lot to do with the client's goals—what it is that the client wants to happen. These goals may have much to do with, for example, a particular verdict in a lawsuit. On the other hand, a client may also have goals that are important for the lawyer to understand, and yet entirely outside the province of the judge or jury.

3.10.1   Immediate Goals

"Immediate goals" are the desires a client has related to the solution of some particular problem or concern. Put simply, an immediate goal may be a particular verdict in a lawsuit or the negotiation of a particular transaction. A lawyer needs the client to articulate immediate goals so the lawyer can determine whether they can be achieved and, if so, to guide the lawyer's activities and efforts on the client's behalf.

Immediate goals have a lot to do with the substantive outcome of the concern that brings the client to the lawyer.

Sometimes the client may define the immediate goal narrowly, for example, in terms of dollars obtained, deals made, or policies revised. Sometimes the client may define the immediate goal more broadly, in terms of the client's sense of a just or acceptable outcome. Often, a client will articulate an immediate goal subject to certain time constraints. For example, a client might tell a lawyer to complete a particular transaction, but only if it is possible to do so before the end of the year. The time constraint "before the end of the year" is part and parcel of the client's immediate goal.

3.10.2 Overarching Goals

In addition to immediate goals, all clients also have "overarching goals." These are the goals that the client will want to achieve even after the lawyer has helped achieve the immediate goals. For a corporate client, one of the principle overarching goals is maximizing profit. An individual client might have an overarching goal of maintaining a working relationship with the opposing party or avoiding publicity.

A lawyer needs to develop an understanding of a client's overarching goals, as well. Some avenues to a client's immediate goals may run afoul of overarching goals. A lawyer who fails to understand the client's overarching goals runs the risk of winning the battle for the client, while losing the war.

3.10.3 Process Preferences

There may have been a time when lawyers could take for granted the process used to achieve client goals, or make those decisions about process without consulting the client. Those times have come and gone. Today, clients can make more choices about legal processes and about lawyers than ever before—and today, clients are increasingly asking to make those decisions themselves.

Alternative dispute resolution and rising legal costs have certainly played a part in this. There are a growing number of business and corporate clients who not only want to decide whether to arbitrate or litigate a matter, but also want to decide whether to file a summary judgment motion or conduct exhaustive legal research. Factors other than cost, however, also shape client process preferences. Business clients may have preferences influenced by their vision of their own corporate style or culture or by their level of risk adversion. In much the same way, individuals may have ethical, emotional, or personal preferences with respect to particular types of legal process. For example, either a corporation or individual might object to an overly aggressive approach to litigation—not for reasons of cost, but because that approach would create unwanted ill will. A lawyer needs to talk expressly with clients about these types of issues.

3.11 HOW SHOULD A LAWYER ELICIT DIRECTION FROM A CLIENT?

By asking. Too many lawyers don't or don't soon enough. Unfortunately, simply saying to a client, "By the way, what are your goals?" is unlikely to be enough.

3.11.1 Techniques for Eliciting Direction

There are three cardinal rules for eliciting direction from a client: discuss the issue expressly, broadly, and frequently. First and foremost, a lawyer must expressly discuss direction, goals, and preferences with the client. The lawyer's assumptions about what the client wants have no value, and the lawyer that acts on those assumptions invites not only client dissatisfaction but malpractice suits. A lawyer needs to know what a client wants, and the only way to find out is to ask expressly.

Second, a lawyer should discuss the issue broadly. The client may not volunteer any information about overarching goals or process preferences. The lawyer must be sufficiently astute to raise these issues for the client's consideration. It is not enough to talk only about the client's immediate goals. A lawyer may elicit direction in much the same way information is obtained from the client: Begin with an open-ended question raising the issues and then follow-up with more specific questions about immediate and overarching goals, as well as process preferences.

Example: Mr. Lamar, you've told me that you want to sue your landlord to force her to make repairs to the building. Let me ask some additional questions about what is important to you. How important is it for you to remain in the building? ... Would you feel comfortable continuing to lease space from a landlord you had sued? ... You've mentioned you are extremely busy with work at your store. This lawsuit will require some of your time and attention, too. Can you spare that time right now?

The third cardinal rule about eliciting direction is to discuss the issue frequently. Clients' lives and businesses change; so too, do their goals and preferences. What seemed most important to the client at the initial meeting with the lawyer may later become only a secondary consideration. Some clients may volunteer information about these sorts of changes, to be sure, but it is the lawyer's responsibility to update this understanding about what it is the client wants.

3.11.2   Limits on Client Direction

It would be easier to be a lawyer if we could refer all the hard decisions to our clients. Alas, we cannot. There are many decisions that a lawyer will typically make and, in fact, may be inappropriate to ask a client to make. These boundaries may differ from client to client. Some clients—particularly those with a great deal of experience dealing with lawyers—may want to give direction to the lawyer on a variety of issues that other clients prefer to leave to the lawyer's discretion.

The lawyer should elicit direction from the client, but the lawyer should not necessarily accept that direction at face value. Sometimes the client may offer direction that the lawyer believes is ethically wrong. The lawyer should not follow directions that would violate the law or the Rules of Professional Responsibility. If the lawyer believes that the client has goals that seem to the lawyer to be unethical or immoral, then the lawyer may also wish to refuse the client's direction.

Beyond ethical reservations, the lawyer has the responsibility to alert a client if the client's overarching goals seem inconsistent with the client's immediate goals and process preferences. The lawyer also has the responsibility to "reality test" the client's immediate goals. If those immediate goals are not realistic, then the lawyer should discuss these reservations with the client. This process of client decision-making is discussed in greater depth in the next chapter, "What a Client Needs from the Lawyer."

E.   FORMING A BUSINESS AGREEMENT

The hardest subject for new lawyers to discuss with clients is fees. Yet every lawyer in private practice needs to be able to talk confidently and responsibly about fees. Every lawyer—whether in private practice or not—also needs to talk with clients about the practical limitations of legal representation. Discussion and accord about these issues is necessary for a successful business agreement between lawyer and client. Section 2.6 explained fees, costs, and retainers, and is "worth" another look now. Sorry.

3.12   RESPONSIBILITY ISSUES

The business agreement between a lawyer and client needs to cover more than the payment of fees. The lawyer and the client also need to reach an understanding of issues such as:

- The identity of the individual lawyer or lawyers who will actually perform the work on the client's behalf.
- The responsibilities the client may have, such as keeping the lawyer apprised of any change of address.
- The reasons for which either the client or the lawyer can terminate the agreement.
- The method by which fee disputes or other disagreements can be resolved, such as the inclusion of a pre-dispute arbitration clause.

This list is not, of course, complete. A lawyer should give attention to additional issues that need discussion and agreement at the outset of work for any new client and, in all likelihood, at the outset of new work for any existing client. These are issues that need to be considered by lawyers even when they are handling matters on a pro bono basis.

3.13   WHY IS A BUSINESS AGREEMENT WITH A CLIENT IMPORTANT?

The work lawyers do for clients is the basis of their livelihood. The business agreement is one very important part of the contract between lawyer and client. Early discussion and agreement with respect to business issues will make it easier for a lawyer to collect fees and can also prevent serious problems of misunderstanding and dissatisfaction later on.

From the client's standpoint, no one wants to agree to buy anything without knowing what the cost will be. The client purchasing legal services has a right to understand the cost of those services and the contractual obligations of the attorney-client relationship. This will allow the client to make informed consumer decisions about hiring a lawyer and will also allow the client to make more realistic decisions about immediate goals and process preferences.

3.13.1 How Should a Lawyer Discuss Business With a Client?

Many new lawyers find it difficult to talk about the business aspects of lawyering with clients. A good starting point for new lawyers is to remember that a lawyer owes the client the same duties of candor and competence whether talking about torts or talking about fees. A client is entitled to open and straightforward discussion of the business aspect of the attorney-client relationship.

3.13.2 Talking About Fees and Costs

The growing literature on marketing of legal services is rife with suggestions about how to "sell" fee arrangements to clients. Mercifully, that topic is beyond the scope of this chapter. Instead, we offer these Four Commandments:

Be candid. Explain fully and accurately the fee arrangement (hourly, contingent, flat, or a combination of these) and other costs.

Make sure the client understands this explanation.

Give the client the chance to ask questions. People paying money for services have a right to ask questions. Client questions are an opportunity to clear up possible misunderstandings that could be devastating later in the relationship.

Don't be apologetic. A lawyer is a professional who earns a livelihood by selling legal services. There is no reason to apologize.

A client has the right to expect that a lawyer will adhere to these four rules. Doing anything less courts disaster.

3.13.3   Express Agreement and Authorization

Before doing anything on a client's behalf, the lawyer should make certain that the client has hired the lawyer and agreed to the terms of representation. The best way to make certain of this point is to ask the client directly.

Example: Mr. Lamar, I've explained my fees to you and talked with you about my retainer agreement. I need to know if you want me to represent you. If you do, you should sign the retainer agreement.

The lawyer's notes of the meeting should also reflect this discussion and agreement.

3.13.4   Written Representation Agreement

The best way to finalize the business agreement between the client and lawyer is to put it in writing. Section 2.6 explained the requirements and advantages of doing so. A written agreement helps the client understand what will happen and reduces the chances that future billing problems will arise.

F.   THE FIRST MEETING WITH A CLIENT

First impressions are important. The first meeting between the lawyer and a new client is the lawyer's opportunity to assess the client and determine whether it makes sense to accept representation of the client. It is the client's opportunity to learn whether it makes sense to hire a lawyer and whether this is the lawyer to hire.

3.14   PREPARING FOR THE MEETING

A lawyer usually does not have a great deal of information about a new client prior to the first meeting. Typically, the lawyer or someone from the lawyer's office will have spoken to the client to arrange the time and place for the first meeting.

During this conversation, the client may have given some information about legal concerns. Some lawyers have legal assistants screen clients more thoroughly before the first meeting. If this is the case, then the lawyer can make a more detailed plan for the initial interview. If not, there are still things the lawyer can and should do to prepare for the first meeting.

Review available information about the client. At a minimum, the lawyer will know the client's name, and this gives the lawyer a basis for making a preliminary check for conflicts of interest by reviewing past and current files.

Review available information about the client's concern. The lawyer will typically have some information about the reason the client is seeking legal advice. With this information, the lawyer could, for example, briefly research the basic elements of the legal claim, as well as the common defenses to the claim.

Plan questions. With some information about the client's concern, the lawyer can begin to outline the topics that will need to be covered during the meeting.

Create an agenda. For new lawyers especially, it is helpful to outline not only topics for information-gathering, but all other issues to be covered during the first meeting. The lawyer can look over the retainer agreement and any other documents the client will need to review during the first meeting.

3.15 CHAIRS AND DESKS; PENCILS AND PAPER

Part of successful preparation for any meeting with a client is arranging to have an appropriate place to talk with the client. Often, the client will meet at the lawyer's office. This is undoubtedly more convenient for the lawyer, but may be inconvenient or pose difficulties for the client. If it does, the lawyer can make an "office or house call" or meet at some mutually convenient place. Wherever the meeting occurs, the lawyer should make sure that the interview will take place at a location with:

Privacy. It will be difficult to talk with a client in any location where there is a chance of being overheard. Likewise, the meeting will be more successful if the chances of interruption are minimized. For example, if possible, the lawyer should avoid telephone calls during the interview.

A place for both the client and lawyer to sit and write. A lawyer can carry a clipboard or pad to write on if conducting a meeting at a client's place. In-office interviews eliminate this concern, but create questions about who should sit where. Some lawyers believe that sitting behind a desk during an interview seems unduly remote or even pompous. They may sit on the same side of the desk as the client, offer the client a seat at the side of the desk, or conduct the interview at a table. Other lawyers feel that this is too informal or invasive and may be intimidating to the client. Lawyers should be thoughtful about these issues, and there is probably no single solution that is best. The key is to provide a comfortable environment that will allow *both* the client and the lawyer to do the work needed during the meeting.

Materials to keep notes. Few of us have photographic memories, so note keeping is a necessity for most. Clients may also wish to take notes during the meeting, so it is a good idea to keep a spare pad and pen or pencil available for client use, and share your crayons.

Copies of any necessary documents. The lawyer should be certain to have a copy of the retainer agreement, as well as any other needed forms such as information releases.

G. STRUCTURING THE MEETING

3.16 A SUGGESTION FOR STRUCTURE

Different clients have different concerns, and good lawyers keep their plans and agendas flexible to accommodate these differences. Consequently, this agenda is a suggestion, not a recipe:

1. *Introduction.* After some welcoming talk (how much depends on the client), the lawyer can briefly describe the agenda for the meeting and the amount of time that is available. This gives the client a sense of what will happen. Many clients also appreciate a brief discussion of fees, so they at least know whether they are being charged for the meeting.

2. *Snapshot of concern.* The lawyer can ask the client for a brief overview of the reason the client is seeking legal advice.

3. *Snapshot of immediate goals.* The lawyer can then also ask the client for a brief overview of what the client would like the lawyer to do about this concern.

4. *Narrative "video."* After the lawyer has a concise picture of the client's concerns and goals, the client and lawyer can then develop a more complete narrative "video" of relevant events. When appropriate, the lawyer can recap this narrative.

5. *Probing via "flashback" and "slow-motion."* The lawyer can then seek additional information on a topic-by-topic basis.

6. *More complete discussion of direction.* Once the lawyer has obtained the necessary information, the lawyer and client can have a fuller discussion of immediate and overarching goals, as well as process preferences.

7. *"Next-step" planning.* At this stage, it usually makes sense for the lawyer to give the client some suggestions about what work the lawyer needs to do next or would like to do next. It is usually too soon to give the client a complete description of legal options, but the client needs to have some sense of what the lawyer can do.

8. *Business agreement.* The lawyer can explain the fee structure and agreement, and give the client a chance to ask any questions. If the client chooses to retain the lawyer, then the lawyer can obtain authority from the client to do "next-step" work.

9. *Arrange next contact.* No client should leave a lawyer's office without knowing when the next communication with the lawyer will be. After talking about what will be done next, the lawyer should make a commitment to the client about the next contact.

10. *Barter.* Consider bartering your fees for a trip to your client's cabin on Lake Superior, apartment in Brooklyn, or villa in Casablanca. Or just rent the movie.

Chapter Four
COUNSELING: WHAT CLIENTS NEED FROM US

I need legal help. I don't know what I should do, I'm not sure what I want to do. So here I am waiting to talk to "my" lawyer.

I feel a little uncomfortable because I have criticized the legal profession for having too many lawyers doing unnecessary things. I used to joke about them a lot. My favorite is ... no, now is not the time when I need something done and a lawyer is the best person to do it.

I wonder what to expect? I do want to decide what I should do, but I'd like some guidance on alternatives and costs. Maybe I'll get the lawyer to decide for me ... but only I really know what is best for me.

I hope this one acts like a real lawyer and a real person. I'm willing to pay for expertise, but I also want someone who cares and understands what I need.

What will I do? Well, here comes my lawyer now.... That's my lawyer?

A. WORKING AS A LAWYER: A RANGE OF PERSPECTIVES

Chapter Three discussed what a lawyer needs from the client. In this chapter, our focus shifts to what a client needs from the lawyer. As the lawyer-client relationship develops beyond the initial stages, the lawyer's role becomes more active and, consequently, the client expects to see tangible benefits from the lawyer's services. The primary thing a client expects from a lawyer is sound legal advice. This chapter discusses the process of advising clients and assisting clients in making decisions.

4.1 WHAT IS LEGAL ADVICE?

When a client seeks legal advice from a lawyer, the client has the right to expect the lawyer to do four things:

- Make an assessment of the client's legal problem or concern.

- Suggest options for dealing with that problem or concern.

- Predict the advantages and disadvantages associated with each of those options, including the likelihood of success.

- Assist the client in making decisions about those options.

B. ASSESSMENT

When a person who is ill visits a doctor, that person usually expects the doctor to do two things: diagnose the illness and then cure it. People visiting lawyers have similar expectations. When clients seek legal advice, clients of course hope that the lawyer will "cure" their legal problems. But before those problems or concerns can be dealt with, they must be identified.

4.2 WHAT IS ASSESSMENT?

The process of assessment involves more than listing the issues of concern to the client. Of course, the client and lawyer must work together to identify these issues, but the lawyer must also work to do two additional things. First, the lawyer must determine which issues are ripe for legal advice. Second, the lawyer must determine whether it is possible to represent the client with respect to all of these legal issues, or whether there are issues on the list beyond the lawyer's professional capability.

Clients seldom arrive at the lawyer's office with a detailed list of legal problems, accurately categorized by type, and conveniently matched with the lawyer's area of expertise. More typically, clients come to a lawyer with either a narrative explanation of a problem they would like solved or with a narrative description of a goal they would like achieved. In either situation, the client's concern may potentially trigger several legal and non-legal problems. The lawyer needs to identify these problems and—ultimately—make a decision with the client regarding which problems will be the subject of the lawyer's advice.

Example: Ms. Overholt, you've told me that you're planning on purchasing this land and building a distillery. You have concerns about negotiating and drafting the purchase agreement. I have experience in real estate law, and can help you in that area. It seems to me that you may also need a license to run a distillery. I'm not familiar with licensing procedures for distilleries, so I don't feel I can help you with that. I'd like to talk with another lawyer here in our firm who can help with that problem.

Example: Mr. Bingham, you've told me that your employer fired you. It sounds like you may have a claim for wrongful termination, and we should talk about that further. You've also mentioned that you're very concerned about being unemployed. I wish I could do something that would help you with that concern right away, but of course I can't. You may want to file a claim for unemployment benefits and talk with some job counselors.

4.2.1 Why Is Assessment Important?

The process of legal "diagnosis" is less scientific than medical diagnosis, but it is just as important and, at times, just as complicated. There are three reasons why assessment is an important part of legal advice. First, assessment identifies the legal issues that are the subject of the lawyer's representation of the client. Identification of these issues helps frame the business agreement between the lawyer and the client and also serves as a lodestar for the client and the lawyer. This certainly does not mean that the lawyer should be blind to all other legal concerns. It does mean, however, that the work the lawyer does for the client should be oriented toward the resolution of these identified issues.

Second, assessment also identifies other legal issues that may need attention from some other lawyer. Sometimes new lawyers believe that they have no responsibility to tell clients about legal problems unless the client asks for assistance with those problems, particularly if those problems are outside the scope of the lawyer's professional competence. This view is extremely short-sighted. An internist who detects symptoms of glaucoma has a responsibility to refer the patient to an ophthalmologist. In the same way, a litigator who "diagnoses" a potential tax problem, should make sure the client is aware of the problem and make an appropriate referral. Failure to identify these other legal concerns is not simply a disservice to a client; it may also be malpractice. No lawyer is capable of handling every brand of legal trouble. Consequently, sometimes the most helpful advice a lawyer can give a client is a referral to another lawyer.

Third, it is important for lawyers to expressly recognize some of the problems that a client mentions even when there are no good legal solutions for those problems. One of the most important things you can tell a client is: "You do have a problem, but I'm afraid it's not the kind of problem a lawyer can help you with." Expressly recognizing a client's problem is an appropriate way to signal empathy and a lawyer's failure to at least mention the problem may make the lawyer seem cold and inhuman. In addition, even though it may seem perfectly obvious, it is helpful to actually tell a client that you cannot help with a particular kind of problem. Making this kind of statement will help avoid later problems of dissatisfaction and may prompt the client to seek alternative solutions for the problem.

4.2.2 How Should a Lawyer Assess a Client's Legal Concerns?

Capable and effective assessment depends on a lawyer's ability to identify problems both inside and outside the lawyer's particular area of expertise. This means that it is a lawyer's responsibility to be familiar with a broad range of legal issues, and to keep abreast of new case law, legislation, and legal developments in the jurisdiction. Good assessment skills depend on more than the lawyer's store of knowledge, however. These skills are also dependent on the lawyer's ability to listen and talk to clients about legal problems and concerns.

4.3 LISTENING TO THE CLIENT

Careful listening is the single most important factor in making a competent assessment of a client's legal concerns. Listening would be easy if clients came to our office and said things like: "I have a breach of warranty claim and a possible quantum meruit claim I'd like you to take a look at." They don't, and consequently a lawyer's listening needs to involve more than making an accurate and complete list of the problems the clients mention.

A client will, however, often make a statement about what the client believes the legal problem or concern to be. The first step in careful listening is to take this statement seriously and discuss it with the client. The second step in careful listening is to take this statement as nothing more than what it is—the client's best guess about the legal problem. Listening to the client's statement with a technician's ears may be disastrous. A client cannot fairly be expected to identify all relevant legal concerns and expressly ask for help with each.

A lawyer needs to hear a client as if the lawyer were a wise counselor or problem solver. The lawyer should listen to the client's narrative description of events and goals and determine if there are issues that need attention, even though the client has not identified these issues as concerns.

> **Example:** Ms. Montoya, you've told me about the car accident you had last month and the problems you've had at your job as a result. You said you wanted to bring a lawsuit against the other driver, and we've talked about that. It also sounds to me like your employer has asked you to do work that has made your injury worse. I'd like to talk with you about that also.

All that time spent taking issue-spotter exams pays off at last. The lawyer should, at a minimum, mention each additional issue to the client. Whether the lawyer undertakes to advise the client about every legal concern depends on the client, the nature of the concern, and the lawyer's conception of what is appropriate.

4.4 TALKING TO THE CLIENT

Sometimes careful listening is not enough. On occasion a lawyer will need to elicit information from a client about problems the client has not mentioned, but the lawyer suspects may exist. Additional probing may be necessary.

> **Example:** Now Ms. Montoya, when I asked you about your earnings the last three years, you mentioned you didn't have any tax returns. This is something I need to ask you about.

Did you mean that you didn't have copies of tax returns or did you mean that you didn't file tax returns for those years?

Needless to say, unmentioned legal problems may involve sensitive or embarrassing issues. A lawyer should deal with these concerns carefully, as with any sensitive issues.

C. OPTIONS

4.5 CLIENTS NEED CHOICES

In many situations, the difference between good lawyering and adequate lawyering lies in the ability of the lawyer to generate additional options for the client. The ability to generate choices for clients can spring from many sources. Many lawyers rely on a solid knowledge of the law coupled with years of experience in practice. Novice lawyers must substitute creative and productive thinking for experience. See how in Section 1.10.

4.6 PRESENTING OPTIONS TO THE CLIENT

A client cannot be expected to make an effective choice among options unless the client truly understands those options. Put another way, even the most creative and productive thinking is for naught if the lawyer does a bad job explaining the options born of that thinking. The acid test for presenting options to a client is this: Has the lawyer given the client enough information so that the client can be an effective decision-maker? If not, then the lawyer needs to expand the explanation of that option.

This section reviews some of the most important points a lawyer needs to raise when talking with a client about options and choices. One of the most important items is not included, however. A lawyer not only needs to describe options, a lawyer must also give the client some sense of the likelihood of success of those options. This topic is covered separately at Section 4.7.

4.6.1 Describe the Process

Having created a brilliant list of options for a client, it is not enough for the lawyer to simply name the options and ask the client for a decision. Few clients are likely to know an option by its name. It is the lawyer's responsibility to introduce the option to the client and to remember that the client will need more than a passing familiarity with the option in order to make an effective decision.

One of the easiest mistakes to make while describing an option is to assume that the client understands the intricacies of the legal process. If a lawyer is listing "litigation" as an option, then the lawyer needs to explain what that option means for this client in this case—and the lawyer needs to make that explanation in a language comprehensible to the client. We all know enough not to throw around terms like "res ipsa loquitur" or "original issue discounts" when talking with clients. This is legalese from the 100 proof bottle, and clients resent having it poured down their throats. But we also need to remember that "legalese lite" can be equally offensive and baffling to clients. A lawyer's description of "litigation" may do a client little good if the description is full of terms like "work product" or "summary judgment," or sprinkled with statements such as "Maybe you saw me in The Client and The Pelican Brief?"

> **Example:** Mr. Lamar, if we sue your landlord she will probably want to take your deposition. You've told me you've never had your deposition taken so let me explain what a deposition is. Your landlord's lawyer will probably ask you to come to her office. I will go with you. The lawyer will have a chance to ask you all the questions she thinks she needs to. There won't be a judge there, but there will be a court reporter who will take down all the lawyer's questions and all your answers. The deposition may take several hours.

We do not advise lawyers to talk down to clients. Condescension is also offensive, and some clients have a great deal of familiarity with any number of legal terms of art. A client who knows what a deposition is does not need a full explanation of the process. What we do recommend is that the lawyer remember who the client is and what the client's level of experience is, and make sure that the description of options is appropriate for that client. One of the best ways to help that happen is to invite questions from the client about each option described.

4.6.2 Explain How the Option Fits the Goals

Clients also need to hear why the lawyer believes a particular option is a realistic choice for the client. The lawyer should take the time to explain how the option fits with the client's immediate and overarching goals and the client's process preferences. This may seem obvious to the lawyer, but it may not be as immediately apparent to the client. It is also helpful for the lawyer to give this explanation, because it gives the client an excellent opportunity to correct any misapprehensions the lawyer may have about the client's goals.

> **Example:** Ms. Cullen, I've told you what arbitration is, let me explain why I think it may be an option for you. You've said that it is important to you to resolve this dispute quickly, and you feel that any further negotiation with your tenant would be a waste of time. One of the advantages of arbitration is that it usually takes less time than a lawsuit.

4.6.3 Talk Openly About the Downside

Clients also need to hear about an option's disadvantages. These disadvantages, drawbacks, and downsides must be discussed openly and completely before the client makes a decision. Lawyers need to remember that the client's definition of a disadvantage may not coincide with the lawyer's own. For example, a client may believe that disclosure of personal medical history is enormously invasive and embarrassing. The lawyer may have considered the production of medical records as a fact of life in litigation, and failed to talk about it with the client. Complete discussion of client goals and complete description of options will help avoid these kind of problems.

> **Example:** One of the problems with suing the coal company is that lawsuits are public. If we sue the coal company, Mr. Peevyhouse, your neighbors could find out about the lawsuit and the problems you had with the coal company. The lawsuit might be reported in the newspaper. That could be helpful, but I can see it might cause problems for you. We need to talk about that.

4.6.4 How Much Will It Cost? How Long Will It Take?

No client should ever have to ask these questions. A lawyer should give a client as full and accurate estimate as possible of the cost of an option and the amount of time the option will take to complete. Without this information, no client can be an effective decision maker. A lawyer will seldom know the exact answers to these questions. The client needs to know that the lawyer's answers are estimates, and if those estimates are little more than guesses then the client needs to know that too.

> **Example:** Mr. Peevyhouse, I can't tell you exactly how long a lawsuit might take. It may take two years or more before we can go to trial, and if we win and the coal company appeals, it may take another year or even two before you get a final decision from the courts. Now, there are things we will try to do to speed the process. We can try to convince the company to settle, or we can try to convince the court to decide in your favor without a trial. But if we decide to sue the coal company, I want you to understand that it may take a very long time.

When it comes to costs, more and more clients are insisting on something more than guesses, however. Clients today are far more sensitive to issues relating to legal fees and far more knowledgeable. Many institutional clients, such as insurance companies or corporations, insist on detailed estimates of fees before agreeing to hire counsel. One lawyer might choose to be responsive to this request and view it as an opportunity to involve the client in making decisions about the legal work. Another lawyer might see this kind of client concern as a nuisance. It will be easy for the client to choose between the two.

D. PREDICTIONS

Not all options are equal. Some fit better with a client's goals, some entail fewer disadvantages, and some are more likely to succeed. One of the most important things a client needs to know is which options are more likely to produce successful results. For the client to be an effective decision-maker, the lawyer needs to provide this information.

4.7 PREDICTING SUCCESS

Lawyers cannot write guarantees, and almost all clients understand and accept this. Even the most experienced lawyer cannot give a client a truly accurate assessment of the odds of a particular option resulting in a successful outcome. Clients do need information about an option's relative likelihood of success, and at least some of this information must come from the lawyer.

When lawyers assess an option's likelihood of success there are a wide variety of factors to take into account:

- Has the option proved successful in similar situations in the past (for example, does case law suggest the option is likely to be well-received by the courts or other decision makers)?

- Does the option seem to produce an equitable result? Does it seem fair? Fairer than other alternatives?

- Does the option seem grounded in good public policy?

- Who is likely to oppose the option? Is the opposition willing to compromise? Is the opposition founded on strong legal, equitable, or policy arguments?

Weighing these factors to produce an assessment of the likelihood of success is an art, and it is an art largely learned in the studio of experience. A new lawyer may want to check assessments with another, more experienced lawyer, however, before voicing those assessments to the client. Even an inexperienced lawyer can help a client weigh these factors objectively to estimate which options are relatively more likely to produce successful results, and to estimate whether chances of success are fairly good or fairly remote. All lawyers should also remember that their client's views on some of the factors influencing success (gauging—not gagging—the opposition, for instance) may be more valuable than the lawyer's own.

4.7.1 Describing Success

An estimate of the likelihood of success is not enough. A lawyer also needs to hear a description of success. Too often, lawyers fail to give clients the information necessary to understand what success means. Civil litigation is a perfect example of this problem.

There is nothing like the thrill of winning a jury trial—for the trial lawyer. Many clients, however, find civil litigation and a verdict at trial disappointing. Why? Part of the explanation is that clients are strongly motivated by justice, and trial seldom provides a client with a satisfying experience of justice triumphant. Part of the explanation is that often a civil jury verdict does not result in any immediate tangible benefit for a client. Victorious defendants face the possibility of appeal; victorious plaintiffs face the possibility of appeal and the difficulty of collecting judgment. This is one reason why alternative dispute resolution methods, such as mediation and arbitration, are becoming much more popular: clients prefer them to the end result of litigation.

This doesn't mean that litigation isn't a good option for clients. Sometimes it is. It does mean that part of what a lawyer needs to do is describe what success means. The client needs to hear a description of the immediate results success may yield, and the client also needs to hear a description of the impact success may have on the client's goals. Very few legal solutions prove to be panaceas. Most legal solutions do not achieve client goals, instead they make achievement of those goals easier or possible. Clients who do not understand this limited quality of legal success have difficulty being effective decision makers. For example, many good settlements have been foregone by clients who mistakenly believed that successful verdicts would bring a greater sense of justice and vindication.

4.8 DEVELOPING A LANGUAGE OF PREDICTION

The language of prediction needs to balance competing concerns of certainty and flexibility. Clients would like certainty because they have to make difficult choices and they want as much assurance as possible that those decisions are correct. Lawyers want flexibility because lawyers make predictions in a world where outcomes depend on variables that cannot always be controlled or even identified. Often, a discussion about prediction results in the client pressing for more certainty than the lawyer has given and the lawyer creating more flexibility by hedging on the original answer. This kind of discussion is frustrating for both the lawyer and the client. Jeanne Dixon, where are you?

4.8.1 Establish the Necessity of Flexibility

A lawyer can avoid this dynamic by telling the client that accurate predictions are not possible, and explaining why that is so. Some clients may need to hear this message more than once, but every client should hear this message before any detailed discussion of the likelihood of any option's success.

> **Example:** Ms. Traver, you've asked me whether you think the marketing company will accept our licensing offer. I can't tell you the answer to that question because I don't know the answer. It may depend on whether the company would prefer an outright purchase to a licensing arrangement. That's not something we know right now. That being said, I can tell you....

If the lawyer establishes why flexibility is necessary at the beginning of the discussion, it will help prevent later hedging that is troubling to the client.

4.8.2 Give the Client Reasonably Definite Information

Telling a client "There is a 43.6 percent chance of winning this lawsuit" would be ridiculous (unless you work with Attorney Spock). Lawyers cannot make predictions to that level of certainty. On the other hand, telling a client "I have no idea whether you'll win this suit, your guess is as good as mine" is unfair to the client. Lawyers can make better predictions than that, and have a duty to provide the client with reasonably definite predictions that the client can use to make decisions.

One area where lawyers can offer reasonably definite information is the relative ranking of options. A lawyer may not be able to quantify success, but the lawyer should be able to give the client information about which of a set of options is most likely to yield success.

> **Example:** We can make the offer now or wait. I can't predict the exact odds of our offer being accepted. I can tell you, though, that our offer is more likely to be accepted now

than it would be if we made it after two more months of negotiation. Here's why I believe that. . . .

In most situations, a lawyer can also give a client reasonably definite information about whether chances of success are good or remote.

Example: I think there is a good chance that we will win this motion. In fact, I would be surprised if we lost. Here's why I believe that. . . .

Explaining the factors underlying the prediction gives the client at least some basis for assessing the accuracy of the prediction. A client may, of course, push for a more definitive prediction. Many clients like lawyers to quantify answers. Before quantifying any prediction, a lawyer should consider whether the answer will really be sufficiently accurate to improve the client's decision-making ability. If the lawyer believes a more exact prediction is possible, the lawyer may want to give the client a range of probabilities.

Example: What are our chances of winning the appeal? I can't tell you exactly. I can tell you that I think our chances are better than one in ten, I don't think our chances are as good as one in three. I believe our chances depend on. . . .

Once again, identifying the factors that influence success will give the client an ability to assess the prediction. Just make sure you don't give a written guarantee along with the retainer agreement.

E.   MAKING DECISIONS

4.9   THE LAWYER'S ROLE IN DECISION MAKING

There is a great deal of writing and writhing about the lawyer's involvement in client decision-making. Some lawyers believe that it is dangerous for a lawyer to make suggestions to a client because the client will be unduly swayed by the lawyer's recommendation. This issue of lawyer recommendations has taken a central position in much of the writing about advising clients. We believe too much is made of this issue.

Make no mistake, we believe that clients need to make decisions for themselves. The central question is not, however, whether the lawyer can make a recommendation to clients. The central question is whether the lawyer has provided the information necessary for the client to be an effective decision maker. Our experience—in a wide variety of practice settings, with corporate clients, with indigent clients, with small businesses— leads us to believe that a client who is an effective decision maker is capable of listening to a lawyer's recommendations without being bowled over. Our experience also leads us to believe that with appropriate information from the lawyer— information about assessment, options, and predictions—most clients can be effective decision makers.

4.10　CLIENT DECISIONS, LAWYER DECISIONS

Clients need to make decisions for themselves, but do they need to make all the decisions? Certainly not. In the course of handling a client's legal problem or concern, there are some decisions that are clearly the lawyer's responsibility. Typically, there are additional decisions that the client will wish to delegate to the lawyer.

The line between lawyer decisions and client decisions is neither straight nor unvarying. It is easy to articulate the types of decisions that fall far from the line on either side. For example, the client needs to choose whether or not to file a lawsuit. The client needs to choose whether or not to accept an offer to close a deal. Some authors have characterized these decisions as strategic. These are the types of decisions the client must make to direct the lawyer's work.

On the other side of the line are the decisions lawyers can make on their own. Some authors have described these decisions as tactical. A lawyer will typically decide, for example, how to cross-examine a witness or when to make a counter-offer during negotiation. Often clients will have little or no input into these types of decisions.

Closer to the line, it becomes difficult to say whether a decision is the lawyer's to make or the client's. Where that line is drawn will often depend on the view of the lawyer's role. A client who hires a lawyer to be a technician may want the lawyer to make all decisions within the lawyer's area of expertise and ask for very little lawyer input on matters outside the area of the lawyer's technical competence. On the other hand, a client who wants the lawyer to serve as counselor may welcome more participation from the lawyer with respect to the entire range of decisions the client needs to make. These are issues that each lawyer must sort out with each client. Though this sorting process must continue throughout the course of representation of the client, a lawyer is well-advised to discuss some of these issues with the client during the early stages of representation.

4.11 HELPING THE CLIENT REACH A CONCLUSION

Typically, during the early stages of representation, the lawyer will need the client to make a decision directing the lawyer to follow one course of action rather than another. By the time this juncture is reached, the lawyer should have given the client sufficient information so that the client can act as an effective decision maker. The lawyer should have given the client an assessment of the legal position, described various options for the client, including the cost and likelihood of success of each option. At this point, some clients are ready to choose one of the options. (Our assumption here is that it may be necessary for the client to choose a single option, although remember that isn't always the case.) On the other hand, some clients may be uncertain, unable to select one particular option. At this stage, the lawyer may be able to assist the client in making a decision.

4.11.1 Match Goals and Options

One of the most helpful things a lawyer can do during the decision-making process is to match options with client goals and preferences. Usually a particular legal option will help the client achieve one goal, but not another. A different option may be more likely to help the client achieve this other goal. Matching options with goals can help the client make a decision. It may also help clarify misunderstandings the lawyer has about the client's goals, and help sharpen the lawyer's sense of the relative importance the client attaches to the different goals and preferences.

Example: Mr. Peevyhouse, you've told me that you would like to recover as much money from the coal company as possible. Suing the company for fraud is probably the option that gives you the best chance of recovering the most money from the company. On the other hand, you've also told me that you want to finish this matter just as soon as possible. Trying to negotiate a better settlement is likely to take much less time than a lawsuit....

4.11.2 Winnow the List

Some clients find it difficult to pick a single option from a list of many. These clients are, however, often able to strike some options off the list. Winnowing or paring down the list in this way can help decision-making because it will focus the client's attention on the remaining options. Some lawyers, reluctant to have clients make decisions too quickly, refrain from asking the client to select a single option. Instead, these lawyers ask the client to strike unacceptable options, and then talk further with the client about the remaining choices. This allows the lawyer a better chance to learn about the client's goals and preferences, and gives the client an opportunity to make more considered decisions.

4.11.3 Reframe the Choice

Once a list of options has been pared to two or three, it is frequently helpful to reframe the client's choice. Rather than asking the client to choose between two legal courses of action, the lawyer can identify the options with the client goals they serve and ask the client to choose between the goals.

Example: Mr. Peevyhouse, we need to decide between going ahead with a lawsuit or trying to negotiate a settlement. I think the choice you need to make is between your feeling that you want to have this over and done with quickly and your hope for a larger recovery. You need to decide which of those goals is more important to you.

Reframing the choice this way usually helps clients clarify their own understanding of their goals and then reach a decision. Reframing the choice this way also illustrates why this is a decision the client must make and the lawyer cannot.

4.12 CHOOSE TWO. CHANGE YOUR MIND.

The discussion of decision-making is written with the assumption that when a client makes a choice, the client is selecting one course of action, one single option. This is sometimes true, but often it is possible for a lawyer to follow one course of action and reserve another as a backup plan or even pursue several courses of action simultaneously. Obviously, if this is the situation, it makes no sense to press the client to choose a single option. The lawyer may need to explain that pursuing multiple courses of action may, however, make accomplishment of one of the options less likely.

> **Example:** Mr. Hakkim, we can go ahead and file the lawsuit against the company and then try to negotiate a settlement. It may be that filing the lawsuit will make the company more willing to negotiate a settlement. In this case, I think it may make settlement more difficult....

Lawyers also need to remember that client decisions do not necessarily last forever. Lives change, business plans change, and clients change their minds. Hopefully, they won't change lawyers. This is one reason that it is important to remember, as discussed in Chapter Three, that obtaining direction from a client is a process that continues throughout the course of representation. It is also a reason to build in plenty of flexibility into any option the client and lawyer decide to pursue.

F. PREPARING FOR THE MEETING

Clients come to lawyers seeking legal advice and they usually hope to obtain it just as soon as possible. Sometimes it is possible to give clients the advice they seek at the first meeting with the client. Sometimes the lawyer will need additional time for investigation, planning, and thinking. When this is the case, it will be necessary to have a subsequent meeting with the client.

A meeting to advise a client is, in some ways, no different from any other meeting with a client. You may want to review the discussion in Chapter Three about first meetings with a client, if you didn't memorize it. There is no standard formula for a meeting to advise a client, but we do offer the following suggestions for preparing for this type of meeting.

4.13 WHAT A LAWYER NEEDS FROM THE CLIENT

Seek information, direction, a business agreement, and trust—just like it says in Chapter Three. Without information and direction, it will not be possible for the lawyer to think productively about client options. A business agreement is necessary because developing options for a client may take a substantial amount of time and effort. It is important for the lawyer and the client to have reached some agreement before the lawyer begins this work. Finally, it makes little sense to try to advise a client who feels no trust in the lawyer.

4.14 THINKING AND PLANNING

As emphasized earlier, clients need choices and it is often up to the lawyer to provide those choices for the client. Thinking creatively and productively—matching what the lawyer knows about the client's concern, the client's goals, and the law—is a critical part of the process of advising the client. Unless the lawyer is experienced in dealing with concerns similar to the client's concerns it is difficult to do this thinking and planning while the client sits and waits, or while you are sitting and talking. Some results of this process depend upon your legal and factual research.

4.14.1 Legal Investigation

Legal investigation is another critical part of preparing to advise a client. The lawyer should do the legal research necessary to learn what the traditional approaches to the client's concern have been, and what new approaches might be plausible. Visit the library, or boot up that computer your family got you for graduation. Aren't you glad you didn't return it? In most situations, there is a record of past approaches taken in similar situations. Sometimes this record is found in appellate decisions; sometimes, in agency rules; sometimes, in settlement reports; sometimes, in past agreements between the parties; sometimes, in the Enquirer. A review of this record will also help the lawyer begin to estimate the likelihood of success of the available options.

The depth and amount of investigation will depend in part on the lawyer's own expertise, but also on the agreement between the lawyer and the client. A lawyer should not devote more time and expense to investigation than the client has authorized.

4.14.2 Fact Investigation

At times, it may be necessary to do fact investigation to prepare to advise a client. A lawyer may want to interview other witnesses or obtain financial records or other documents. See or visit Chapter Ten. This investigation may help the lawyer fill in gaps in the information obtained from the client. It may also help the lawyer begin to move beyond "lawyer" approaches to the client's concern. The depth and amount of investigation will again depend on the agreement between the lawyer and the client, as well as the lawyer's own expertise. It is particularly important that the lawyer have the client's express agreement before contacting any other witnesses during a supplemental fact investigation.

4.15 CHECKING YOUR WORK

Novice lawyers should remember that experienced lawyers are often a very valuable resource of information, plus a source of new friends to replace those lost during law school. A lawyer who has not dealt with a concern similar to the client's may want to discuss particular options with a more seasoned attorney. More experienced lawyers can be particularly helpful in providing guidance about the likelihood of success with different options. Depending on the depth of discussion, the lawyer may want to have the client's permission before talking to a colleague. If the lawyer seeks advice from an attorney outside the lawyer's firm, care should be taken to safeguard the attorney-client privilege.

4.16 AGENDAS AND LISTS

Before meeting with the client, the lawyer should prepare an agenda for the meeting which, at a minimum, lists the different options to be discussed. The lawyer should consider giving the client a copy of this agenda. For some clients, it may be helpful to have the lawyer make a list or chart matching the different options and goals. In fact, some corporate clients routinely ask lawyers to prepare elaborate "decision trees" matching each option with the likelihood of success and the client's goals.

G. STRUCTURING THE MEETING

4.17 A SUGGESTED STRUCTURE

Once again we remind you, as we did in Chapter Three, that different clients have different concerns, and good lawyers keep their plans and agendas flexible to accommodate these differences. Consequently, use this suggestion about structure as a guideline or checklist, rather than a recipe.

1. *Update.* As time passes, things happen. This may be the world's most obvious truism, but many lawyers conduct subsequent meetings with clients as if facts and plans were set in stone at the first meeting. Find out if something new has happened or if the client's goals have changed.

2. *Assessment.* A lawyer needs to give a client an assessment of the client's legal situation. It usually makes sense to do this before discussing the client's options.

3. *Description of Options.* Some lawyers like to give clients a quick overview of all the different options and then discuss each separately. Other lawyers prefer simply to move through options one by one. The lawyer should give the client the opportunity to ask questions about each option, and should discuss the cost of each option and likelihood of success.

4. *Review of Options.* After a full discussion of the individual options, it is generally helpful to briefly recap the list. For many clients, it is helpful if this recap includes a reference to the goals the option is well-suited to help achieve, the likelihood of the option's chances of achieving those goals, and the cost of the option.

5. *Decision.* After the client has discussed the available options, the client will typically need to choose one or more. If the client is not ready to make a decision, the lawyer can help by matching goals and options, winnowing the list, or reframing the choice.

6. *Discussion of next step.* After the client has made a decision, the lawyer and client should discuss what the lawyer plans to do next to implement the decision.

7. *Arrange next contact.* Before the close of the meeting, the lawyer should tell the client when the client will next hear from the lawyer.

8. *Update critical information.* See if your client has started a band that can play at your next office party or has acquired a yacht you can use for work with the client.

Part Two
PLANNING AND NEGOTIATIONS

Chapter Five
PLANNING THE TRANSACTION: THE OTHER SIDE OF PRACTICE

I don't really like lawyers much. It seems to me they cause as many problems as they solve. Blocking deals, delaying progress, twisting the truth, making people look like jerks. I don't need that.

That's why I didn't hire a lawyer when I bought my house. I figured that I could do everything I needed without any help. I just signed the papers people put in front of me and crossed my fingers. I haven't had any problems—so far.

I also drafted my own will. I bought one of those "Do It Yourself" kits, and just filled out the forms. And I haven't died, yet.

Now I'm planning on starting my own business. Maybe it's time for a lawyer. I want to make sure I'm doing it right. I've got some questions I'd like to get answered.

I wish I knew a lawyer that understood reality. Maybe this law firm has one. Their advertisement said something about being expert planners.

A. INTRODUCTION
5.1 THE PRACTICE WITHOUT A NAME

Fiction shapes our vision of reality. A half-century of movies, books, and television programs have largely defined our conception of what it means to be a lawyer. Say the word "lawyer" to people today, and most will think of Susan Dey playing Grace Van Owen from TV's *L.A. Law* or Gregory Peck as Atticus Finch in *To Kill a Mockingbird*, or any of the other trial lawyers that dominate Hollywood's vision of lawyers.

That vision is, however, only half of the story. Many lawyers have never set foot inside a courtroom and never plan to. These are the lawyers that do the legal work needed for corporate mergers, real estate sales, contract drafting, and a variety of other tasks. Some attorneys call this work "corporate practice," but that is a misnomer, because this work is done for individuals, partnerships, and sole proprietorships just as often as it is done for large publicly traded corporations. Some attorneys call this work "office practice" or "advisorial practice," but those dreary names fall far short of capturing the challenges and excitement inherent in this work. In the end, "transactional practice" is the best of a batch of poor choices, but is itself misleading, because this work involves a far greater range of activities than negotiating and crafting deals.

5.2 THE NATURE OF THE WORK: TRANSLATION, DEFINITION, AND TRANSACTION

By whatever name it is called, much of lawyering involves work that has little to do with the resolution of disputes. The breadth of this practice defies easy categorization, but in the main, legal work outside the realm of dispute-resolution involves translating the law, creating and defining relationships, and structuring transactions.

5.2.1 Translation: Bringing the Law to Clients

One of the most important tasks any lawyer can perform is to make the law accessible to clients. As the law has grown more complex, it has become increasingly difficult for clients to have a first-hand understanding of the rules, regulations, and statutes that govern their actions. Consequently, one of the big parts of any lawyer's job is finding and explaining to a client the law that bears upon that particular client's problem.

The importance of this task is heightened when the client needs legal advice in order to guide future behavior. A large part of transactional practice involves "translating" a sophisticated body of law and advising clients about that law so that the clients can make effective decisions. Clients come to lawyers for advice about tax laws, securities regulations, estate planning, or intellectual property. In fact, in the day-to-day practice of law, many lawyers who consider themselves litigators find that they spend a great deal of time translating the law and advising clients outside the context of a particular dispute. For example, a small business owner might seek advice from an employment lawyer about the Americans with Disabilities Act; a corporation's general counsel might call an antitrust lawyer for an opinion about the Robinson–Patman Act; a tenant in a housing project might consult a legal aid lawyer about lease provisions. All of this work involves "translation" of complex bodies of law and regulations, and all of this work could be described as "transactional," because none of it necessarily involves the resolution of existing disputes.

5.2.2   Creation and Definition: Making the Law Work for Clients

Transactional practice also often entails the creation of new relationships or the definition of existing relationships. The web of the law is filled with categories of different types of relationships between people: agent and principal; landlord and tenant; licensor and licensee; settler, trustee, and beneficiary; employer and employee; lender and borrower; buyer and seller. At each juncture, the creation and definition of these relationships is work often done by transactional lawyers.

When these relationships are created or defined, a client will typically seek help from a lawyer in understanding the rights and responsibilities the law imposes. The lawyer may need to "translate" the relevant law so that the client can make effective decisions. That translation is, however, only part of the lawyer's work. There is more to transactional practice than telling the client the law and then reaching for the appropriate forms. An important part of the lawyer's job involves developing a deep enough understanding of the client's goals to offer meaningful advice about how the law may help the client accomplish those goals. Rather than trimming the client's goals to fit the law, the creative lawyer will work to tailor the law to fit the client's needs.

For example, a client who wishes to start a business and comes to a lawyer asking for information about forming a corporation certainly needs to understand the requirements of incorporation, and may also need advice about the rights and responsibilities of directors and shareholders. "Translating" corporate law for the client is a part of the lawyer's work, but only a part.

That same client may be better served by the lawyer who takes the time to explore the client's goals, and then works with the client to determine whether it might be wiser, for example, for the client to form a limited liability partnership rather than a corporation.

Creation and definition of relationships usually entails drafting documents that spell out the rights, responsibilities, and limits of the relationship. Whether that document is a lease, a will, an employment manual, or a contract, the transactional lawyer must make sure that the document comports with the existing law governing the relationship. And whether the client is an individual, a small business, or a multi-national corporation, the transactional lawyer must insure that the document will give the client useful guidance during the course of the relationship.

5.2.3 Transaction: Using the Law to Work With Others

Sometimes a transactional lawyer is called on to create or define a relationship that a client can create or define largely at will. For example, an employer may ask a lawyer to draft a manual that spells out the rights and responsibilities of the workplace. A large manufacturer may want legal help in creating policies governing the distribution of its products. While the interests of the employees or purchasers are important, in these types of situations the employer or manufacturer may be able to create or define relationships unilaterally.

More often, transactional lawyers find themselves called upon to create or define relationships in which other parties have a voice in the costs, benefits, and design of that relationship. Every transaction involves this sort of negotiation. Mergers, securities offerings, real estate purchases, employment contracts, sales of goods—all of these require the parties involved to reach mutually agreed-upon resolutions of a whole host of questions about legal relationships. The transactional lawyer is responsible for making sure that the right questions are asked and, to the extent possible, that those questions are answered in a way that accomplishes the client's goals.

When other parties come to the table, the challenge of transactional practice increases exponentially. To complete a transaction successfully, a lawyer must be able to translate the law for a client and create and define a new relationship. That lawyer must also be able to work with other parties who have interests and goals at odds with the interests and goals of the lawyer's clients. The ultimate challenge of transactional lawyering is convincing a variety of parties to balance competing interests in a fashion that serves the interests of the lawyer's client. To do this, the transactional lawyer must not only be an effective negotiator, the transactional lawyer must also have a deep understanding of the client's goals.

B. DIFFERENCES AMONG DISTINCTIONS
5.3 IT'S THE SAME, BUT IT ISN'T

In some sense, all law is much the same and lawyers have more in common with each other than with anyone else. Being a litigator is more like being a transactional lawyer than being a doctor, stockbroker, locksmith, or wedding planner. Still, there are important differences between the work of the litigator and the work of the transactional lawyer. These distinctions shed some light on the different sets of skills necessary to be an effective transactional lawyer.

5.4 I GOT HERE AS SOON AS I COULD, AND I'M NOT PLANNING ON LEAVING ANY TIME SOON

The first set of distinctions between litigation and transactional practice concerns the points in time in which the client seeks assistance from the lawyer. Every lawyer who has tried lawsuits, arbitrated disputes, or negotiated settlements has, at one time or another, thought: "If only this client had called me sooner, none of this ever would have had to happen." These thoughts are commonplace because, quite often, a client will not sense a need for legal assistance until a dispute has arisen—for example, the client is sued. The lawyer who is summoned once a dispute has flared is in the position of a fire fighter. The dispute may be a manageable blaze or an enormous conflagration, but either way, a crisis has occurred and it is the lawyer's job to help the client extinguish that crisis.

By contrast, the transactional lawyer is often in a position more akin to a fire inspector. The client summoning a lawyer before a dispute has arisen is not interested in putting out fires; instead, the client wishes to prevent fires altogether. Like a fire inspector, it is the transactional lawyer's job to seek out potential trouble areas, and suggest changes (through artful planning or drafting) that will prevent future problems. To be sure, good litigation practice also requires some of these same skills, since sound strategic planning is important in solving crises. Transactional practice is more heavily reliant upon these skills, however, since good transactional practice is built upon a lawyer's ability to see trouble before it happens and help a client take steps to forestall that potential trouble.

The litigator arrives when the client calls for assistance in resolving a crisis. At the end of a trial, a litigator may be called upon to work on an appeal or assist with collection of the judgment, but, for the most part, a litigator's work is done once the crisis is resolved. Transactional lawyers not only arrive on the scene earlier than litigators, they stay around longer. Since transactional work is not focused on the resolution of a dispute, there is no "natural" stopping point for much of the work transactional lawyers do. There are certainly exceptions to this rubric; at the end of a negotiated deal, a client may no longer need or want legal assistance. More often, however, a client will want continued advice and assistance from a transactional lawyer across an extended period of time. Consequently, the transactional lawyer must be able to foresee future problems and help solve them.

5.5 EXCUSE ME, COULD YOU DIRECT ME TO THE FEDERAL RULES OF TRANSACTIONAL PROCEDURE?

There aren't any. And that fact—perhaps as much as any other—makes for the difference between the life of the transactional lawyer and the life of the litigator. When the litigator submits a dispute to the jurisdiction of the courts, the applicable rules of practice and procedure dictate to that lawyer the conduct and structure of the lawsuit. Those rules will determine (it is hoped) how the lawyers will discover facts and information from each other; what sanctions will be assessed if those rules are broken; in short, when, where, and how that dispute will be resolved. When these same lawyers step into the courtroom, the applicable rules of evidence will determine what those lawyers can say and what they cannot. The world of the litigator is bounded by rules that govern lawyer behavior.

No such rules exist for the transactional lawyer. To be sure, the transactional lawyer must answer to the same ethical standards as the litigator—but read through those rules and see how many seem to have been drafted with only the litigator in mind. To be sure, the transactional lawyer must heed the statutes and cases that govern the relevant legal concerns of the client—but these laws do not govern lawyer behavior. When a client asks for legal advice, there is no rule that tells the transactional lawyer that the client's question must be answered in thirty days. When two parties agree to the terms of a contract, there is no rule that tells the transactional lawyer the size and color of the paper on which that contract is to be written. If a deal turns sour and negotiations become bitter and hostile, the transactional lawyer cannot ask a judge to sanction opposing counsel.

All this can be very freeing. Transactional lawyers can mold the law to shape clients' needs unfettered by rules that mandate process. This leaves much room for innovation and creativity. It also leaves much room for headaches and frustration. A popular law school myth holds that the life of the transactional lawyer is much less hectic than the life of the litigator. A little thought about the difference between the two practices dispels that myth. If a client comes to a litigator and asks that the lawyer sue someone and collect a judgment before next Thursday, the lawyer can patiently explain that America's court system doesn't work that quickly. The client may not like the explanation, but the client will blame the system for the delay, not the lawyer. On the other hand, a client who comes to a transactional lawyer and asks that a contract be drafted before next Thursday need not listen to explanations about the wheels of justice grinding slowly. If this lawyer can't do the work, the client can find someone else who will. Ultimately, transactional law is a process that is driven and administered by the participants, not by some outside authority—and it has all the joys and frustrations of a process that is self-driven and self-administered.

5.6   I DON'T HAVE TO IF I DON'T WANT TO

In the final analysis, the most important distinction between transactional work and litigation is that the participants in transactional work are all there voluntarily and, typically, any of them can leave whenever they want to. The realm of litigation is far different: in litigation, at least one and sometimes all the participants are there against their will and, typically, none can leave without the assent of the judge or the other parties. It is this distinction that makes for much of the charm and challenge of transactional practice.

The right to walk away is an enormous power. In most transactional settings, it is a power that each of the participants has. In almost every transactional negotiation, any of the parties to the deal could simply decide to take their capital, their business, their services somewhere else and walk out of the room. In litigation, if a party walks away from a settlement negotiation, that party walks straight into the courtroom. The alternative to settlement is suit. In transactional work, the alternative to the transaction is either no deal or another deal with someone else. During litigation, the lawyer works—in a sense—to make the other side go away. During a transaction, the lawyer must work—in a sense—to keep the other side at the table. Consequently, it is not enough that the transactional lawyer have a good understanding of the client's goals. The transactional lawyer also needs to be attuned to the interests, motivations, and goals of all the other parties at the table.

C.   TRANSACTIONAL GOALS

5.7   DOING TRANSACTIONAL WORK: TAKING GOALS SERIOUSLY

The skills that a transactional lawyer uses in practice are not that different than the skills a litigator uses. Like the litigator, the transactional lawyer interviews clients, advises clients, researches the law, negotiates with other parties, and drafts agreements. Like the litigator, the transactional lawyer must be a good listener, a thoughtful and knowledgeable interpreter of the law, a creative and lucid drafter, and a persuasive and patient negotiator. But because of the differences between litigation and transactional practice, there are distinctions in the skills needed to be an effective practitioner. The most important of these distinctions centers around the understanding the transactional lawyer must have about the goals and motivations of the different parties to a transaction.

5.7.1 Immediate Goals: Clarify and Condense

A great deal of transactional work involves intensive work with clients—a cycle of interviewing, advising, and drafting— that is repeated until the clients' goals are accomplished. Time, patience, and sanity are best preserved when the lawyer has a solid understanding of what it is that the client wants. Pity the new lawyer who drafts an opinion letter for a client and then is told by the senior lawyer on the file: "This is fine, but it doesn't answer two of the questions the client has, and this last section answers a question the client didn't ask." This kind of misunderstanding usually occurs when the lawyer has a firm grasp of the legal issues, but only a vague sense of the client's goals.

The best way to obtain a solid sense of the client's immediate goals is to ask the client. Unfortunately, simply asking, "Oh client, what are your immediate goals?" seldom yields enough information. Instead, the transactional lawyer needs to ask a whole gamut of who, what, where, and when questions. The lawyer writing the opinion letter should, for example, ask:

- Who will be reading this opinion letter?
- What kinds of decisions will they be making on the basis of this letter?
- Where does this letter fit in with other legal or business advice the client may already have?
- When does the client need this opinion? When will it be used?

As these questions are answered, the lawyer can begin to clarify the understanding of the client's immediate goals. And as that understanding is clarified and condensed, it is usually true that the work the lawyer does for the client will be more efficient and more valuable.

5.7.2 Overarching Goals: Learn and Serve

A lawsuit is a crisis, and crises can be easy to understand. Clients don't like crises; clients want crises solved. Clients call litigators to deal with crises, and are happy once the crises—and the litigators—are gone.

Transactional practice presents a different calculus of desire. Clients typically do not seek out a transactional lawyer for crisis management. Instead, clients hire transactional lawyers to do work the clients have chosen to do in order to promote long-range or overarching goals, although some of these goals may need to be addressed with great dispatch. Often, the true measure of the value of the transactional lawyer's work is whether that work has helped advance the client's overarching goals. The lawyer who drafts an employment manual for a client may have helped that client achieve the immediate goal of creating written policies for the workplace. Whether that work is of any value, however, will depend on whether the employment manual accomplishes overarching goals such as harmony in the workplace or minimization of litigation.

It takes time—and often experience—for a lawyer to understand how the work the lawyer is doing for the client fits into the client's long term plans, the client's business, the client's life. While the question "why do you want to do this?" is hardly out of place in the litigator's office, it must become a staple of the transactional lawyer's practice. That question is usually the first step on the road to understanding the client's overarching goals. One of the joys of transactional practice is that a lawyer will typically work with many of the same clients across several years. As the lawyer accumulates experience with a client, the lawyer's understanding of the client's goals will deepen, and the lawyer will be better able to tailor legal work to meet the client's interests, needs, and goals.

D. THE ROLE OF THE CLIENT

5.8 PROCESS PREFERENCES: PASSENGER, DRIVER, OR MAP–MAKER

Since there are no rules for transactional procedure and since participation in most transactions is completely voluntary, the client's level of participation in transactional work can vary enormously. Litigators know that during trial and during discovery there are times in which the client's participation is not simply desirable, but actually required by law. In transactional work, the client's level of participation in the process is largely left to the decision of the client and the lawyer. Consequently, the transactional lawyer must spend more time with the client learning about the client's own process preferences.

In transactional practice, it is possible for a lawyer to serve a wide range of functions—map-maker, driver, passenger. Some clients come to lawyers with a firm idea of what it is they want to accomplish. These clients need lawyers who can function as "drivers," steering through difficult patches of road, suggesting alternative routes, finally bringing the client safely to a destination that client has determined. Other clients may need lawyers to function as "map-makers." These are the clients that need a wider range of assistance from their lawyers. The new business owner who comes to a lawyer to ask for assistance negotiating a commercial lease may also need the lawyer to point out the need for the client to do some tax planning. In fact, this client may not only need the lawyer to do this, but expect it. The lawyer who fails to understand this client's process-preferences risks future malpractice claims.

Just as some clients are sophisticated parties to litigation (insurance companies, for example), some clients are sophisticated parties to transactions. These clients may neither expect nor want questions from lawyers about the whys and wherefores of a particular transaction. For example, a client may hire a lawyer to complete a particular type of real estate transaction, having already made informed decisions about whether the transaction serves immediate and overarching goals. Persistent and repeated questions from the lawyer about whether the client's decisions are well-grounded may only serve to convince the client to hire a different lawyer next time. This client needs neither a map-maker, nor a driver. This client simply needs a valuable passenger—a lawyer with the technical expertise to implement decisions the client has already made. In transactional practice, this is a reasonable process preference and it is the lawyer's responsibility to ask the questions necessary to learn about this process preference.

5.9 THE OTHER SIDE: ALL THE SAME ISSUES SQUARED

The transactional lawyer needs a solid understanding of the client's goals and preferences. When dealing with other parties with competing interests, the transactional lawyer needs as firm an understanding of the other side's goals and preferences. That understanding is helpful to the litigator, but critical for the transactional lawyer. Litigation makes captives of the participants. In a transaction, a party will be present only as long as that party sees participation in the transaction as consistent with the party's goals. A transactional lawyer needs to understand those goals. Absent that understanding, the transactional lawyer lacks the basic information necessary to keep the other side at the bargaining table while still protecting the client's interests.

How does a transactional lawyer learn about the other party's goals? Fact investigation can yield some information about other's immediate and overarching goals, but it is often possible to obtain that information directly from the other party's lawyer. Can lawyers get that information from opposing counsel? At first glance, it seems the answer must be no, but in a sense, negotiation is the opportunity to do exactly that. The transactional lawyer must use negotiation as an exchange of information, as well as an exchange of positions.

5.10 WHY DON'T MY CLIENTS SMILE WHEN I WALK IN THE ROOM?

Lawyer jokes aren't just about litigators. Just as some clients resent having to hire lawyers to resolve disputes, some clients may dislike transactional lawyers. Clients may mutter to themselves, or we hope, discuss with us concerns about:

The Deal Killer. Clients may perceive that lawyers view themselves as deal killers instead of deal makers. The lawyer who is overly negative about a situation or who continually raises roadblocks instead of suggesting bridges to close gaps may rightly be perceived as interfering with the process instead of constructing a deal.

The Detail Chewer. The lawyer who focuses on what seems to the client to be petty issues and details that can only be revealed by a legal microscope may view the lawyer as being focused on irrelevant matters. This is not to say that a devotion to minute details may not be critical to the success of a project, but a lawyer who seems overly obsessed with these details may not be what the client needs or expects. The danger is that the lawyer who dwells on the minutia may lose sight of the broader goals of the transaction, to the dissatisfaction of the client.

The Legalese Expert. The lawyer who drafts terms that only another lawyer can understand may cause the client to wonder if the lawyer speaks the same language as the client. Drafting legal provisions may require the use of legalese, but the terms should also be drafted plainly enough so all can understand.

The Apocalypse Predictor. It is appropriate and necessary for lawyers to point out to clients worst case scenarios and to draft accordingly. For example, good lawyering involves discussing with the client the inclusion of a pre-dispute resolution clause in agreements in case disputes arise in the future. However, the lawyer who is primarily worried about unlikely potential disasters and tries to negotiate or draft for these contingencies will wrap the client in a tangle of paper and red tape and may unnecessarily interfere with the completion of a deal.

These concerns can be avoided by understanding the proper role of the lawyer and by open communication between the client and attorney. The goal of the lawyer is to help the client and not create unnecessary problems. It should be the client's choice, in consultation with the lawyer, how this can best be accomplished.

Chapter Six
PLANNING FOR DISPUTE RESOLUTION: WHAT ARE WE TO DO?

It's happening.

It shouldn't be, but it is.

A problem. No. A disagreement. No. Worse, a real bona fide dispute.

What to do?

There must be a way to resolve it without costing a bundle and wasting years of time.

I want this solved as quickly and inexpensively as possible. I don't want to be emotionally and physically drained at the end of it. I want it done reasonably and fairly—as long as I get what I want.

Now, where is that lawyer who can make this happen?

A. INTRODUCTION
6.1 PLANNING WHAT TO DO

It has happened. Your client is involved in a dispute—and comes to you for help. You know what lawyers initially need to do to help. They need to:

- Assess the dispute
- Determine the remedy
- Seek relief
- Select a dispute resolution method

B. ASSESSING THE DISPUTE
6.2 DISPUTE RESOLUTION PLANNING

A lawyer representing a client involved in a dispute needs to consider the nature of the dispute. The first assessment is whether the client has a claim to make or must respond to a claim brought by someone else. If the client has a claim then affirmative steps may need to be taken. If a client only has a defense, the client may not need to do anything but wait, or the client may need to take affirmative action to preserve or enhance the merits of the defense.

6.3 CAN A CLAIM BE MADE?

Not every problem lends itself to legal resolution, or even legal action. For example, even nasty behavior that causes tangible hurt to a victim will not be actionable in tort if the law does not recognize a duty on the part of the perpetrator or does not recognize the resulting injury as significantly concrete to justify legal relief. To take a fairly obvious example, if Harry and Sally develop a personal relationship and if Sally jilts Harry, there is unlikely to be any cause of action for intentional infliction of emotional distress (Sally has no duty to stay with Harry) no matter how sad Harry becomes (romantic heartbreak is not sufficiently tangible), even if Sally terminates the relationship with harsh words.

In real life, more complex situations are presented. What if Sally, knowing Harry has just finished treatment for alcoholism, delivers a case of his favorite beer and a long speech informing Harry that he's so repulsive that no other woman will so much as look at him in the future? Will Sally be liable if Harry downs a case of beer and runs into a school bus, killing himself and several children? To Harry's estate? To the children's families? To the school district for damage to the bus? To the state for road repairs necessitated by the crash? Substantive tort law provides the answers to these sorts of questions and will vary by jurisdiction, requiring the lawyer to obtain sufficient facts and then conduct appropriate research, the depth of which will vary according to the novelty of litigation, the stakes involved, and the ability and willingness of the client to pay.

To take the preceding "breaking up is hard to do" scenario one step further, consider how a few changes in the facts can have major legal consequences. If Harry and Sally were not merely in love but husband and wife, the law regulates their relationship much more closely. If they break up, they will need the government's "permission," obtained via divorce, and each may have a claim against the other for a share of property, child support, or maintenance. Whether the client is Harry-the-jilted-lover or Harry-the-abandoned-husband will have a dramatic impact on the appropriate lawyering response.

6.3.1 Should the Claim Be Brought?

Even if the law provides a right of relief, reality may not. For example, a tortfeasor may lack financial resources. Even in cases of relatively great harm, it may simply be not worthwhile to pursue a civil judgment against an impecunious defendant. "Spite" litigation—pursing a legal claim just to make life difficult for the defendant without any realistic hope for recompense—is both ethically suspect and out of reach for any but the most well-healed spite litigants. However, some litigation against judgment-proof wrong doers is objectively justified. For example, if the tortfeasor has caused numerous accidents in many states and continues to drive without a license or insurance, this person is a menace endangering the lives of the innocent. A relative of a recent victim may want a lawyer to urge government prosecutors to act or to seek an unsatisfied judgment as grounds for contempt of court resulting in imprisonment in order to remove the defendant driver from the road. More benignly, the plaintiff may wish to force the defendant into a settlement that requires treatment for alcohol abuse, the underlying cause of the automobile accident.

6.3.2 What Type of Claim Can Be Brought?

The substantive law will have much to say about what claims can actually be brought. You will need to attend your other classes or research those areas you missed when you were enjoying yourself away from your classes.

C. DETERMINING REMEDIES

6.4 WHAT REMEDIES CAN BE SOUGHT?

The law recognizes the following remedies:

6.4.1 Money, That's What We Want

The client who has been wronged may want the wrong to be righted by monetary compensation. A money judgment or award requires the losing party to pay money to the victor. The law generally has a preference for monetary relief because this type of relief normally ends a matter and because most people are content with money. Most people pay their debts, at least after they have lost fair and square, so the victimized party is usually satisfied.

6.4.2 Stop, in the Name of the Law

A client may want to stop someone from doing something or to require them to do something else. This is known as equitable relief which involves a court order requiring a party from refraining to do something (stop dumping sewage in the river) or to affirmatively do something (fix the fence you ran over in the monster truck). This type of relief is called "equitable," not because the court is necessarily trying to be fair when it makes these orders (although one certainly hopes this is the case). Instead, we call the relief equitable because it first developed in Anglo–American law in the courts of equity, rather than in the courts of law which essentially rendered money judgments. In modern America, the courts of law and equity are now merged virtually everywhere, but the old terminology continues to be used to describe differences in the types of relief. Modern lawyers may find it better to think in terms of "compensatory" relief (rather than legal) and "injunctive" relief (rather than equitable). Injunctive relief is normally only ordered when monetary relief is ineffective or problematic. Injunctive relief requires more judicial effort to enforce compliance and frequently requires ongoing judicial involvement.

6.4.3 Just Decide

A related equitable remedy is "declaratory" relief which results in a decision maker deciding the status of something. For example, declaratory relief may determine who owns real estate, or whether an insurance policy covers a specific loss. A declaration can have monetary ramifications and can be enforced by an injunction.

6.4.4 Pay My Lawyer, Too

A party may also seek to recover costs and fees incurred in pursuing claims and defenses. The losing party usually has to pay the winning party for costs and expenses involved in a case. These costs include expenses such as filing fees, discovery expenses, expert witness fees, and related transaction costs. Attorney's fees may be recoverable in three limited situations: if a statute allows for the recovery of attorney's fees, if a contract or an agreement between the parties allows them to recover these fees, or if a party acts in such bad faith that a decision maker determines it is an appropriate remedy. Whatever the amount of attorney's fees that may be recoverable, they do not include the recovery of law school tuition.

6.5 WHAT ARE THE LEGAL AND PRACTICAL LIMITS ON SEEKING RELIEF?

Legal doctrines place limits upon available remedies in addition to the economic reality of seeking certain types of relief. For example, the statute of limitations may prevent a claim from being brought if it is too old. Or, an injured party may forego a remedy if to do so would cause unnecessary family strife or severe adverse community responses.

D. SEEKING RELIEF

6.6 WHO CAN SEEK RELIEF?

Anyone who has a legal claim for relief can do something about it. The party must be involved in an actual controversy with an opponent and must seek a recognizable judicial remedy. We lawyers call this "standing." But not everyone can get what they want. An outraged citizen cannot sue the president to "do something about ethnic bloodshed abroad," and a distant relative of yours can not sue your professors for teaching malpractice. At least, not yet.

People can join together to do something. More than one person or entity can be joined together in one action to seek relief against defendants individually or all together. Only a civil procedure instructor can really enjoy and make sense of joinder.

Lots of people can also get together. In litigation, this is called a class action. A representative plaintiff (Mother Theresa) or plaintiffs represent numerous unnamed class members (all persons affected by a religious swindle). Class action litigation can be complex, difficult, and risky. Federal Rule of Civil Procedure 23 and similar state court rules establish criteria for class litigation.

Class actions may provide relief to victims who otherwise would remain victims. Class actions when properly administered by counsel and the courts can vindicate the rights of a large number of people who have losses significant in the aggregate but individually too small to justify the costs of litigation. Class suits have been criticized as encouraging the named plaintiffs and counsel to use this device to pocket a sizable settlement and substantial counsel fees while selling out the class interests. Class actions can also result in questionable settlements because of the extensive transaction costs of defending them and the sheer risk of an adverse judgment.

6.7　FROM WHOM CAN YOU SEEK RELIEF?

Anyone or any entity who is legally responsible can be a proper defendant or respondent. Not everyone who does something wrong can be civilly liable for wrongdoing, not even in this country. The reach of the law determines who may be held accountable for their actions. You learned in contract law that relief may be sought against a party who breached a contract. You learned in tort law that anyone breaching a legal duty of care may be sued. You learned in property law about future interests, but who really cares? You will learn in practice that your client will usually want to pay you to sue someone who can pay them. Adam Smith was right.

Some potential defendants may not be worth suing. They may be unable to pay damages and consequently will be judgment proof. Others may be entities with which the claimant may wish to do future business. Still others may be friends or family with whom the plaintiff wants to maintain a relationship (at least through the holidays). Some defendants in litigation may be bypassed because they may create problems of jurisdiction or venue. A decision to make a claim against someone should be something more than a reflexive shotgun blast at all imagined enemies. Now there is an odd metaphor.

E. SELECTING A DISPUTE RESOLUTION METHOD

Parties involved in or anticipating a dispute have a number of methods to choose from to resolve their problems:

- They can negotiate on their own and settle their disputes.
- They can have an impartial forum and decision maker decide their case.
- They can have a neutral person mediate their dispute.
- They can have someone provide an opinion or an evaluation of their case.
- They can create their own dispute resolution process.

6.8 NEGOTIATING YOUR OWN ACCORD

Parties can negotiate on their own or through their attorneys to reach an agreement. Chapters Seven and Eight describe this process in detail. Now there's something to look forward to.

6.9 AVAILABLE DISPUTE RESOLUTION FORUMS

There are at least three different impartial forums that can decide disputes: judicial, arbitral, and administrative. We exclude open fields at dawn and saloons. You may or may not have a choice where to bring or defend a case. A binding arbitration clause may require that a claim be filed with a specific arbitration organization (e.g. National Arbitration Forum or American Arbitration Association) which will administer the case and appoint an arbitrator who will conduct the hearing. The law may require that you bring a claim in an exclusive forum. You have to file a bankruptcy petition in federal bankruptcy court, a divorce action in state court, and a workers compensation claim in a state administrative forum. If there is a choice, you will need to consider the ability and power of the forum to decide the case. This is what is called jurisdiction. More on that in Chapter Eleven.

6.9.1 Enforceability

The initial issue you must resolve is to make certain that a judgment or award you win will be enforceable. It does your client little good to win something that is unenforceable. It does your client less good to have the losing party rightfully refuse to pay money. Proper jurisdiction is what makes your judgment or award enforceable. If the forum has jurisdiction to hear and decide the case, your decision will be enforceable. See, all that time you were studying jurisdiction may be worth it after all.

A related issue which you must consider is *where* you will seek to enforce the judgment or award. It will do you no good to seek to enforce your victory in a place where it is unenforceable. In this country, judicial, arbitral, and administrative decisions made by a forum with proper jurisdiction will be enforceable everywhere. The Federal Arbitration Act allows a party to force a recalcitrant party to arbitrate and to enforce an award if the agreement is in writing and involves interstate commerce. State arbitration laws have similar provisions for enforcing and policing arbitration agreements and outcomes. In other countries, treaties and conventions determine the reach of enforceable judgments and awards. The vast majority of countries readily recognize and enforce arbitration awards. Most countries recognize and enforce judicial judgments entered in the United States. You need to do legal research and planning to determine these issues before you seek any remedy for your client anywhere. You may become an international lawyer before you know it.

6.9.2 Litigation

Lawsuits may be brought in federal or state court, whichever has jurisdiction over the defendant. Federal courts resolve disputes involving federal statutes and the federal constitution, disputes between citizens in different states in excess of $50,000, and special cases such as patent disputes and bankruptcy. State courts are courts with general jurisdiction and hear the vast majority of disputes.

A plaintiff can serve a summons and complaint on the defendant who can reply with an answer. Litigation proceeds with the parties conducting discovery and bringing motions eventually resulting in a trial. Parties have a right to a jury or a bench trial. Federal and state constitutional and statutory provisions provide parties with the right to a jury trial in most civil cases, particularly those involving money damages. Other cases, including injunctive relief cases, are tried in a bench trial. Any party with grounds may appeal to an appellate court.

Litigation is usually the remedy available to the parties if they are unable to agree to another dispute resolution method. Litigation is often the last resort parties rely on to have their dispute resolved because the trial process can be very expensive, slow, time consuming and painful. Only lawyers think it's a real fun process.

Parties may decide to litigate and then agree to submit their dispute to a private judge who makes a decision after a trial. Parties may prefer a private judge instead of a public judge because the private judge may have experience resolving the type of dispute and the trial may be able to be scheduled much more quickly than a public trial. In some jurisdictions, the decision by the private judge (special magistrate or referee can be enforced as if it were a judgment and can also be appealable.

6.9.3 Arbitration

An arbitration resolves a dispute between parties by the issuance of an award after a hearing. One type of hearing is called a document hearing in which the parties submit their case to the arbitrator in writing through documents, records, and affidavits. Another type of hearing is called a participatory hearing in which parties present evidence through witnesses and exhibits and make arguments before the arbitrator.

Arbitration proceedings operate under rules administered by the arbitration organization conducting the arbitration proceeding, e.g., The Code of Procedure of the National Arbitration Forum. The arbitration organization, which can be public or private, is selected by the parties before or after the dispute. The organization appoints the arbitrator and administers the arbitration procedure. Arbitrations begin by a claimant filing a written arbitration claim with the arbitration organization and serving it on a respondent, who answers and may counterclaim. Arbitration proceedings are less formal than judicial proceedings, with limited discovery and motions and less strict rules of procedure and evidence. The procedures involved in litigation, arbitration, and administrative hearings are explained in detail in the companion book entitled *Advocacy by Roger Haydock and John Sonsteng,* Book One: Planning to Win, Chapter 2, Section C (West, 1994).

The arbitrator or panel of arbitrators decides a case by issuing a written arbitration award following the hearing. The award in a binding arbitration proceeding is final and there is usually no appeal, although the award can be vacated in a few circumstances such as a corrupt arbitrator or an illegal award. A binding arbitration award is as effective as a judgment entered after a judicial trial. Arbitration awards are legally enforceable in all fifty states and in the federal courts. State and federal laws allow parties to "confirm" an arbitration award into a judgment. A non-binding arbitration proceeding operates similarly to a binding arbitration process, with the exception that the award is only advisory and not final. A court may and can mandate parties use non-binding arbitration before proceeding to trial. Any party can refuse to accept the decision and have the dispute resolved through another dispute resolution method. Costs of arbitration include the filing fee and the fee for the arbitrator, usually computed on a hourly basis. And, no, arbitration cannot be used to resolve disputes you have about your grades.

6.9.4 Administrative Hearings

Administrative hearings typically resolve disputes involving statutory remedies. A party may file a petition with an administrative tribunal, and an administrative judge holds a hearing and decides the case. Administrative proceedings are similar to bench trials in litigation. The availability of discovery and the use of motions may be limited.

Controversies resolved through federal and state administrative hearings include workers compensation claims, unemployment compensation claims, tax claims, social security claims, welfare claims, and other rule based claims. Administrative claims may also involve regulatory procedures. Parties involved in a dispute regarding the enactment or enforcement of government regulations may appear before administrative bodies to present their case. Examples include utility rate setting cases and environmental cases, but exclude any claims you may have against your law school administration.

6.10 MEDIATION

Mediation involves disputing parties resolving their differences with the assistance of a mediator who facilitates a settlement in a private, confidential setting. Participants in mediation include the parties, their attorneys or representatives, and an impartial mediator. Mediators can clarify what the parties want, focus on their needs and interests, exchange information, and suggest alternative ways to reach an accord. It's acceptable to be nice in mediation.

Parties may mediate voluntarily by agreement, entered into either before or after a dispute arises, or as mandated by a court. Mediation differs from litigation and arbitration in that no decision is issued that involuntarily binds the parties. Mediation may take only a couple of hours, several hours, or a number of days, depending upon the complexity of the issues and the position of the parties. The cost of mediation includes the mediator's hourly fees and, in most mediations, an administrative fee.

Parties may use mediation by itself or before resorting to other forums to resolve a dispute. Parties may first attempt to mediate the dispute, and if that fails, they can then litigate, arbitrate, or administrate. The neutral who mediates the dispute with the parties is usually not the judge or arbitrator, but may be. The mediation process may not resolve the entire dispute, but may resolve some substantive and procedural issues.

The most common form of mediation involves one neutral mediator. Mediation may also be conducted by a team of mediators, known as a moderated settlement conference. All the mediators may be impartial, or one of them may be impartial and the others selected by each of the parties. Team mediation may be useful in complex cases or situations where the involvement of additional individuals may accelerate the mediation process. You will learn much more about mediation in Chapter 9, which will be reason enough to keep this book.

A combination mediation and arbitration proceeding is known as a med-arb proceeding. Mediation occurs first, followed by arbitration, if necessary. A combination arbitration and mediation is known as a arb-med proceeding (clever, huh?) A neutral acts as an arbitrator, conducts a hearing, and issues an advisory decision. This opinion becomes the basis for a mediation which follows the arbitration proceeding.

6.11 CASE EVALUATIONS AND OPINIONS

Parties may find it useful to obtain an independent evaluation of their case. There are three primary ways parties can obtain an evaluation from other persons.

6.11.1 Minitrial

Minitrial is a proceeding where each party makes a short presentation before a panel who then issues a written or oral evaluation of the case. The panel may consist of one or more neutrals or one neutral and a representative from each party. The non-binding decision may resolve the dispute or may be a basis for negotiation or mediation.

6.11.2 Summary Jury Trial

A summary jury trial is what it sounds like: the parties present a summary of their evidence and arguments to a mock jury. The jurors may be selected from a jury pool or may be obtained from a jury consulting organization. The jury, after hearing the evidence and presentation, deliberates and returns a recommended verdict. This advisory verdict provides the parties with a basis to predict what a jury would do after a complete trial. The lawyers may question the jurors about their verdict and learn why the jurors reached the decision they did. The verdict may also be a basis for negotiation and mediation.

6.11.3 Early Neutral Evaluation

This process involves a neutral who, early in the dispute resolution process, obtains information from the parties and evaluates the case. The recommendations of the neutral may become the basis for resolution by negotiation or mediation, may narrow the issues to be resolved, or may suggest a dispute resolution method or combination of methods to use. The neutral may also act as a mediator or arbitrator. Fact finding can be useful in resolving complex scientific, technical, or economic issues.

6.12 CREATING YOUR OWN DISPUTE RESOLUTION PROCESS

Parties involved in a dispute can create their own dispute resolution system instead of using an existing process. They can reach an agreement which provides the details and mechanics of the system to be used. This power to decide their own fate is based upon contract law and applicable federal and state statutes, including the Federal Arbitration Act. The parties need to consent to whatever system they wish to use, and their contractual agreement binds them to this process and makes the result enforceable.

The type of system used depends upon the needs of the parties. The parties may select one method or a combination of methods. For example, parties can agree to mediate, and if mediation is unsuccessful, agree to submit the dispute to binding arbitration. Parties often prefer to use fast, affordable, private, and fair resolution methods. They may reach an agreement before a dispute arises, known as a pre-dispute resolution agreement (e.g. a pre-dispute binding arbitration clause). Or parties can fashion their own process after a dispute arises, known as a post-dispute resolution agreement.

6.13 FORTUNE TELLER

Parties can visit a modern automated fortune teller machine (AFTM).

F. DISPUTE RESOLUTION GOALS

6.14 GOALS OF DISPUTE RESOLUTION METHOD

Parties should consider the following goals in designing or selecting a dispute resolution system:

Speed. How quickly do the parties need a resolution? How long can they wait?

Cost. What can the parties afford? What are the transaction costs? For example, in litigation, parties will need to have an attorney represent them. In arbitration or administrative hearings, the parties may reasonably represent themselves.

Exchange of Information. How should information be disclosed and exchanged between the parties? Is formal discovery necessary?

Discovery. In litigation, discovery includes depositions, interrogatories, document production requests, and admissions. In arbitration and administrative hearings, discovery may be much more limited, or the parties can agree to use specific discovery devices.

Availability of Motions. Do the parties need to bring motions which can resolve part or all of a case? In litigation, there are hundreds of motions that can be brought. In arbitration and administrative hearings, a limited number of motions may be available.

Hearing and Trial Procedures. All forums generally allow opening statements, direct and cross-examination of witnesses, submission of exhibits, use of expert witnesses, and closing arguments.

Decision Maker. Who should be the decision maker? Should it be an expert, like an arbitrator or administrative judge? Should it be a public judge? Should it be lay persons on a jury?

Finality. Should the decision be final and binding? Should there be broad appeal rights? Should there be limited circumstances to challenge the decision?

Privacy. Do the parties want the proceedings private? Do they prefer a public trial?

Enforceability. How will the final decision be enforced? Mediation settlements can be enforced as contracts. Arbitration, administrative, and judicial decisions can all be enforced as judgments.

Fairness and Satisfaction. Whatever the method used, the process must be fair and one in which the parties can be satisfied with the process if not with the result.

Mercenary Armies. Oh ... we're now well beyond that.

6.15 MANDATED ALTERNATIVE DISPUTE RESOLUTION

Alternative dispute resolution (ADR) is a popular description of non-litigation methods used to resolve disputes. The most common ADR methods are mediation and arbitration, previously described. A growing number of federal and state court systems mandate parties to use mediation or non-binding arbitration before they will be allowed to go to trial. A growing number of legislative enactments substitute ADR methods instead of litigation to resolve problems. Administrative agencies may require the parties to attempt to mediate a problem before a hearing is conducted.

These developments are occurring for a number of reasons. ADR methods are usually much faster and much less expensive than litigation. The use of ADR may result in a resolution that better meets the needs of the parties and that may not be available through a judicial or administrative decision. The transaction costs and attorney fees involved in ADR are significantly less than judicial proceedings. For many disputes, the litigation system can cause more problems that it resolves. But that's part of its ... charm?, and why so many cases settle through negotiations.

Chapter Seven
PLANNING FOR NEGOTIATION: WHAT IS IT YOUR CLIENT WANTS?

I'm ready to negotiate.

I'm going to demand what my client wants....

Well, maybe I should first....

What is it I want to do first? And then next?

I'll go by instinct....

Well, maybe I should plan.... Plan what?

I'll just use good negotiation tactics I've read about.

Where did I read about them?

Where is that book?

A. INTRODUCTION

7.1 THE STAGES OF NEGOTIATION PLANNING

Lawyers negotiate for clients to create transactions and to resolve disputes. Every client need or desire creates the potential for negotiated results. Successful negotiators:

- Establish goals based on their client's needs and wants and the other side's interests.

- Analyze effective approaches and factors that influence the negotiation.

- Effectively evaluate a situation or case.

- Assess ethical issues and concerns.

- Exchange information by disclosing and seeking information from the other side.

- Employ effective negotiation strategies and tactics, seek solutions that satisfy the client, propose alternative options, and explore creative and mutually satisfying solutions.

- Conclude the negotiation with an agreement that meets the client's needs and interests, or decide not to reach an accord.

This chapter focuses on the first four of these stages, and Chapter Eight explains the other three stages.

B. ESTABLISHING GOALS

7.2 NEGOTIATION GOALS

The first step before beginning a negotiation is to understand the goals of the client and the interests and needs of the other side.

7.2.1 Goals of the Client

What is it that the client really wants and needs from the negotiation? Determining this is discussed in Chapter Four. Now is a good time to review it, or read it for the first or fifth time, depending upon how much you enjoyed it.

Clients' wishes are both tangible and intangible. Tangible wishes include money, position, power, and having the other party do something. Intangible wishes include dignity, justice, psychological satisfaction, community cohesion, being heard, saving face, seeking revenge, promoting values, and insisting on principles. It is often more difficult to uncover and understand a client's intangible goals than the tangible ones, and efforts need to be made to do so.

A variety of factors—such as cultural, social, ethnic, economic, and religious—may also exert significant influence on client goals. For example, many clients behave primarily as entrepreneurs with the goal of maximizing profits in the marketplace. Other clients are not motivated primarily by money or do not act as competitively. Lawyers need to cultivate awareness of their clients' attitudes if they are to understand their goals.

Some client goals may be unreasonable or unethical, and attorneys must develop a way of reconsidering or transforming these goals (now be sure to re-read Chapter Four). This determination may be easy and obvious or difficult to discern. But it must be done.

Client interests often shift in the course of representation. Life goes on, the odds of winning at trial can change, business opportunities open and close, injuries heal or fester, personal and community situations change. Periodic discussions with clients may reveal these changes.

The goals of a client include past, present, and future interests. Clients may want something resolved from the past, may need something now, or may wish something in the future. Parties to a negotiation may get everything they want if their past, present, and future needs differ. If one side wants something now and another side wants something later, they both may get what they want. Negotiations that involve parties who want the same thing at the same time will require compromise.

7.2.2 Goals of the Other Side

It is equally critical to find out what the other side wants. If one side in a negotiation focuses only on getting what they want, they are much less likely to be successful than when they also focus on satisfying the other side. It is easy in a negotiation to demand or offer what a client wants. It is more challenging to make a proposal that will both get what one's client wants and satisfy the other side. The ultimate goal is to seek a negotiated solution which satisfies both sides.

7.2.3 Understanding Different Perceptions

Perceptions that parties have dramatically affect negotiation goals. Two examples demonstrate this impact of differing perceptions.

In a sale/purchase transaction, a buyer and seller may have significantly different perceptions about the value of a piece of land. A variety of objective and subjective perceptions may influence the parties:

Buyer	Seller
This land is going to be worth a lot more in the future.	This land is worth more now than I thought it would be when I bought it.
I can resell this land for more money tomorrow.	This property is not going to be worth any more tomorrow than it is today.
I have always wanted to own this piece of land.	I want to get rid of this and buy something else.
I can get this land re-zoned and make a huge profit.	I tried getting it re-zoned, and it can't be done.
I can keep some of this land for my own use, and sell part of it for the same price I'm paying for all of it.	No one else has offered me anywhere near this amount of money.
This land will skyrocket in value when the adjacent land is developed.	The bridge and highway are not going to be built making this land almost useless.

In litigation, adverse parties may have markedly different views about the case. The following views reflect what a plaintiff, who was injured in a golf cart accident, and the defendant golf course, who owns and leased the golf cart, might have in a personal injury lawsuit:

Plaintiff	Defendant
I expect something I lease to be safe and the defendant owes me, a consumer, special care.	The cart was recently inspected and was in excellent shape.
We carefully used the cart the same way other golfers use it.	The driver didn't know how to drive the cart and should have been more careful.
Special brakes should be placed on such carts, but the golf course is too cheap to do so.	The brakes didn't stop the cart because the tree did first.
If the defendant wants protection he should sell insurance with the cart. I would have bought some.	She was hurt because she stupidly stood up while the cart was moving.

Plaintiff	Defendant
I suffered a lot of pain and can't enjoy golf now, and they will pay me a lot.	She sues me instead of her friend who was driving because I have money.
This has never happened to me before, and I'll never be the same.	This has never happened on our course before, and the bad publicity has hurt my business.

These differing beliefs can be based on objective data, hearsay, speculation, or dreams. Both sides can be very satisfied when the negotiation is completed if their differing perceptions can be mixed and matched.

7.2.4   Why Not Reach an Agreement?

Parties will agree to a transaction or settlement because it will be better for them than not agreeing. To assess whether it is better or not, each party must assess what their alternatives are to a specific negotiated result. The key question to ask is: what will the client do, or be able to do, if the negotiation fails? Hopefully, they won't blame you.

There may be very good reasons not to reach an agreement. A seller may have other buyers who will submit bids. An employee may have more than one job offer. A plaintiff can engage in further discovery. A defendant can decide to go to trial. Much of the success of a negotiated accord will depend upon the extent to which one or both parties have considered realistic alternatives to the agreement or settlement. Whether or not something is accomplished during negotiation depends upon the attractiveness and appropriateness of other alternatives, known as BATNA: best alternatives available.

Options that a party has will affect how the party perceives interests and needs and what approaches or strategies a lawyer will adopt as the negotiation proceeds. These options will appear in various ways during a negotiation. In litigation, the parties may choose to have a judge or a jury resolve a dispute. In lease negotiations, the lessor may have other potential lessees, and the lessee may be able to lease from other lessors. In an employment setting, the availability of several potential employees will strengthen the bargaining position of the employer.

The negotiating lawyer has to prepare properly for the failure of negotiations. Lawyers can prepare a list of all possible actions that could be taken if negotiations fail, can evaluate each of the options, can attempt to creatively merge or modify the options, and can have the client select one which appears to be the best option. To do otherwise may mean that a negotiated accord may be reached primarily because the attorney has not seriously considered or prepared for other options and because the client is desperate.

The options available to the other side also need to be considered. Parties may not fully participate in negotiations because they believe that they have more attractive alternatives to satisfy their interests. A negotiator facing these situations will need to analyze and critique the alternatives available to the other side, to explain why such options do not adequately satisfy the other side's needs, and to otherwise persuade the other party that a negotiated accord is the best possible solution.

7.3 AUTHORITY TO NEGOTIATE AN ACCORD

The client makes the final decision to accept or reject a negotiated accord. A lawyer must receive explicit authority from the client as to what will be an acceptable result and needs to discuss the range of acceptable resolutions to the negotiation. This may be a preliminary assessment with the client, subject to revision as the lawyer and client gain information through the course of the negotiation. Or the client may have a firm minimum need or demand that is unlikely to change. In most negotiations, it is very important to have a clear understanding of the minimum and maximum amount of money or other benefits to be received or paid by a client and the upper and lower limits of probable recovery.

It is essential to have a client clearly define the boundaries of the lawyer's authority to reach an agreement. This prevents misunderstandings between lawyer and client—misunderstandings that can have serious repercussions for both. Attorneys should not assume they have authority to get the "best" deal possible. Of course, nothing should ever be assumed, except a really good mortgage for your first law office.

There are a variety of degrees of authority clients may delegate to their lawyer:

Unlimited Authority. The client may prefer or insist that the attorney make negotiation decisions. The client, or the lawyer, may want the lawyer to have complete control over what occurs and delegate all decision making, subject to the final approval of the client.

Range of Authority. The client may provide the attorney with instructions that delineate the range within which an attorney can accept or reject a proposition. The extent of authority may be general, providing the attorney with authority regarding major issues and with flexibility for minor issues.

Alternative Authority. Negotiations will invariably include alternative solutions to reach an accord. A lawyer will need to obtain the client's preferences regarding various optional solutions.

Specific Authority. Clients may know exactly what they want. An attorney will be guided during negotiations by specific instructions received from a client.

No Authority. The lawyer may be involved in negotiation discussions with the permission of a client but without any authority from a client to accept an agreement or resolve a problem. The attorney will need to discuss any proposed solutions with the client before a result can be obtained.

The client may confer authority upon the attorney either in writing or orally. A written understanding may prevent future misunderstandings. Oral authority will be appropriate as long as there is a clear communication between the client and attorney. Authority limits will often need to be modified, and ongoing contacts between the lawyer and client permit such changes.

C. SELECTING A NEGOTIATION APPROACH
7.4 NEGOTIATION APPROACHES

Negotiation results depend in large part on the approaches taken by the negotiators. A useful assessment may be to consider four general approaches to negotiations. It is common for lawyers to use a mix of these approaches in a negotiation:

The Competitive Approach. The competitive negotiator attempts to maximize a client's position and to minimize the opponent's position. These negotiators want to win and want the opponent to lose.

The Individualistic Approach. This negotiator seeks to maximize a client's position and is neutral about the opponent's position. These negotiators are self-centered about their interests and indifferent to the other side's needs.

The Diminishment Approach. A negotiator may attempt to minimize the other side's position while remaining relatively neutral about a client's position. These negotiators want the other side to lose while preserving the status quo for their client.

The Cooperative Approach. The cooperative negotiator seeks to maximize gains for both parties. These negotiators are interested in the needs and wants of both sides.

The Guilt Approach. This negotiator has no idea what approach to use and tries to shame the other side into feeling guilty and giving up everything. These negotiators are ineffective negotiating for clients, but may be successful in family negotiations.

7.5 TRADITIONAL AND MODERN BARGAINING MODELS

Another useful assessment is to analyze the negotiation process from two broad perspectives: the positional bargaining model and the interest based model.

The bargaining model generally involves a pattern of positions and concessions. Bargainers begin with high aspirations and opposing positions, exchange concessions, and reach a result at some undetermined point. More specifically, these lawyers usually establish extreme offers or demands, commit themselves to positions, argue issues, seek to persuade each other, make concessions, employ threats, and ultimately reach an agreement. This process represents a traditional way to create agreements and resolve disputes. Lawyers have long been engaged in this bargaining process and have achieved very acceptable agreements and satisfactory settlements for countless clients. These results contribute to the continued use and vitality of this process.

The interest based model generally involves the parties focusing on their differing and mutual interests. These negotiators explain their client's primary interests, seek information to discover the other side's interests, attempt to establish trust, avoid asserting or inviting extreme positions, seek cooperation, explore alternative options that may benefit both sides, and ultimately reach a mutually satisfactory agreement. This process reflects a popular way to reach a negotiated accord. A growing number of negotiators attempt to use this model in place of the more traditional bargaining process.

Both these approaches have advantages and disadvantages. What doesn't? Subsequent sections of this chapter will discuss the advantages. The following section explains the disadvantages.

Disadvantages of the positional bargaining model are:

It's a game. Elements of the bargaining form resemble a game. Both negotiators know that each will begin with an extreme position, that both will assert their positions to be firm yet will soon make concessions, that both will employ tactics that attempt to persuade or manipulate the other, and that a result will be reached despite recurring threats to the contrary. And, we don't want to encourage lawyers to play even more games.

It's adversarial. Aspects of the bargaining process also reflect an adversarial approach to negotiations. Whether it is a lease agreement, an employment contract, or a lawsuit settlement negotiation, many negotiators will view the other side as an "opponent" and engage in advocacy strategies, argumentative tactics, and aggressive behavior.

It promotes exaggeration. The bargaining process encourages negotiators to be selective, cautious, and suspicious in communicating information. The assertion of extreme offers and demands forces lawyers to fashion positions based on exaggerations or distortions.

It fosters distrust. The need to establish firm positions and to flexibly modify these positions as a negotiation progresses requires attorneys to carefully phrase disclosures. The realization by both lawyers that each is disclosing information that does not accurately reflect the true interests of a client fosters an aura of distrust between the negotiators.

It's a wasteful ritual. Facets of the bargaining process also constitute inefficient rituals which waste time, energy, and money. A competitive or disparaging strategy may initially be adopted for the primary purpose of establishing significant differences with the other side. Bargaining talks may be conducted as argumentative debates. Threats and bluffs may be employed to coerce the opponent into a concession.

It's too rigid. Various misconceptions about negotiations plague the bargaining process. It is presumed by many lawyers that the best way to achieve success at a negotiation is to demand a lot, concede little, control what happens, and take advantage of the other side as much as possible. This viewpoint holds that effective negotiators are secretive, conniving, and ruthless. These traits may be useful for spying, but not for negotiating.

Disadvantages of the interest based model are:

It exchanges misinformation. Negotiators who disclose their clients real interests may reveal too much information, providing the other side with too much helpful information. Instead of reciprocating with similar disclosures the other side may fudge their real interests. And, we don't want to encourage lawyers to fudge even more.

It promotes distrust. Mutual trust may be difficult to establish. A totally open and honest approach to a negotiation may not be reciprocated. Suspicion and distrust may overcome efforts to maintain a trusting relationship.

It's too inflexible. The lawyer concerned for the other side's interest may appear too generous or flexible. The other attorney may be inclined to take advantage of this approach leading to a one sided agreement. This method may also exacerbate risks in the negotiation process. The "opposing" lawyer may exploit the cooperative nature of the other negotiator and increase demands, exaggerate differences or refuse to cooperate.

It's a change. Lawyers used to the traditional bargaining model may have difficulty in changing their approach. They may revert to asserting positions or making threats which destroy mutual trust. Other lawyers may have difficulty considering alternative solutions that benefit both parties because of their inclination to want to "win" the negotiation. They may prefer to be competitive instead of cooperative.

It may be inappropriate. This model may not be appropriate for all situations. A party to a potential deal may be more effective being firm and insistent. A defendant in a lawsuit who faces frivolous or weak claims may be better off adopting a principled take-it-or-leave-it position. Those of you who majored in philosophy may have an advantage here.

Which approach—or combination of approaches—works best depends upon the circumstances. Negotiators should avoid focusing on positional bargaining and concentrate on reconciling interests where best. Negotiations should also avoid the interest based approach if the other side is unwilling to reciprocate and cooperate.

7.6 ASSESSING NEGOTIATION INFLUENCES

Three primary factors influence negotiations:

- Power and how it is balanced
- The level of mutual trust
- The level of experience of the negotiators

7.6.1 Power, Power, Power

Power is the capacity or ability to accomplish things. The effectiveness of a negotiation approach depends upon the capacity or ability of the negotiator to achieve the desired result. Power is derived from many sources. Money, time, needs, threats, and perception, as well as gas turbines create power. A defendant may have money to pay a settlement now, or may have more money in the future. A plaintiff may be desperate for money now, or may be willing to wait until the jury verdict. A buyer may need critical supplies immediately, or may be able to negotiate with other sources. A seller may not want to risk market fluctuation, or may threaten to sell to someone else later.

Power often can be created by perception. The appearance of power or the ability to use power appropriately can be an important tactic in negotiations. A party with more power may dominate the negotiation and get what they want. A party without power may be at a great disadvantage. Balancing power—both actual and perceived—is the goal of an effective negotiator.

Lawyers in the litigation process have a substantial amount of power derived from the adversary system, the reality of expenses, discovery methods, the threat of trial, and other factors. Lawyers in negotiations involving agreements also have sources of substantial power; although, again, the degree of power may be largely a matter of perception. For example, consider a negotiation between a corporation attorney and a bank attorney regarding a commercial loan agreement. Many corporate attorneys view their role as a "beggar" who would have to "plead" a case before the bank's attorney. The bank will invariably receive favorable loan terms in these negotiations. Other corporate attorneys assume a contrary attitude. They approach the bank's attorney with the view that the bank has a need to loan some of its money and ask the bank attorney why the corporation should decide to borrow money from that bank. In these situations the corporation will invariably obtain favorable terms. The roles, attitudes, and perceived power displayed by the lawyers may be the product of their assumptions regarding stereotypical negotiation situations. The corporate negotiators who pierce the traditional stereotype that the bank has more power promote their client's interests more effectively.

7.6.2 It's Always Been a Matter of Trust

Negotiations between lawyers who trust each other may proceed differently from negotiations where distrust prevails. Lawyers who have mutually negotiated previous agreements or who have tried many cases with each other may have developed a level of mutual trust. They may respect each other's judgment, more often than not. They understand that their word is their bond. A high level of trust may permit them to arrive at a mutually satisfactory settlement without having to spend a lot of time negotiating. Lawyers who distrust each other—or the other party—will have difficulty communicating and negotiating. Trust may need to be developed to achieve a successful result. Bringing a reputation of honesty to a negotiation is an essential attribute. You can start forming your reputation now by not exaggerating your G.P.A and class rank.

7.6.3 The Experience of a Lifetime

Negotiation experience is derived in significant part from the life experiences of the lawyer-negotiator. Before a lawyer negotiates on behalf of a client, that lawyer has negotiated a lot. Consider yourself: you have been negotiating since birth. Every time you wanted or needed something, you used some negotiation tactic to get it. You have a lot of negotiation experience with your family and friends and obtained from work, hobbies, and shopping experiences. Just look at your Visa balance.

Lawyers will draw on the negotiation approaches developed on their own in negotiating on behalf of a client. These experiences may or may not be useful in a legal situation. Another primary source of experience comes from negotiating specific transactions and cases again and again. These repeated professional experiences provide knowledge, information, credibility, and confidence.

The level of experience of the negotiators may affect the process. Experienced lawyers who have negotiated previous agreements or tried many cases are able to negotiate more efficiently toward results which reflect past negotiations and which will be comparable to future situations. This wealth of experience may allow them to arrive at a mutually satisfactory settlement fairly quickly.

Inexperienced lawyers may proceed differently. If both negotiators are inexperienced, they may use unfamiliar, cumbersome or time consuming approaches to negotiate. Their unfamiliarity or uncertainty may cause them to be very cautious in reaching a result. The better prepared they are, and the more information they can obtain from experienced negotiators, the easier it will be for them to avoid these problems.

An inexperienced negotiator who is negotiating with an experienced negotiator has some disadvantages and advantages. The lack of experience may make inexperienced negotiators vulnerable to certain tactics and may cause them to miss opportunities. Some experienced lawyers may attempt to exploit inexperience by using unfamiliar tactics, being condescending, using peer pressure, and offering friendly advice. The inexperienced lawyer needs to counter these approaches.

Thorough preparation and continual planning may make up for the lack of experience. The more experienced negotiator may take for granted the inexperienced negotiator or assume that experience will overcome this extra preparation. Lack of experience can be balanced by hard work and the confidence to succeed.

The novice attorney can involve the other attorney as a mentor by asking questions and appearing to use the other lawyer's experience as a resource in shaping a result. Comments such as "In twenty years of practice that position has never been taken" or "Well, I have tried this type of case thirty times and this is your first one" can take their toll. The novice lawyer can demonstrate energy and enthusiasm the more experienced lawyer may not have, can say they will devote all their available time to this case, and can comment: "I can't imagine anything more satisfying than winning this case with you on the other side." The novice lawyer should exercise restraint and *not* say: "This is the beginning of the end of your long career. You're mine."

Friendly advice should be ignored. While it may appear easy to reject this advice, lawyers who practice in small communities or specialized areas may have a difficult time resisting threats implicit in the advice. If experienced lawyers really want to be friendly, test that assertion by asking for (more) information or (more) money. Or, if they're real friendly, ask if they'll adopt you after the negotiation and pay off your VISA balance.

D. EVALUATING THE NEGOTIATION

7.7 A CHECKLIST

A thorough evaluation of a case includes an analysis of various factors that effect the preparation and presentation of a case. The following checklist lists factors that need to be considered:

Interest and Needs

What interests and needs does the client have?

What interests and needs does the other side have?

What mutual interests do the parties have?

What will satisfy the parties?

Exchange of Information

What information and documents should be disclosed to the other side?

What questions should be asked and information sought from the other side?

Financial concerns

What are the financial interests and needs of each party?

How are the attorneys being compensated and how much?

Negotiation approaches

What negotiation approaches should or will be used by each side?

What experience does each party have with this type of negotiation?

How effective is each attorney as a negotiator?

Sources of satisfaction

Why does each side want to reach a negotiated accord?

Who will have the ultimate authority to reach an accord?

Will the negotiation result in an accord which matches the values of each party and negotiator?

How will the result affect the reputation of the party and the negotiators?

Relationships

How does the existence or lack of a relationship between the parties affect the negotiation, past and future?

Will the like or dislike of the negotiators for each other affect the negotiations?

How will the negotiation affect future cases or business for the parties and the lawyers?

Time

Do time considerations or a deadline affect either side?

Are the parties and negotiators available or are there conflicts with other transactions, cases, vacations?

Alternatives to Negotiation

If the negotiation fails, what will each party do?

First Aid Kit

Oops. Wrong checklist

This evaluation preparation continues throughout a negotiation. An ongoing assessment includes what is being said and what is not being said, what is being done and not being done, and predicting what will happen in the future. Cases vary in the degree to which an attorney can predict outcomes. Some cases will be relatively easy to evaluate; many others will only permit "guesstimates." Lawyers also differ in their ability to predict what may or will happen in the future (or not).

The evaluation of a case includes both a general evaluation and a specific evaluation. Specific evaluation depends on the facts, client interests, and issues to be negotiated. General evaluation depends upon whether the case is a transaction or a lawsuit to be negotiated.

7.8   GENERAL EVALUATION OF A TRANSACTION

Evaluating a transaction includes a consideration of the following issues:

What amounts of money have been exchanged in similar transactions? Parties may be influenced by what others have done in previous transactions.

What is the market value? There may be a variety of sources of market value depending upon the type of land, goods, or services involved.

What are the total direct and indirect costs involved in the transaction? Direct expenses may be easy to determine, and indirect costs may be more difficult to ascertain but significant.

How else can this transaction be completed? There may be other businesses or individuals with whom to negotiate the same transaction.

What will happen if this transaction does not occur? What will the client do with the money not spent or with the deal not completed?

7.9 GENERAL EVALUATION OF A LAWSUIT

The value of a case depends upon the attorney's assessment of the probable outcome. Usually these determinations consist of a range of amounts: a jury is most likely to return a verdict in the range of X to Y, or an arbitrator will probably decide based on factors A and B. Lawyers can effectively evaluate the proof aspects of a case by analyzing what their closing arguments will be.

Lawyers have developed some devices in an attempt to make the evaluation process objective:

Formula. One formula involves the selection of an average damage figure for the case multiplied by a percentage that reflects the probability of success ($100,000 average verdict times 60% chances of success equals $60,000 proposed settlement).

Multiplier. Another formula computes personal injury outcomes as an amount equal to X times the special damages with X being anywhere from three to ten in value. ($8,000 in specials times five equals a $40,000 proposed settlement amount).

Point system. Other lawyers have developed point-system formulas that assign points for various factors such as liability, injury, type of plaintiff, and type of defendant. The point total is then used as a percentage multiplier to produce a figure representing what a jury would award in a perfect case.

Jury verdict reports. Published reports summarizing jury verdicts may also yield comparative information. These reports may be gathered by a national firm, by a local bar or trial lawyers' association, or by governmental or judicial agencies. Verdicts involving similar cases are obtained and compared to the current case with proportionate adjustments made to reflect differences in liability, damages, and other factors.

7.10   EVALUATING YOUR INTERESTS AND VALUES

As mentioned previously, you will need to assess your past personal and professional experiences in determining how they influence your present negotiation approaches. And you will need to consider the following influences.

7.10.1   What Are Your Present Interests and Needs?

Attorneys' personal and professional needs may well influence negotiations. The task is to become conscious of one's values and goals as an attorney and plan to avoid them getting in the way of a client's values and goals. For example, impressing the other side with the ability to be a patient, deliberate negotiator may not be consistent with coming to a quick agreement for a client. Or, an attorney who wants to come to an agreement quickly because of financial or time pressures may not as vigorously represent a client's interests.

All sorts of interests may influence you. Your financial and economic goals may be achieved or adversely affected by an agreement. Your status as an attorney may affect your judgment. Are you in-house counsel for a company with a larger agenda, or are you an attorney in a law firm who needs the client for continuing business? How are you being paid? Will you make more or less if an agreement is reached now? Other needs you may have involve your reputation (how will an agreement or the failure to conclude a deal enhance it?) and your desiring more experience (maybe you want to try a case instead of settling it). The primary way to blunt these potential conflicts of interest is to be aware of them so that you may mitigate their effects and to openly discuss them with a client.

7.10.2　What Are Your Values?

You have developed a set of values, moral principles, norms of behavior, and ethical guidelines for both your personal and professional life. Your clients have also developed their own principles. All these factors will influence your approach to a negotiation and your client's acceptance or rejection of a result. For example, you may believe it wrong to lie about certain things in a negotiation, but a client may believe you should do so. You may think it appropriate to obtain as much money as possible for your client, but your client may perceive that "fairness" requires demanding less money. You need to assess your own personal and professional principles and discuss these with your client when necessary.

7.10.3　Will You Listen to Yourself?

There is a time and place to talk to yourself. Self-evaluation must be done periodically so that you can evolve and improve as an effective negotiator. Taking the time to consider the impact of values, interests, and needs and taking the time to critique actual negotiations to learn from what you did and did not do are critical to being an effective negotiator. Just make sure you listen to what you have to say.

7.11　EVALUATING AND UNDERSTANDING THE OTH-ER SIDE

How the other side negotiates depends upon factors that influence them. Negotiation behavior may be influenced by various factors including experience, age, gender, and other characteristics. Predictions about what a negotiator may say or do based upon conclusions drawn from previous experiences may be helpful. Predictions based on stereotypical evaluations may be dangerous. Speculative assessments about a group of individuals may not be based upon reliable data but may be based on biases and prejudices. For example, some negotiators believe that male lawyers will be more competitive and female lawyers more cooperative. Even if this generalization were reliable, it would be foolhardy to assume an individual male or female negotiator will act according to such a trait. It is better to treat each negotiator as a distinct individual. If you don't, we don't want to be there to watch.

An effective negotiator must also try to understand the other side's position as the other side sees and feels it. They are—or should be—doing the same to you. It is easy to focus on your client's position, especially as an advocate and fail to understand (this does not mean agree with) the other side's position. You can talk with yourself, your clients, and with others who are not involved in the matter (keeping within the confidentiality rules of professional conduct, of course) until the other side's position becomes a bit easier to understand. This is important if one wants to avoid unpleasant surprises during the negotiation. What is motivating the other side if not a strong position? If imagination fails and one cannot understand *how* the other side can seem to feel its position is so strong, keep trying. They could be right, and you could be wrong. It's possible.

Analysis of the strengths and weaknesses of each party's deal or case is a dynamic, ongoing process. In the course of it all, remember that every contact with the other party—whether during a contract negotiation or in a dispute—is a negotiation. Be well prepared.

7.12 PREPARING A THEORY OF THE DEAL OR CASE

A theory of the deal or case is a short, simple, and persuasive explanation of the client's position. If the alternative to a negotiated agreement will be to go to trial, then later the theory will be developed for use in persuading a decision maker such as judge or jury. A good theory of the deal or case should be persuasive to the other side, and it should also aid the attorney and client when they need to justify changes of position as the negotiation proceeds. For example, a lawyer whose client is an artist striving to license a design may have a theory that the design should be purchased because of its strong appeal to the children that the company hopes to attract to buy its product. During negotiations, the lawyer may explain a lowering of the artist's price for the license by referring to the resulting lower prices that children will pay for purchases which will in turn increase sales and profits. Developing an effective theory of the deal or case will also help focus the negotiation on the client's position.

7.13 PREPARING FOR THE NEGOTIATION

Preparation for a negotiation includes rehearsing the negotiation and preparing written materials for use during the negotiation. Rehearsal may be informal or formal. Negotiators may mentally prepare and talk with themselves about what to say. Negotiators may also prepare with their clients, colleagues, or other team negotiators.

7.13.1 Preparing a Negotiation Notebook

A negotiation notebook that contains various types of materials can be a highly useful device. What should be included depends upon the specific requirements of a negotiation. Some generic information includes:

A summary of vital data, facts, events.

A list of documents or exhibits and copies or originals of such writings.

Lists which detail important dates, figures, and objective information.

Summaries and citations of legal authorities.

Questions to be asked of the other side.

Information and documents to be disclosed to the other side.

A summary of strong points or weak points for each side.

A description of the interests and needs of each side.

A comparison of which interests and needs are different, which conflict, and which are complementary.

An overall negotiation plan including the initial offer or demand or response, a description of subsequent positions or concessions, and final positions.

Alternative proposals and solutions.

A draft of written negotiation documents to finalize and formalize the negotiation.

A list of the other side's favorite snacks.

7.13.2 Preparing an Agenda

It is always wise to prepare a negotiation agenda. Some negotiations have a defined agenda. Negotiators may submit a written agenda to the other side which lists topics for discussion and resolution. A contract or lease proposal inherently includes an agenda with its listed clauses and terms. Labor negotiations may involve a list of issues that need to be negotiated before negotiations on the merits occur.

The negotiators may initially agree on a list of all the issues to be negotiated. This single text details the matters that will be discussed and avoids problems with negotiating an unknown number of individual issues. A preliminary comprehensive agenda may operate as a device to prod both sides to engage in discussions without having to take firm positions, so that later discussions can be more productive. Litigated cases do not traditionally present a set agenda, but cases have specific claims, damages, and defenses which can be used as an agenda.

The lack of an agenda creates unorganized discussion. An agenda prepared in advance permits topics and issues to be discussed in a structured, orderly manner. Organized negotiations increase the likelihood that the needs of the parties will be addressed. One clear advantage that an agenda provides is the preclusion of the later introduction of unanticipated matters. Another advantage is that an agenda prevents an attorney from refusing to discuss an issue during the late stages of a negotiation. A tactic some lawyers use is arbitrarily to refuse to discuss an issue because it was not discussed earlier and they assumed it would not be pursued.

7.14 I WANT TO CONTACT THEM. HOW?

Contacts between attorneys occur through letters, over the telephone, and in offices. Initial planning includes deciding which of these contacts will be made.

7.14.1 I Want to Write Them. Why?

Correspondence can be very useful in documenting positions, offers or demands. Letters can explain positions economically.

Statements can be written in a clear and convincing manner that may avoid misunderstandings. They can also be later useful in writing your memoirs. Written contacts also have some disadvantages. They provide the other attorney with time to reflect on what response should be made, and they may involve more time and expense than telephone contacts.

7.14.2 I Want to Call Them. Why?

Telephone negotiations also have advantages and disadvantages. Telephone discussions tend to be shorter than face-to-face negotiations because person-to-person meetings justify taking more time. Misunderstandings or understandings caused by facial expressions are avoided because of the lack of visual feedback. Telephone conversations can be less stressful because the lack of personal contact reduces peer pressure. It is easier to say no over the phone than it is in person because phone contacts tend to be impersonal. The caller almost always has the advantage because of preparation and anticipation. The recipient may reduce this handicap by not making a decision during the initial conversation and by returning the call after planning a response. A written memo summarizing the conversation can be prepared after the conversation and sent to the other side. A collect negotiation call can always be declined.

7.14.3 I Want to See Them? Why?

Many negotiations will be more effectively conducted with the negotiators face to face, sometimes with and sometimes without their clients. These negotiation meetings may occur after letters have been exchanged and telephone negotiations conducted. Which method should be used at what stage of the negotiation depends upon the assessment of which is the most effective, efficient, and economical method to use.

7.15 I WANT TO NEGOTIATE HERE. NO, HERE.

The decision where to negotiate usually focuses on the office of either negotiator. There are advantages to both places. It may be preferable to hold negotiations in one's own office because: it avoids the inconvenience of being removed from other obligations; it saves time and expense; it may provide the one negotiator and client with a psychological advantage over the other negotiator coming to negotiate; it is more convenient to display exhibits, use charts and arrange the room appropriately; it permits access to information and data from files; team negotiations with colleagues may be more convenient to arrange; and it may be easier to establish and maintain the proper atmosphere for the negotiation.

It may be advisable to have the negotiation discussions occur in the other side's office because: it is easier to leave; it is easier to concentrate on the negotiations without being distracted or interrupted; the other side has difficulty in refusing requests for documents and other information at hand; and information and supporting data can be selectively brought or not made available.

Other locations for meetings include a client's office or a neutral site. These alternatives may be appropriate depending upon the type of case, the kind of client, the needs of people involved, the facilities needed, the degree of comfort required, previous negotiation discussions, and the relationship between the attorneys. Negotiations may also occur in mediator offices and in courtroom hallways and judges' chambers.

Seating arrangements also may impact on the process. For example, it may be more conducive to a cooperative relationship to have both lawyers sit on the same side of a conference table rather than across from each other, or it may make no difference.

7.16 I WANT TO NEGOTIATE, TOO. WHAT ABOUT ME?

If more than one attorney is available to negotiate, the choice needs to be made regarding who and how many should negotiate. Obvious considerations are a lawyer's familiarity with the case and with the other negotiators. A single negotiator is always in charge of what is happening and does not have to share decision making or implementing with anyone. The other side does not have the opportunity to create disagreement or dissension among multiple negotiators. Depending upon the complexity of the negotiations, negotiating alone can produce some difficulties and cause things to be missed and overlooked.

Team negotiators make it possible for the work to be divided so that one person can concentrate on observing and listening while another lawyer does the talking, or topics can be divided, allowing the negotiators to concentrate on fewer items. More than one negotiator also permits the use of different tactics: one negotiator may take a hard line and the other a soft line as a technique. Two people working together may also be able to come up with more creative solutions than a lone negotiator. But two lawyers may also have difficulty coordinating their efforts.

Clients may need to or may want to be present. Many negotiations—especially those involving transactions—require the presence of the client to make decisions. Some negotiations can begin without the client who participates in later negotiation sessions. There will be occasions when the client's presence may not assist the negotiation because a frank discussion may be inhibited, particularly if the conversation involves a discussion about the client's conduct. Nevertheless, a client can be an asset during negotiation, whose presence may add an appropriate dimension to the discussions, and who can also provide information or make decisions.

Other participants besides attorneys can be present at some negotiations. It might be helpful to have non-lawyers attend a negotiation. An accountant may provide financial data; a real estate agent may be able to evaluate property values; a tax specialist may provide information regarding tax consequences; a soothsayer may be able to predict the future settlement. These individuals need to understand their role and how the negotiator will communicate with them.

7.17 I WANT TO NEGOTIATE NOW, NOT LATER.

Time is always a factor in negotiations. Many negotiations include a self-contained deadline. The attorneys may have only scheduled one hour to discuss an agreement or a judge may have given litigators thirty minutes to settle a case. Even in negotiations without time limits, lawyers always have limitations placed on their availability. Their other work and clients require their attention. Establishing time limits may be a useful tactic.

These limits may or may not be revealed or discussed with the other attorney.

Negotiation discussions usually fill the amount of time available, with results reached when a deadline looms imminent. This deadline phenomenon matches other life experiences. Many attorneys complete and file briefs on the last day; many taxpayers file income tax returns near the deadline; legislatures enact many laws at the end of sessions. Time deadlines, either intentionally established or caused by the natural course of events, increase the momentum of negotiation discussions.

Negotiators who establish several periodic deadlines within an overall time frame will promote more efficient negotiations. Deadlines impose some discipline upon the negotiating parties precipitating an accord and providing a legitimate reason why a decision should be reached by a certain time. Qualified deadlines, which permit time extensions for certain conditions, provide incentives for the negotiators to reach an accord while reducing the pressures imposed by firm deadlines.

Deadlines nevertheless may cause problems. A deadline accompanied by a party's threat to do or not do something will automatically force that party to fulfill the threat or lose credibility by failing to go through with that threat, unless that party has a very good explanation why such action or inaction is appropriate. Deadlines also create pressures for the negotiators that may be unreasonable or counterproductive. The less time pressure some negotiators feel, the more relaxed, flexible, and creative they may be.

7.18 HOW MUCH TIME DO WE HAVE?

Several timing factors may affect the negotiation:

Strength. Negotiators with time on their side can deal from a position of strength. A party who has time pressures, dates, or deadlines that have to be met may be at a disadvantage. The commercial tenant who has to move by a certain date may become disadvantaged the closer the negotiation discussions approach that date. The negotiator whose schedule has no available time may have a severe time conflict in postponing an agreement.

Immediate Needs. Some parties involved in negotiation discussions may have an immediate need. The stronger this interest is, the weaker a negotiation position may become. The party who needs a job to earn some much needed income will be at a growing disadvantage the longer a prospective employer continues delaying a negotiated agreement. Some parties with potential litigation claims may be at a similar disadvantage. Insurance claims adjusters often succeed with low offers made at times when a claimant needs money.

Effort and Expenses. Early accords may be advantageous to one party if the other party does not want to put the necessary effort, time, and money into further discussions or litigation. Many clients will not be able to afford extensive attorney's fees, requiring a lawyer to accelerate the process of reaching an accord.

Harmful Information. Circumstances in which one party fears the other side might learn about some information which would alter positions may prompt a negotiated agreement. Situations with glaring factual or legal weaknesses unknown to the other side may dictate an early settlement to avoid the discovery of such defects.

Time of Meeting. Early mornings and early afternoons will usually provide more time for protracted negotiation contacts, whereas late morning and late afternoon times may rush the negotiators into a hasty settlement or into a deadlock, to the disadvantage of one or both sides.

Client Instruction. Client needs may dictate timing. A client may instruct the attorney to resolve a matter through negotiation at a time when the client's negotiating posture is weak.

Patience. Patience is the ability to forgo immediate satisfaction in exchange for gaining more satisfaction in the future. Parties may have many reasons for wanting to settle as soon as possible, not the least of which will be to finalize a legal agreement or end the uncertainty surrounding litigation. Some negotiators place too much emphasis on speed. They may be unable to handle anxiety and uncertainty properly or may have a psychological block about time delays. They may unreasonably fear that the other side will walk out or that some unexpected event will intervene. Patience allows a negotiator to take the time to understand the issues, weigh the risks, test the opponent's strength, appear uneager, explore alternative positions, and probe for problem-solving resolutions. A reluctance to negotiate will often strengthen a bargaining position because the negotiator does not appear anxious to resolve a matter.

Patients.... sorry, that's another profession.

E. ASSESSING ETHICAL CONCERNS

Ethical norms—whether from a divine source or otherwise—significantly influence the negotiation process by shaping the actions of negotiating lawyers. Provisions of the Rules of Professional Conduct apply to negotiations. These ethical standards require an attorney to be fully prepared for a negotiation, to accept only those negotiations which the attorney has the competency to handle, to represent a client zealously, and to be truthful in statements to others in the course of representing clients. The lack of time, the commitment to other clients, the lack of knowledge of specialized substantive law, or the absence of sufficient negotiation experience may prompt a lawyer either to refer a negotiation to another lawyer or seek assistance from a specialist.

7.19 ETHICAL RULES

Ethical rules prohibit an attorney from threatening criminal prosecution in a civil case, representing a client regarding a matter in which the attorney previously served as arbitrator or mediator, acquiring any interest in the negotiated matter, compromising a matter because of the effect it might have on the attorney's reputation, and negotiating an agreement that restricts the right to practice law. Conduct that is generally prohibited in the negotiation of contract disputes includes: conjuring up a pretended dispute, asserting an interpretation contrary to a client's understanding, falsifying information, and making harassing demands. Some jurisdictions may impose obligations of good faith and fair dealings in certain types of negotiations.

7.19.1 Ethical Norms

Like all of lawyering, negotiation will challenge a lawyer's morals even when the lawyer has complied with all legal ethics rules. What threats are acceptable—morally, personally, socially, legally? What tactics are acceptable: Scorched earth approach? Appeals to bias? Can one make a deal that one doubts the client can or will honor? Can one try to get out of a deal arguing that it's unfair after agreeing to it? If it might help the strategy to plan to portray one's client in an unfavorable light— e.g. as having unrealistically high expectations, or being particularly bellicose or greedy or stupid—must one reveal that to the client? Good lawyers plan for these challenges, resolve them when they occur, and try in any event to live their lives in harmony with their personal codes of conduct. For most, it will be too high a price to sacrifice personal values for anticipated professional advancement.

The lack of accountability for statements made during negotiations accounts for some questionable ethical conduct. The lack of publicity surrounding negotiation discussions, the unlikelihood that a misrepresentation will be discovered, the lack of opportunity by the other side to investigate the accuracy of a representation, and the fact that an accord is reached, all tempt some negotiators to take advantage of the situation and stretch ethical standards.

7.20 THE TRUTH?

Ethical considerations on truth telling in negotiations present probably the greatest quandary for lawyers. Considered opinions about the propriety of lying during negotiations range from the position that a lawyer should never resort to lies, to the position that certain situations may justify lies, to the position that a lawyer must lie in some circumstances to protect client interests. What is Aristotle's e-mail address?

Whether an attorney must tell the truth may depend upon the type of "lie" asserted by the lawyer, the position of the lawyer regarding the propriety of "lying," and the situation which prompts the "lie." Untruthful statements range from the very direct to the very indirect: a person may volunteer a statement that contains a blatant untruth, exaggerate some information through puffing, remain silent in a situation to avoid having to provide correct information, be asked a question and answer it evasively and incompletely, or refuse to provide any answer in response to a question. Lawyers' decisions to be untruthful will depend on their views of such practices.

Lawyers may have a duty not to reveal certain information in negotiations and a duty not to lie. These conflicting obligations complicate the process of deciding ethically which should be done. It is an inadequate answer to say that if the other side has no right to the information or if the attorney has an obligation to withhold the information, the attorney should remain silent. The very act of silence may reveal the nature of the adverse information. The only way for the attorney to respond effectively will be to say something. The damage in saying something is the creation of a false statement or false impression. There is no easy or quick ethical resolution of these problems. It may be that in such a situation a lawyer will feel duty bound to mislead the other side. The situation within which the opportunity to "lie" arises determines the appropriateness of such conduct.

Many practitioners do not believe they engage in lying when they negotiate. Yet the nature of negotiation often seems to force lawyers to engage in forms of misrepresentation. The following subsections describe three negotiation scenarios that produce different answers to this quandary.

7.20.1 Facts, Data, and Evidence

It is unethical and improper for a lawyer knowingly to manufacture facts, falsify data, and make up evidence. These are obvious instances of lies. It may be appropriate for a lawyer to present an exaggerated statement of facts, to interpret questionable data, or to describe possible evidence that may be available. These instances reflect borderline situations of proper/improper conduct. Valid differences of opinions exist regarding what is a permissible exaggeration, what is an appropriate interpretation, and how likely it is that evidence will be available. Considered differences of opinion will exist regarding what is and what is not a fact.

Facts may be divided into past facts, present facts, and future facts. Past and present facts are actual facts, but future facts are really more in the nature of opinions. Informed differences of opinion may exist justifying the "misrepresentation" of facts, as long as those facts are not material or relevant to the negotiation. This position mirrors contract fraud analysis that establishes fraud only if the facts involved were material to the case. It also reflects the provisions of Model Rule of Professional Conduct 4 which refers to truthful disclosures of "material" and relevant facts. These borderline decisions will be resolved differently by negotiators based upon their personal and professional ethical norms.

7.20.2   Law, Precedent, Cases

A lawyer has an obligation to accurately disclose and present the law to a judge. A lawyer cannot knowingly falsify or make up legal precedent. A lawyer may have to disclose adverse legal precedents to a judge but not to the other negotiator during a negotiation. These duties become confused when mixed with other obligations to interpret the law in a light that supports a client's position, to argue that legal precedent supports a certain result, and to advocate that new law should be created. These obligations of interpretation, argument, and advocacy may conflict with the duties to be accurate and complete in disclosing and presenting black and white law. Different lawyers will resolve these conflicts differently based on their assessment of the "grayness" of the law and their obligations to their clients.

7.20.3   Opinions, Tactics, and Positions.

Our negotiation process countenances the misrepresentation of opinions, tactics, and positions. An attorney may deceive the other negotiator regarding these sorts of information either because such misrepresentation constitutes strategic tactics and is not a lie or because our system permits and requires lawyers to lie in some situations. The former explanation sounds more appropriate because the latter explanation appears to advocate that attorneys lie, a position which bothers many. Model Rule of Professional Conduct 4.1 recognizes differences between misrepresentations of facts and misrepresentations of opinions. The comments to the rule explain this difference in part:

> This Rule refers to statements of fact. Whether a particular element should be regarded as one of fact can depend on the circumstances. Under generally accepted conventions in negotiation, certain types of statements ordinarily are not taken as statements of material fact. Estimates of price or value placed on the subject of a transaction and a party's intentions as to an acceptable settlement of a claim are in this category, and so is the existence of an undisclosed principal except where nondisclosure of the principal would constitute fraud.

Regardless of the explanation of this phenomenon, the reality is that some negotiators routinely mislead and deceive other negotiators concerning certain information. Examples abound in negotiations. Lawyers will:

> Render an opinion about a matter that does not reflect their true opinion.

> Make an exaggerated claim that some property or injury is worth a certain value.

> Assert a threat which they or their client have no real intention to carry through.

> Present a false demand which does not reflect their client's goals or needs.

> Describe a position of their client which they have manufactured.

> Pretend to be interested in reaching an accord when their real intent is to delay or deadlock proceedings.

155

These and other common statements and conduct that constitute misrepresentations appear to be essential to the negotiation process. But must they be? Their frequency can be dramatically reduced and the need for lawyers to rely on such tactics can be substantially eliminated by employing different negotiation strategies and tactics. With effective preparation, a lawyer can:

> Base an opinion or evaluation not on the attorney's inflated perception of something but on objective criteria obtained from reliable, impartial sources.

> Avoid having to assert threats and instead encourage the other side to reach a negotiated accord by focusing on how negotiations can result in mutual gains for both sides.

> Delay obtaining specific authority from a client until alternative proposals have been considered and evaluated by both negotiators.

> Discuss the interests and needs of both clients instead of establishing and arguing the legitimacy of set positions.

7.21 REMAINING AN ETHICAL CHARACTER

It is a major premise of this book that lawyers need not and should not lie, mislead, deceive, or otherwise misrepresent information during negotiations. Deceitful conduct is both unethical and risky strategy. Lying may be discovered, resulting in deadlocked negotiations or providing a cause of action to set aside an agreement. Lying may also destroy the reputation of attorneys and render them inefficient as negotiators. Lying should be avoided for professional business reasons as well as for ethical reasons.

One major reason that lawyers engage in misleading and deceitful conduct is their failure to prepare thoroughly for a negotiation and to consider creative options and alternative solutions. Laziness and unimaginative assessments will account for lawyers' reliance on the easier and simpler tactics of lying. Be prepared, and then some. And when you don't know what to do, call your mentor day or night.

Chapter Eight
NEGOTIATIONS: GETTING WHAT YOUR CLIENT WANTS

Both sides want me. It seems I'm very popular.

Well, one side says they want me, but I wonder if they really do. And the other side has something like me already, and I'm curious why they would want more.

Fortunately, I have a split personality and I can reproduce myself on demand. So there should be enough for everyone.

It will be interesting to see how they go about divvying me up. Here they go.

A. PLANNING INFORMATION EXCHANGE

Every contact with the other side should be seen as an opportunity to gain and give information. Always consider: What is it you want to say? What is it you want to ask?

8.1 INFORMATION YOU WANT THE OTHER SIDE TO HAVE

A negotiator needs to consider how best to disclose information. Many negotiations involve specific, formal documents. Significant business transactions typically involve a prospectus. Some of the written information may be required by the law; other information may be presented in a manner to impress the other negotiator with the merits of the offering.

Litigators in major cases often use a settlement brochure. Such a brochure in a personal injury lawsuit typically includes a biographical resume of the injured person, a statement of the facts surrounding the injury, a description of the medical history of the injuries, an itemization of the damages, and an explanation of the theory of liability. Another technique for presenting information to the other side involves the use of the client or witness. Their appearance during a negotiation discussion may be effective as well as satisfying to the client.

8.2 LEGAL EFFECTS OF DISCLOSURES

Disclosure of information may have important legal effects. What an attorney says may (or may not) constitute an "admission" that has legal consequences. In transactional work, this concern exists during discussions. In litigation work, the common law and current evidence rules reflect a public policy that favors and encourages settlements. Typical privilege rules render all offers of compromise and all factual statements inadmissible. These rules reflect a broad social policy that encourages frank negotiation discussions and attempts to resolve litigation.

8.3 PROTECTING INFORMATION FROM DISCLOSURE

An attorney must plan ahead about what information to reveal and what information to withhold from the other party. Planning helps prevent the unconscious or unnecessary revelation of client confidences or secrets, the disclosure of which may reveal information to the client's ultimate detriment. All disclosures and non-disclosures should be planned.

8.3.1 Using Non–Disclosure Approaches

It will be a rare negotiation in which a lawyer does not have some information to protect. There are a number of ethical approaches that a lawyer can take to withhold information:

- Ignore the question and shift to another topic.
- Refuse to answer and explain why.
- Admit the question deserves a response but delay the response until later.
- Answer only a part of the question.
- Provide a general and not a specific answer.
- Ask questions and refuse to answer until these questions are answered.
- Make an admission or concede a point to avoid any elaboration.
- Postpone the negotiations to obtain the information.

- Feint or faint.

These techniques can also be useful when asked to respond to disclosures of surprise information by the other side. In general, the less perturbed an attorney appears in response to a difficult question, the more likely the response will be accepted by the other lawyer.

8.3.2 Obtaining Information From the Other Side

In every negotiation, there is information the other side has that is valuable to learn. For example:

- The interests of the other side.
- The positions of the other side.
- The strong points and weak points of the other side.
- Facts and law underlying the deal or case.
- The other side's perception of your client's position.
- The extent of the other lawyer's preparation and available time.
- The other negotiator's style, experience, strengths and weaknesses.
- Alternatives for the other side if the deal is not made or the case settled.
- How the other lawyer is being paid.
- The authority limits of the negotiator for the other side.
- Time pressures or deadlines.
- The interests of any third parties affected by the results.
- What they really think about your multi-faceted talents.

The best way to obtain information in most situations is simply to ask for it. The most direct approach may well produce the most reliable information. An efficient way to conduct the information exchange in negotiations is to conduct it as if it were an interview and combine active listening with a mix of open and closed ended questions.

Negotiators who ask indirect questions may be able to mask their real motives successfully. A negotiator may mix innocuous questions with important questions. For example, apparently innocent questions about the attorney's practice, experience, or workload assist in evaluating that attorney's abilities and situation.

It is useful to keep an ongoing list of information that is needed from the other side. That way, when the other side calls unexpectedly, one has a ready reference in an attempt to get information in every communication with the other side. And if they won't give you the right answer, try playing Jeopardy to see if you can get the right question.

8.3.3 Maintaining Accountability

It is important to hold the other negotiator accountable for information revealed. Some negotiators are prone to exaggerate or misrepresent facts or the law. An effective way of holding negotiators accountable for the accuracy of statements is to ask for the source of the information, for the name, address, and telephone number of the witness, for the identity or location of documents, or for the citation to the law. Requesting sources will hold the other negotiator responsible for what is said and decrease the chances that misstatements will be made.

8.3.4 Assessing Responses

When deciding upon the accuracy of responses to questions, the reaction of the negotiator can be observed in face to face negotiations. Hesitations, facial reactions, gestures, and nervous movements may provide a more reliable answer than the verbal response. This is why face to face exchanges—if they are possible—can be invaluable to negotiations. Another gauge of accuracy is to compare the response to a question with explanations or positions made before and after the response.

8.4 INFORMING AND UPDATING THE CLIENT

For the reasons explained in Chapter 7, it is vital to keep the client fully informed about the progress, or lack of progress, of a negotiation. Lawyers may fail to keep clients adequately informed because of all that is happening and other demands on the lawyer's time. Some clients may not want what seems to be constant communications; and others do not want to pay the attorney for the time it takes. It usually will be most effective to continue to discuss the negotiation plan with the client unless the client expressly declines to have this discussion.

B. ENGAGING IN THE NEGOTIATION

During negotiations, negotiators can discuss: the past (what has happened and why), the present (what the client wants now), and the future (what will be, will be). Negotiators can make three general types of statements about the past, present, and future. They can:

- *Make a wish.*
- *Make a persuasive statement.*
- *Make a threat.*

8.5 MAKING A WISH

Negotiators make a wish when they discuss what it is their clients want or need. Specific "making a wish" statements include offers and demands. When to make a wish, what to say, and how to respond are discussed in this section.

8.5.1 How Should A Negotiation Begin?

How negotiations open may affect how they end. The attorney deciding to initiate settlement discussions may need a legitimate reason for broaching the negotiation dialogue, such as:

- Your client has some interests that can be met if we talk.
- We have a proposal to present to you and your client that we think you will find attractive.
- Both parties have some complementary and mutual needs that can be satisfied.
- Our firm has a policy of contacting the other side to determine whether there is any desire to resolve the problem.
- You represent the plaintiff and it is only appropriate that you tell me what you want; or, you represent the defendant who is responsible for what happened and it is only appropriate that you make an offer.

- Both our clients will gain by saving expenses if this case settles. Cases like this may be better resolved to both sides' satisfaction through settlement.

- We will be required to attempt to mediate this dispute. Why don't we try to settle it ourselves?

- The judge will expect us to have discussed settlement, so perhaps we should begin now to determine whether the case can be settled.

- I have no other clients and nothing else to do so I thought we could chat.

8.5.2 What Are the Advantages and Disadvantages in Making or Receiving the First Proposal?

One of the negotiators must either make the first offer or demand, or initially explain the specifics of a position.

Going First: The Pros

An initial proposal may set the initial tone of the negotiation or may provide the negotiator with more control of the process.

The initial offer or demand indicates to the other side the exact position of the negotiator, which may strengthen that position.

A large demand or small offer may focus discussions at one end of the concession-bargaining spectrum and make any responsive small offer or large demand seem unreasonable in comparison.

A position may gain credibility by being the first to be advanced and by becoming the focus of the discussion.

The initial request may accelerate the reaching of an agreement or settlement.

Advancing the first position allows the negotiator to obtain and analyze a reaction from the other side which may help reveal the opponent's bargaining position.

Going First: The Cons

The initial demand may be lower than expected or the initial offer higher than anticipated.

The opponent can more accurately assess both ends of the concession spectrum.

The other side can measure the first offer and modify a counteroffer based on that information.

An initial position may unwittingly give away too much if the interests of the parties significantly overlap.

It may be easier to respond and fashion a more effective negotiation approach after knowing the opposition's initial position.

The offer or demand may be described as unreasonable.

The opponent can refuse to make a counteroffer unless the first demand is reduced or first offer increased.

8.5.3   How Should Positions Be Expressed?

Several considerations affect how clear and how firm a position need be. The circumstances and the issues may dictate how to describe an offer or demand. The type of negotiation, the simplicity of the issues, and the nature of the provisions all affect how resolute the position need be. General types of offers and demands may be appropriate. Market valuation in a contract or lease situation may be flexible. A range of prices or costs may be all that an attorney can propose, with a mid-range figure used as a specific amount. A range approach to offers also may be proper in situations in which flexibility is necessary to resolve a dispute. It may make sense to take elastic positions when the negotiators have not previously had a full discussion of their clients' interests. The major consideration in determining when to take a clear and firm position is timing. Describing positions too early may cause a deadlock or cause a lawyer to defend a poor position, but a clear and firm description that is made too late may be too late.

Many negotiators round off negotiation figures because it is often difficult to make a firm commitment to a specific amount, and because round numbers may seem easier to use. Other negotiators prefer to use precise amounts relating to specific factors in a case. While both of these approaches are valid, negotiators should take care to calculate the monetary impact on the client before any commitments are made.

8.5.4 How Should Component Issues Be Discussed?

Most items involved in negotiations can be divided into components and sub-issues. An attorney representing an employee in an employment contract case can describe the amount owed to the employee in terms of a single sum of money or in terms of multiple components measured as lost wages, vacation time, pension amounts, insurance premiums, and other benefits.

When should the component approach be used? Attorneys must consider whether the component or the unit approach benefits their position and their client's interests when preparing an offer. Component demands may favor the plaintiff or seller, while lump sum, single-unit offers may favor the defendant or buyer. Positions consisting of components allow an attorney to appear to be asking for less, may lull the other attorney into perceiving that the component amounts are not that significant, and provide an agenda for discussion.

8.5.5 What Responses Can Be Made?

How a negotiator responds to proposals has a substantial impact on the final settlement. Both verbal and nonverbal reactions may reveal more than what the lawyer wishes to disclose. The reaction displayed should be consistent with the interests and positions disclosed. Negotiators can respond to an offer or demand by:

- Asking questions to clarify the position.
- Accepting it and ending the negotiations.
- Rejecting the offer or demand and continuing negotiations.
- Rejecting it and walking out or deadlocking negotiations.
- Postponing consideration of it and discussing other matters first.
- Searching for mutual client interests.
- Having the negotiator explain the basis of it.
- Making a verbal counteroffer or concession.
- Insisting on a larger offer or reduced demand.
- Laughing hysterically (not highly recommended).

Some negotiators will be tempted to accept a proposal made early during the negotiation process that falls within the range of settlement. These negotiators may be relieved to have reached this position and accept the offer or demand in order to avoid further anxiety or tension. Other negotiators will ask themselves: Can a more favorable accord be reached? Many negotiators instinctively avoid accepting an early offer even if the demand falls within settlement range because it is early in the process and they anticipate that an exchange of counteroffers will most probably result in an even better settlement.

8.5.6 How Should Positions Be Adjusted?

It can be a difficult task to make a high demand or a low offer in a negotiation. Attorneys who are confident and sure about their position have little difficulty in taking a firm, tactical position. However, attorneys who fail properly to evaluate a situation and vacillate in constructing a position have difficulty in expressing an extreme, but appropriate, demand or offer.

It can be difficult for a negotiator to make a proposal only to have the other lawyer react by either appearing incredulous, claiming the proposal is unreasonable or blaming the negotiator for attempting to deadlock the negotiation. Some offers and demands may genuinely appear unreasonable to the other attorney and produce such a reaction. The negotiator must be able to reasonably explain the position and provide substantial reasons to weather this reaction.

8.6 MAKING A PERSUASIVE STATEMENT

Negotiators make persuasive statements when they suggest reasons why the other side should be satisfied. The purpose of the statement is to convince the other side to accept an offer or demand. As stated earlier, the process of a negotiation is an effort to have the parties reach an agreement that satisfies their interests. The focus needs to be on interests which negotiators express as positions. The process of negotiation is an enterprise which blends the different and mutual interests of the parties.

The following sections suggest ways to make statements persuasive and convincing.

8.6.1 Focus on Complementary Interests

One side may demand Y, and the other side will offer X, resulting in a substantial gap and requiring sides to make concessions. It is often presumed that, since the positions advanced by the parties conflict, their interests conflict as well. Parties may also have some related needs and wants. For example:

> A consumer plaintiff who demands her money back through a breach of warranty action may want the product replaced; the defendant manufacturer may want the original product returned to determine the cause of the defect to prevent future problems.

> A corporate plaintiff who demands an injunction and damages in a contract dispute may prefer re-negotiated contract terms and prices; the defendant may wish to continue the business relationship based on modified terms.

> A corporate vice president may support the construction of a one-story office addition while another vice president insists on a two-story addition. These two vice presidents may discover that they have related interests if they focus on what corporate functions need how much space, instead of their set positions.

> A lessor may want a five-year lease while a lessee only wants a three-year lease. Both may be interested in a three-year lease with options and liquidated damage clauses.

> A landlord needs to charge market-value rent that will attract tenants who will pay regularly; a tenant wants to pay market-value rent to a landlord who can afford to provide regular maintenance and repairs.

Parties will typically have some complementary interests and needs that can form the basis for negotiation. In sales negotiations, complementary interests exist because the buyers want the goods and the sellers need the money. In litigation negotiations, the plaintiffs want money and the defendants want to resolve the dispute. The redefinition of interests may turn what appear to be conflicting interests into complementary ones.

8.6.2 Focus on the Real Interests of the Party

The reasons that attorneys give to support positions also disclose the underlying interests of their clients. It is common for negotiators to include in offers and demands items that have little or no value to their clients. These negotiators mix ficti- tious needs with real interests, or artificially create interests when their clients have no needs and then concede the contrived interests in exchange for something that has value. This false demand tactic has substantial drawbacks. The client may have no interest in what the attorney has demanded and such an explanation of the client's needs might be an outright falsehood. This result can be avoided by counseling discussions between client and attorney.

8.6.3 Exchange Valuable Concessions

A concession is the giving up of something of value. A reaction to an offer or demand may appropriately be a concession which will prompt the other side to counter with an equal concession. Whether a trade-off should be made depends upon the negotiation approach employed and the best interests of the client. Concessions are a common technique to bridge differ- ences in competitive negotiations. They may also be appropriate to reach an accord in collaborative negotiations.

A goal of many negotiators is, or should be, the promotion of mutual gains for both sides. A gain is a relative proposition. It may mean that a party obtains more of something as a result of a negotiated accord. It may also mean that a party does not lose as much. To the extent that a party has to give something up in negotiations, then concessions may be appropriate. These con- cessions should be made contingent upon the other side cooperat- ing and making compromises equal in value and with the same frequency.

8.6.4 Propose Alternative Positions

The manner in which a party presents a position will influ- ence the receptivity of the other side. A single proposition provides a party with two alternative responses, usually yes or no. A multi-pronged proposition will provide alternatives one or more of which may be more likely to be acceptable to the other side. An employee negotiating a restrictive covenant contract clause may present to the prospective employer three alternative provisions instead of just one provision. For example, an employee may suggest that acceptable restrictions include (1) a three-year prohibition within a 10–mile radius, (2) a two-year prohibition within a 20–mile radius, or (3) a one-year prohibition within a 30–mile radius. An employer interested in a long term prohibition or a broad, geographic restriction may perceive one of the alternatives to be more acceptable.

8.6.5 Say What You Mean

Most negotiators perceive an offer or demand to be more valuable if an explanation supports that position or interest. Why? Because positions consist of two parts: the extrinsic value (usually money) and the intrinsic value which the negotiator attaches to the reasons or explanation. An offer or demand that is supported by an intrinsic reason is more effective and persuasive than one from which an explanation is omitted. For example, it is more effective for a negotiator to demand $10,000 and to explain how that demand was arrived at instead of just demanding $7,500 without any explanation.

8.6.6 Use Objective Explanations and Reasons

Every position should be supported by some explanation. It is more persuasive and efficient to gain the acceptance of the other lawyer by relying on solid, firm criteria rather than on the negotiator's own self-serving opinions and conclusions. For example, if a lessor and a lessee concern themselves with the fair market value of leased space rather than their own valuation, they will be more likely to reach a reasonable accord. Relying on objective criteria shifts the focus of the negotiation to more useful matters.

Each situation needs to be analyzed to determine what specific, objective reasons support positions. The following paragraphs detail some of the more common supportive explanations.

Facts. Every situation will have some persuasive facts supporting the issues. Whether undisputed or disputed, persuasive facts can effectively be used as reasons.

Component Positions. The component parts of many monetary demands may be used as reasons. A consumer contract obligation will comprise X number of dollars for the amount financed, Y number of dollars for the finance charge, and Z number of dollars for other charges. Positions or concessions may be pegged to these specific amounts: "We will reduce our demand by dropping our claim for the unearned finance charge."

Law. Every case will have some supportive law. These legal claims may be employed to explain a position: "We will not pay anything for the punitive damages claims because the law does not permit such recovery," or "We included this term because the law requires us to include it in the lease."

Precedent. Precedent will often provide support for counteroffers: "This case will provide our client with a legal ruling that, regardless of the decision, will clear up this problem once and for all," or "Our client refuses to include those terms for your client because then everyone else will expect the same terms."

Verdicts. Prior jury verdicts or judicial determinations in similar cases are a good source of objective criteria. These sources may be obtained from independent jury verdict research reports, from local jurisdiction records, or from the lawyer's experience.

Economic Data. The economic value of property or damages may be based upon some objective sources like market value. The more reliable the economic source, the more likely the other side will accept it as authoritative: "Valuation can be accurately determined by using the standard price list (or consumer price index) in effect at this time."

Tax Consequences. The tax consequences of an agreement or settlement may well affect the scope and terms of an agreement. The consideration of these issues may support a larger or smaller negotiable amount. See Section 8.6.7.

Structured Settlements. The lower present payout by a defendant will provide a larger settlement to the plaintiff paid over a period of years through a tax-free annuity.

Business Concerns. There may exist business practices and procedures that affect proposals. Accounting procedures, corporate practices, and other business concerns need to be reviewed to determine what support they provide for particular positions.

Expert Opinions. Expert judgment will often be a source of support. The more objective the data that supports the expert's opinion, the more authoritative the support will be.

Principles. Principles and moral standards will explain some positions asserted. A client may insist on a certain demand purely on principle: "Our client wants, for security reasons, to be completely protected and insists on this position," or "Our client, as a matter of principle, will not agree to an offer equal to the nuisance value of this case because it gives the appearance of liability."

Fairness. Being fair will explain a compromise. For example, in a multi-party case in which all parties have agreed except one, fairness may provide a basis for agreement by the holdout so as not to spoil the settlement reached by the other parties. "Just to be reasonable, we will offer," or "For the sake of fairness to everyone concerned, we will...."

Tradition. Custom, usage, unwritten rules, and tradition sometimes provide a basis for settlement. The strict legal rules may not be as important as doing things consistently with the way things have always been done. "These contracts have always included the following terms...."

Reciprocity. Reciprocity will usually produce a counteroffer in negotiations. Most attorneys expect to exchange concessions in sequence: "We have made this concession, now it's your turn."

Splitting the Difference. This reason may be effective in cases close to settlement or an agreement. It will be inappropriate if it bears no logical relationship to the positions.

Peripheral Issues. Peripheral claims will often explain away a concession without conceding much in fact. In transactions, certain language, the structure of the agreement, and its effective date may be exchanged for more valuable interests. In litigation, attorney's fees, court costs, and settlement payment schedules may be exchanged for a more valuable counteroffer from the other side: "We will drop our request for attorney's fees if you...."

Risks. Elimination of risks and costs may be alluded to as a rationale for a concession. Threats made by the negotiators, the additional time and effort necessary to close a deal with someone else or further prepare the case for trial, and future expenses will support a concession: "Your client cannot afford to lose this deal," or "Your client runs the risk of an unknown jury verdict, so...."

Client Satisfaction. Clients will derive satisfaction for a variety of reasons as discussed in Chapter 7. These sources of satisfaction will support a bargain: "My client will be satisfied if they receive this, so we demand ..." or "Your client is anxious to reach an agreement and will be satisfied if...."

Publicity. Public visibility or the lack of sufficient privacy may have an effect on one or both parties. A provision that the terms of the agreement not be made public may have significant value to a party.

Specific types of negotiations may lend themselves to additional explanations to support a position. For example, in commercial negotiations the seller may be able to explain to a prospective buyer why certain terms or a specific price is appropriate, employing such reasons as:

Identity and Reputation. The seller has created a popular and attractive reputation for the product or service which buyers identify with and which will make it easier for the wholesale buyer to sell in turn to retail buyers.

Promotion. The seller has aggressively advertised the product or service, created a market for it, and forged a highly visible position in the marketplace.

Warranties and Guarantees. The seller warrants its product or service, and will stand behind what it sells.

Good Service. The seller provides quality repair services in case any problems arise.

Credit Advantages. The seller offers favorable credit terms that make it economically more feasible for the purchaser to buy the product or services.

8.6.7 Assess the Effect of Tax Considerations

Tax aspects affect the structure and provisions of nearly every negotiation transaction involving a contract or lease agreement. An attorney must be familiar with applicable laws, how those laws apply to a negotiation, what effect those laws will have upon a proposed agreement, and whether the tax consequences of an alternative proposal better serve the interests of one or both parties. For example, an attorney advising a business client regarding the purchase or lease of a $50,000 machine will need to examine the tax ramifications of alternative purchase and lease agreements and advise the client concerning feasible options. Another example explains the importance of considering tax consequences before making any proposals. A spouse involved in a divorce situation may receive tax benefits or incur tax liabilities as a result of the terms of a stipulated agreement.

Other negotiation situations highlight the importance of considering tax consequences. A client may express a desire to purchase some land, but it may be that tax considerations will influence that client to reconsider and decide that a long-term lease better serves the client's tax interests. The effect of income, sales, estate, and gift taxes may be complex, requiring the negotiating attorney to consult with tax lawyers and accountants.

Litigators must consider the tax treatment afforded by litigation settlements and must review and analyze the impact tax laws and regulations have upon a proposed settlement before finalizing an agreement. Additional factors in assessing tax consequences of a settlement agreement are the timing of when it is signed, when the settlement is paid, and when the income has to be reported.

Personal Injuries or Illness. The Internal Revenue Code states that gross income does not include the amount of any damages received on account of "personal injuries or sickness."

These damages encompass a broad variety of claims. Damages resulting from claims based on physical injury, wrongful death, invasion of privacy, and defamation have been held to fall within excludable gross income.

Property Damage. Recoveries for injury to property will be taxable as income only to the extent they exceed the taxpayer's basis in the damaged property.

Lost Wages, Profits, Income. Damages received for lost wages, profits, or income may be taxable as ordinary income, unless the damage money reimburses a party for lost wages, profits, or income caused by personal injury or sickness.

Interest. Interest a party receives computed from the time a cause of action arises until it is settled will constitute taxable income.

Expenses, Costs, and Fees. Part of the settlement may reimburse the claimant for attorney's fees, expenses, or other costs. Under the broad definition of income, this portion of the settlement may be taxable income (and a deduction) to the claimant since, in effect, the other party to the settlement is paying the claimant's expenses. Even if that portion of the settlement is paid directly to the claimant's attorney, it may still constitute taxable income (and a deduction) for the claimant.

Deductibility. The deductibility of settlement payments from taxable income will be another factor in shaping a negotiated agreement. The party paying settlement recoveries may be able to deduct from taxable income the amounts paid. A taxpayer may deduct settlement payments as ordinary and necessary business expenses if the payer can establish that the payment was directly related to the conduct of the payer's business.

8.6.8 Consider a Structured Settlement in Litigation Negotiations

A structured settlement is a financial package settlement in which lump sum or periodic annuity payments are used with resulting tax benefits. Structured settlements can provide recipients with tax-free income and payers with tax gains. This settlement approach has been primarily used in personal injury litigation where a plaintiff has legitimate claims for substantial damages. The most important factor influencing courts in interpreting the nature of the settlement recovery is the payer's basic reason for making the payments. Why the payer has settled will largely determine the nature of the payments for tax purposes.

8.7 MAKING A THREAT

Negotiators can make a threat in an effort to get a result. A *threat* is an avowal to do or not do something. It may be stated as a promise ("we will withdraw an offer") or it may be stated as a conditional declaration ("bankruptcy is a probability depending upon the amount of a trial verdict"). Threats are designed to persuade the other negotiator that a failure to reach an accord will result in unpleasant consequences. Some lawyers may not negotiate unless some potential consequences exist. Threats may occur in both competitive and cooperative negotiation approaches as incentives for parties to reach an agreement or settle a case.

Threats can be used both effectively and ineffectively. To be effective, threats must be credible, involve something of value, and be supported by the threatening party's resolve. Tactically, threats will be most effective under the following conditions:

- Actions support the verbal threat.
- Reasons support the threatened action.
- The threat is effectively communicated.
- Multiple, varied, and incremental threats are made.
- The threats are substantial.
- The size of the threat is scaled to the size of the problem.

8.7.1 How to Respond to Threats

A negotiator may respond in a variety of ways to a threat:

- Clarify what was said to make certain a threat was intentionally asserted.
- Be silent for a while and consider an appropriate response.
- Express disbelief or bewilderment.
- Empathize with the other side's situation.

- Explain how the threat adversely affects the threatening party.
- Seek to defer the threat and focus the discussion on another matter.
- Counter the threat with a threat.
- Call the other side on the threat and determine if they are bluffing.
- Walk out or deadlock negotiations.

8.7.2 How to Resolve Problems

The following techniques summarize ways to reduce problem situations that arise during negotiations:

- Recognizing that a problem exists and identifying the problem.
- Assuming appropriate responsibility for the problem and not blaming the other negotiator.
- Resisting the tendency to exaggerate a problem caused by the other side.
- Viewing the problem from the perspective of the other negotiator.
- Considering possible solutions to the problems and selecting the most mutually effective solution.

8.7.3 How to Gain the Cooperation of the Other Negotiator

During negotiations, one negotiator may refuse to engage in reasonable negotiation discussions. This refusal may occur at any stage of negotiations, with the negotiator preferring to take a competitive approach rather than a collaborative approach. It is critical at these stages for an attorney who prefers the cooperative approach to attempt to make an ally of someone who prefers to act like an adversary by:

- Adopting a friendly approach and explaining why cooperation will work.
- Focusing on the merits of the negotiation.
- Persisting in efforts to reach an agreement.

- Focusing on the parties' best interests.

- Controlling the urge to be defensive.

- Avoiding gambits and ploys.

8.7.4 How to Respond to Gambits

Some negotiators may use diversions or gambits. Many of these techniques involve ploys and manipulation. When used during negotiations, such tactics turn that part of the process into a game. Many lawyers deplore the use of these techniques, while other attorneys endorse these ploys on the basis that the end justifies the means. It is easy to scoff at and dismiss these tactics when reading about them. It may be another thing to avoid using them during a negotiation when difficulties arise.

Examples of gambits include:

- Acting as if a position is ridiculous.

- Being condescending or rude.

- Pretending not to have sufficient authority.

- Delaying negotiation talks for no good reason.

Negotiators who face these ploys may be able to deflect these adverse influences effectively by: (1) recognizing the gambit, (2) informing the other negotiator that the tactic has been recognized, and (3) diplomatically requesting that the discussion shift to a more productive topic. Some negotiators may not be aware of their gaming techniques and quickly accede to such a request. Other negotiators who have consciously tried to be manipulative may stop such attempts if they perceive such efforts to be unproductive. It may not be advisable, in some situations, to ask the other side to desist if the negotiator can effectively counter such ploys. In all situations negotiators should not yield or accede to gambits and ploys and should make clear that they will only be influenced by legitimate reasons and objective factors.

8.7.5 How to Unlock a Deadlock

Deadlocks may occur when one or more negotiators engage in a pattern of threats, but can occur at any time during a negotiation. There are numerous alternatives to prevent dead-locks or to restart deadlocked negotiations. Negotiators may:

- Discuss the reasoning behind the position that led to the deadlock.

- Describe how the parties benefit from continued negotiations.

- Detail the practical effects of failing to settle.

- Agree to reconsider the last position if the opponent will do likewise.

- Take a short break instead of ending the negotiation.

- Seek agreement on some issue to which both sides can readily agree.

- Display some understanding and empathy with the other side's quandary.

- Concede something; make an offer; reduce a demand.

- Table the deadlocked issue.

- Change something about the negotiation process, such as its location.

- Ask: "Do we agree we should continue to talk in the future?"

- Seek assistance from a mediator.

8.7.6 Whether to Use the Take-It-or-Leave-It Approach

One approach that is used in some situations is the firm-offer/single-demand approach, also known as the take-it-or-leave-it position. One attorney sets a position that must be met for settlement to occur. It may have its best effect when both parties are nearing settlement but for some reason are unable to reach final agreement. Many attorneys attempt to use this threat as a bluff, which can be determined with a counter offer or demand. Still other lawyers use the approach to deadlock a negotiation or as a means to refuse to negotiate in good faith.

8.7.7 Whether to Walk Out

The tactic of walking out may be a planned tactic, or it may be a spontaneous, ill-advised reaction. Some negotiators will intentionally test the opponent by staging a walkout to see how the opponent reacts. If time permits, they believe that there is no need to make quick, early concessions. They prefer to be obstinate early, often hoping to disturb the opponent to see what will happen. They know that some opponents fear deadlocked situations and will be willing to make major concessions to prevent deadlocks. What approach is taken should be decided upon in a reflective, cautious, and responsible way. Some deadlocks and walkouts are precipitated by emotional interchanges and reactions. Effective negotiators stop, consider, and decide before reacting.

8.8 EMPLOYING CREATIVE APPROACHES

Effective negotiators use a blend of wishes, persuasive statements, and threats to craft creative resolutions. Creative approaches to the formation of an agreement or the resolution of a dispute may provide both sides with mutually satisfactory results. Negotiators may best serve their clients' interests through creative brainstorming. See Section 1.10. The following examples demonstrate creative negotiation solutions.

8.8.1 The Consumer Camper Case

A consumer purchased a new, $32,000 motor home and began a one week vacation. After driving only 500 miles, transmission problems developed and he returned to the dealer to have the transmission repaired under the warranty. The repair work took one day. He decided to shorten his trip and left again, only to encounter electrical problems about 100 miles from the dealer. Again he decided to return and have the repairs made. The dealer told him the repairs would take one day but because some of the parts were out of stock, the repairs took three days. He requested a loaner camper, but was turned down. He stayed home during the remainder of his vacation. After visiting his lawyer, he revoked acceptance of the camper, and sued, in part, for $21,600. This amount reflected lost leisure and vacation time computed at a rate of $2,400 a day. This claim represented an issue of first impression in the local courts. Liability was uncertain; damages were speculative. A main issue was: How much is lost vacation time worth? The defense initially refused to offer any money for such damages; the plaintiff stood firm at $21,600. A deadlock occurred. Then the defense reviewed the interests of the plaintiff: the plaintiff wanted to recover his lost vacation time. They then proposed the following: that the plaintiff accept the equivalent of one week's salary ($1000) and use that money to pay for a one-week leave of absence from his job. That way, he would still get his vacation time prospectively. The plaintiff could take a leave of absence from his job, and after further discussions accepted $3,000 in settlement of that portion of his claim for a two-week leave of absence and for the lost week of repairs (plus a completely repaired motor home).

8.8.2 The Surviving Spouse Case

This example comes from the world of jury deliberations which, in effect, are group negotiation processes. A jury was observed on videotape deliberating a verdict in a civil action. In the case being tried, the defendant had negligently killed the wife of the plaintiff in an auto accident. Liability was clear; the real issue in the case concerned damages. The wrongful death statute permitted the husband to recover for loss of love and affection. During closing argument the plaintiff's attorney asked for $1,000,000 for that claim in addition to damages for other claims. During jury deliberations, five jurors were prepared to provide the plaintiff with a substantial recovery on that claim (they mentioned $250,000 to $750,000). One of the jurors resisted. He then began to negotiate with the other five jurors. He told them that if they provided the plaintiff with that amount of money they would "ruin his life!" They literally laughed at him. He further explained that the plaintiff was young, handsome, likely to marry again, earned only $28,000 a year, and a substantial verdict would change his life style. The lone juror then proposed that the interests of the plaintiff and the responsibility of the defendant be analyzed: the plaintiff needed some time to grieve and recover from his loss and some money to compensate for the tragedy; the defendant had the obligation to provide that opportunity and money. The juror then suggested that an award of $75,000 would be sufficient because then the plaintiff could quit work for a year, ($28,000), buy a new car

($12,000), spend the extra money on himself ($10,000), pay off his attorney ($25,000), and start a new life. The other five jurors, after further discussions, agreed that $75,000 satisfied the plaintiff's interest on that claim. They were very pleased with the arrangement and believed they benefited both parties.

8.8.3 The Ski Accident

A college-age student on a skiing weekend was killed in the crash of a ski lift gondola. The ski lift operator recognized the extent of its liability and wanted to settle the case to avoid any adverse publicity. The wealthy parents of the college student brought a wrongful death case, repeatedly refused the offers of a cash settlement, and wanted to proceed with the litigation in part to hold the ski resort publicly accountable and in part to preserve the memory of their son. The attorneys for the defendant began to consider alternative ways to settle the case, because no reasonable amount of money appeared to satisfy the plaintiffs. The attorneys reviewed the real interests of the parents and the needs of their client. They then prepared a professional brochure proposing a solution which required the defendant to: endow with a substantial amount of money a ski safety training program named in honor of the son, establish a college scholarship in the name of the son, publicize the availability of both, and pay litigation expenses and some damages. This proposal was modified, with the endowment and scholarship money increased, and was then accepted by the parents. They received some satisfaction plus money; and the defendant saved trial expenses, avoided the risk of a huge jury verdict, and was able to conduct an effective safety advertising campaign which promoted the name and location of the ski area.

8.8.4 The Seven Percent Solution

A corporation had an interest in limiting salary increases for its employees to no more than 7 percent for the following year. The employees requested a minimum increase of 10 percent to reflect inflationary and merit factors. Both sides had legitimate positions supported by objective criteria. The corporate management relied upon economic data that an increase in excess of 7 percent would adversely hike the cost of its services, shrinking the available consumer market. The employees relied upon economic data that combined the rate of inflation with the average salary of similar employees in the community to produce the 10 percent rate. The following solution satisfied the needs of both sides and provided mutual gains: the corporation totally revised its fringe benefits plan and created a flexible, cafeteria-type plan in which the company provided a certain amount of money to the employees to be used for health insurance, disability benefits, life insurance, and pension plans. The adoption of this plan resulted in the company budgeting employees salaries at a 7 percent increase and the employees receiving a salary increase equal to a 10 percent raise. These differences came about because the company was able to prevent an increase in its fringe benefit costs and because the employees were able to use pre-tax dollars to pay for medical and related expenses.

8.8.5 Selling the Farm

A corporate farmer wanted to expand and offered an adjacent farmer $122,000 for his small farm. The farmer was not anxious to sell to someone outside his family, but was nearing the age of retirement and planned to sell sometime soon. The neighboring farmer set a price of $150,000 for his farm. Neither the farmer nor the buyer wanted to make any major concessions concerning price. The final purchase agreement included these provisions: a $142,000 purchase price, payment terms of an $82,000 initial payment with six annual $10,000 installment payments, the farmer being able to live in the farmhouse for six months after the closing, the farmer retaining a right to store a camper and a boat trailer and to hunt on the land until his death, and the daughter of the farmer having the right of first refusal if the farm were resold. These provisions satisfied the needs of both parties and avoided their having to make major concessions.

C. ENDING THE NEGOTIATION

8.9 CONCLUDING A NEGOTIATION

Reaching an accord concludes many negotiations, but not all. The failure to reach an accord may result in litigation madness or the death of an agreement. Or it may be the best thing to do.

Not all negotiations will, or should, result in an accord. Some legal relationships should not be formed through an agreement. Some cases need to be tried. The trial result may be the best alternative available to both sides because there exists no chance for compromise or no complementary, mutual interests or needs. Other situations may involve several instances that result in temporary deadlocks. Both parties may evaluate the facts so differently that there exist few common perceptions. One or both sides may need to obtain more information, verify some data, or conduct further investigation before negotiations continue. Serious negotiations may begin again after a temporary deadlock at the prompting of a negotiator, party, mediator, or judge.

8.9.1 When Is a Final Position a Final Position?

When a negotiator says "This is my last and final offer" is it? When will a "last" demand really be a final position? The best way to determine the answers to these questions is to analyze the statement's content and context.

How did the lawyer phrase the offer or demand? Was it in absolute terms?

Was any condition included?

Is the final position consistent with previous positions taken by the lawyer?

Does there seem to be additional room for more negotiating?

Is the timing of the final offer or demand reasonable in light of what has occurred to date? Is it too early?

Did the lawyer appear credible in taking such a position or did it appear to be just a tactic?

Did the lawyer become emotionally involved and overreact by stating such a position?

Did it appear that this tactic was planned by the negotiator? Was it inadvertently made?

How does the position reflect the real needs and interests of a party? Of both parties?

Are there other acceptable positions that would produce mutual gains for both sides?

How does the final position compare to alternative options to settle the case?

Does the position appear to reflect the authority limits the client may have provided the negotiator?

A final position should be just that. If a negotiator asserts "This is my final offer," then negotiations should cease or the other side should accept the offer. However, final offers may not be what they seem. A negotiator may employ such a final position as a tactic to gain more for a client. Tactics like this can easily backfire. A negotiator who backs away from a final position without a legitimate reason will lose credibility. Why should the other attorney believe that negotiator the next time the negotiator says: "This is it, and this time I mean it"?

8.9.2 How Can a Negotiation Be Reconvened After a "Final Position"?

There are some effective ways to renew discussions after one or both sides have asserted a final position that is unacceptable to the other side. Either party may attempt to:

- Interpret the statement in a way that makes the offer or demand firm but not final.

- Provide the negotiator with an opportunity to restate the position to eliminate its finality.

- Suggest a new perspective that may cause the other side to reconsider its position.

- Explain that the best interests of both parties will be served by continuing negotiations.

- Directly suggest that the negotiator reconsider the position.

- Recommend that additional authority be obtained from a client.

- Employ some tactic, like splitting the difference, if the existing gap is not large.

- Indicate that it is the other side's turn to make a concession.

- Suggest that negotiations be continued at a later date after both sides reassess their positions.

8.9.3　Has the Accord Been Reduced to Writing?

Before or immediately after an accord is reached, it might be a good practice to prepare a concise memorandum of agreement or letter of understanding which informally summarizes the major negotiated terms.　The purpose of these informal documents is to confirm what has been agreed upon and to provide an outline for drafting a formal agreement.　At the conclusion of multiple negotiation sessions, a written summary or outline of what was agreed upon and what remains to be negotiated can be drafted.

The most effective way to conclude a negotiation is to reduce the agreement to writing formally and have it signed by the parties or the attorneys.　Negotiations that create contractual relationships or that resolve litigation will typically result in a formal written agreement.　Some negotiators will rely on each other's oral promise or statement regarding an agreement, but the preferred practice is to document final agreements in writing or to incorporate a settlement agreement in the record of the case.

There may be an advantage in drafting the document because the words used may be susceptible of various interpretations and the drafter can employ appropriate language favoring a client's interests.　There may also be an advantage in drafting a negotiation agreement when a matter arises during the drafting that the negotiators did not fully discuss.　It might be best to resolve this unresolved issue as neutral or fairly as possible or to contact the other negotiator if the matter is important.

There are several disadvantages in drafting negotiation agreements or settlements.　Drafting will take time and cost a client money.　It might be better strategically to have the other side draft tentative provisions and edit such terms.　Courts usually interpret ambiguous terms of a contract against the interests of the drafter. These and other reasons may prompt a negotiator to have the other negotiator draft an accord.

8.9.4 How Should the Attorney Draft the Accord?

The drafting of an accord may occur at various times in negotiations. Detailed provisions for releases and stipulations in litigation negotiations will probably be drafted after a settlement has been finalized in oral terms. Terms and conditions of contract or lease negotiations may be drafted during the course of negotiations. The steps in memorializing a complete, final agreement include the following steps:

- Preparing an outline of the document
- Drafting all the terms of the accord
- Revising the initial draft
- Completing the final agreement

8.9.5 What Type of Settlement Document Should Be Used?

The contents of a negotiation agreement depend upon the nature of the negotiation. Transaction agreements range from simple contracts to complicated, lengthy documents. Litigation settlement forms include a stipulated dismissal, a release, or a covenant not to sue, often in some combination form. The attorney should check the local statues and law of the applicable jurisdiction for specific requirements and effects of different types of settlement. The following paragraphs explain common litigation documents:

Stipulations. Stipulations to dismiss a case may be created which dispose of a case with or without prejudice. A stipulation of dismissal *without prejudice* leaves the claims and defenses intact and permits the parties to litigate these issues in the future. A stipulation of dismissal *with prejudice* operates as a final disposition of the issues. These latter stipulations are much more common than stipulations without prejudice because their finality will meet the interests of both parties who seek to resolve a dispute once and for all. A *stipulation* consists of a document bearing the caption of the case with a statement similar to the following:

In consideration of mutual promises, the parties, through their undersigned attorneys, stipulate and agree to dismiss this action with prejudice.

Releases. A *release* is the relinquishment of a claim or right to the person against whom the claim exists or against whom the right is to be enforced. It is a discharge of the claim by the voluntary agreement of the parties as opposed to by operation of law. A mutual release has the effect of both sides surrendering all claims and defenses in a compromise settlement. The provisions of a release may include statements such as:

Plaintiff has made certain claims against Defendant, and Defendant has asserted certain defenses and counterclaims against Plaintiff, which claims, defenses, and counterclaims are in issue in a lawsuit (caption).

Although both parties wish to pursue their claims and defenses and both deny liability, they also wish to settle their differences (reasons may be stated, e.g., in the interests of justice, to resolve a dispute, for financial reasons).

In consideration of a dismissal of this lawsuit, mutual promises, monetary consideration, and for (additional terms), the plaintiff and the defendant release each other, their successors and assigns, from all actions, causes of action, claims, defenses, counterclaims, and judgments which the plaintiff and defendant or their heirs, executors, administrators, or assigns ever had or now have.

Covenants Not to Sue. A *covenant not to sue* is an agreement by one who has a right of action at the time of the making against another, by which the party agrees not to sue to enforce a right of action, and may be included as part of a release. A covenant not to sue differs from a release in that it is not necessarily a present abandonment of a claim or right but is an agreement not to sue on the existing claim, which does not extinguish the cause of action. The action is relinquished between the parties to the covenant, but is still viable as to third parties.

Other Settlement Forms. Other types of settlement devices may be available depending upon the settlement terms and the number of defendants in an action. A *confession by judg-*

ment will be appropriate in cases in which a party is making periodic payments to the other party in satisfaction of a compromise. The default by a party of a payment will permit the other party to unilaterally seek a judgment for the unpaid balance or more, after providing the defaulting party with notice. In a *Mary Carter* agreement one or more, but not all, of the multiple defendants may contract with the plaintiff to limit liability and remain a party to the litigation by presenting a defense in court. The agreement guarantees the plaintiff a certain amount of money whether or not the plaintiff recovers anything through a verdict. Jurisdictions which permit *Mary Carter* agreements may require that they be disclosed to the jury. Some jurisdictions prohibit this type of settlement because of public policy considerations. Another type of settlement device used when there are multiple defendants is the *Pierringer release*. This is a release of a portion of the cause of action equal to the part attributable to the settling defendant's liability, with the case continuing against the remaining defendants and the released defendant absent from the trial.

8.9.6 Did I Succeed?

It can be difficult, if not impossible, to determine whether a negotiation result was a "success." This is because success means different things to different parties. Clients will have different goals and expectations, accounting for different perceptions of success.

The following criteria represent some benchmarks to determine whether a negotiation was a reasonable success.

- Did the accord meet the needs and satisfy the interests of the client at the time of the final proposal?
- Did each party achieve most of their objectives?
- Did both sides gain as a result of the negotiation?
- Did the parties through their attorneys sufficiently participate in the negotiation process?
- Did the negotiators consider alternative options to reach an accord and attempt to come up with a creative, innovative result?

187

- How does the final accord compare to the alternative outcomes had the negotiation failed?
- Did the parties learn something from the negotiation discussions?
- Is the accord reasonably enforceable?

D. REVIEWING THE NEGOTIATION PROCESS

8.10 An Overview

The negotiation process may be analyzed from various stages that occur during ongoing negotiations. While all these stages will not occur in every negotiation, it is helpful to have an overview of them:

1. *Analyzing the Situation.* The attorney in consultation with the client analyzes the situation and determines the propriety of negotiating.

2. *Preparing for the Negotiation.* Specifics regarding alternative approaches need to be considered to create a plan for negotiations.

3. *Making Initial Contacts.* Initial contacts establish the beginning tone of the negotiation and resolve procedural matters. Typical introductory remarks reflect social courtesies.

4. *Establishing a Relationship.* The negotiators may spend some time becoming acquainted or renewing the relationship.

5. *Obtaining an Overview.* The negotiators may discuss the background of the situation to obtain an overview.

6. *Creating an Appropriate Atmosphere.* The more trust negotiators establish, the more favorable a climate for discussions occurs.

7. *Establishing an Agenda.* A formal, set agenda may be appropriate in some situations while an informal, unwritten agenda may be more suitable for other negotiations.

8. *Disclosing Information.* The negotiators disclose information to provide each other with facts, opinions, and inferences necessary to assess interests.

9. *Assessing Interests.* Disclosures concerning what the parties want and need help determine mutual and conflicting interests.

10. *Refining Issues.* After initial disclosures, the negotiators may modify the agenda and refine the issues to be negotiated.

11. *Establishing Positions.* Negotiators may communicate general or specific positions supported by reasons explaining these positions.

12. *Debating Positions.* The negotiators may engage in debate and argument in order to attack the legitimacy of the other's position or defend the client's position.

13. *Exchanging Concessions.* The negotiators may make demands, offers, counteroffers, and concessions as part of the bargain and compromise pattern.

14. *Searching for Objective Criteria.* Positions based on objective factors rather than subjective impressions more often provide viable support for solutions.

15. *Considering Alternative and Creative Solutions.* Either negotiator may suggest and consider alternative and creative solutions.

16. *Reaching Agreement.* The conclusion of a negotiation may, or may not, result in an accord.

17. *Drafting the Accord.* The terms and provisions of the negotiated result may need to be composed and memorialized.

18. *Implementing the Accord.* The agreement or settlement may require things to be done.

19. *Ending a Negotiation.* Not all negotiation will result in an agreement or settlement. Negotiation discussions may become futile and terminate because there exists no mutually acceptable common ground.

20. *Celebrate.* If an agreement is reached, go out and celebrate. If an agreement is not reached, you may want to consider the services of a mediator. And then you will have another reason to read Chapter Nine.

Chapter Nine
MEDIATION: HELP!

Need help?
Can't settle by yourself?
Call: 1–900–M–E–D–I–A–T–E

A. INTRODUCTION

9.1 HELP!

You have been unable to close the deal or resolve the dispute by negotiating with the other side. You know from your reading from Chapter Six that help is available. You and the other side can agree to mediation and have a mediator facilitate the reaching of an agreement. In some cases you may have no choice. A pre-dispute mediation clause in an agreement may require that the parties attempt to mediate a settlement before initiating an action. In many jurisdictions, the rules mandate that parties mediate before trying the case.

In any event, mediation is usually a very helpful idea, and the time has come to study it more.

9.2 PARTICIPANTS IN THE MEDIATION PROCESS

Participants in mediation include the parties, their attorneys or representatives, the mediator, and a mediation organization.

Parties. Parties need to be directly and actively involved in the mediation because they must mutually agree to any resolution. The more receptive parties are to the belief that mediation will work for them, and the more effort they are willing to invest in the process, the more successful they will be. An individual who is a party obviously has the authority to agree to a settlement. An agent or employee of a corporation or organization must have or obtain the authority to reach an agreement. Insurance companies which insure a party often send or are required to send an agent to the mediation. This agent must also have full settlement authority.

Attorneys or Representatives. The parties usually are entitled to have a lawyer or representative participate in the mediation process. A lawyer may provide helpful legal advice and counseling to the parties. Another representative may provide information or support to the parties.

The primary role of lawyers in mediations is to promote the best interests of their clients and to increase the chances of a favorable settlement. Lawyers can discuss with their clients the legal issues involved and the legal ramifications of a settlement, provide the parties with alternative strategies, suggest to the mediator approaches which may help in resolving the dispute, and explain the expenses and procedures involved in arbitration and litigation, should mediation fail. The lawyer can also assist in drafting a settlement agreement.

Mediator. Mediators are appointed by an independent mediation organization, or are selected by the parties, or are appointed by the court. Mediators need to be independent and have no real or perceived conflict of interest. Mediators also need to be experts regarding the disputed issues. The most effective mediators are usually professionals who have substantial practice experience or who understand the needs, interests, feelings, thoughts, emotions, and hopes of the parties. Mediators serve various roles during a mediation. An effective mediator should be able to do all the things explained in Section 9.6.

Mediation Organization. The mediation service is the organization used by the parties to administer the mediation. This service may appoint the mediator, assist the parties in preparing for the mediation, answer their questions, schedule the mediation, and handle any administrative matters not handled by the mediator.

Exorcist. Oh, that's a different proceeding.

B. WHY MEDIATE, OR WHY NOT
9.3 REASONS TO MEDIATE

Whether or not a case can or should be mediated depends on multiple factors. The following list details these considerations.

Party preferences. One or both parties realize they need help and may prefer or be eager to engage in mediation and should do so.

Time considerations. Mediation may be able to create an agreement or resolve a problem faster than other methods.

Cost considerations. A mediated agreement may make or save the parties money. The substantial costs of litigation and attorney's fees can be avoided in the mediation process.

The effect of no agreement. Parties may lose an opportunity to create a relationship or produce a profit if no agreement is reached, and mediation allows them to get together and achieve mutual gains.

Relief sought. A judicial or administrative decision may not provide the relief a party wants, and mediated settlement may be the only way parties can have their needs met.

Problems initiating or sustaining negotiation discussions. Neither party may want to suggest negotiation talks or negotiation efforts may have failed, and mediation may overcome the difficulties parties have negotiating on their own.

Substantially different perspectives. There may be substantial gaps between the positions asserted by the opposing sides, and the skills of a mediator are necessary to reduce these differences of perceptions.

The relationship between the parties. Opposing parties may have, or hope to have, a continuing relationship after the dispute is resolved, and mediation offers the parties an opportunity to maintain or create a relationship.

Complex problems or issues. Some matters may be very difficult, time-consuming, and expensive to litigate or otherwise resolve, and mediation provides a much more efficient and economical way to resolve problems.

The need for confidentiality. The process and results of mediation are more private and much less public than other forums, and parties who want matters to remain confidential may prefer to mediate.

The effect of obtaining a judgment. It may be best for a party to avoid the adverse effect of a judgment in a case, and mediation can avoid the permanent effect of a judgment and its precedential value for future cases.

Unusual considerations. Some parties may misperceive why everyone is getting together. They think it's to meditate, instead of to mediate. And, hey, if it works, it works.

9.4 REASONS NOT TO MEDIATE

The following factors suggest that mediation may not be especially productive.

Substantial party resistance. Mediation requires the cooperation of a party to engage in serious and good faith discussions. A party may be so opposed to mediation that it would be useless to mediate. In a multi-party case involving significant persons not interested or available, mediation efforts may be unsuccessful because those who are affected are not involved. However, an effective mediator can successfully involve stubborn parties in productive discussions.

Non-negotiable positions. If a party takes an intractable position regarding a critical mediation issue and states that nothing will change that position, mediation may not be successful. But, simply stating an unyielding position does not necessarily reflect an inflexible position. A party may only be "posturing" and may change a position when faced with "reality."

Sabotage. Usually, parties want a mediation to succeed. There may be occasional situations when a party approaches a mediation with no intent or hope the mediation will succeed. This party may attempt to sabotage the mediation process, and it may be very difficult to attempt to mediate with a party who operates in bad faith.

Financially destitute party. Mediations which involve the payment of money or distribution of assets between parties may be unsuccessful if a party does not have the ability to make the necessary payments or distribution. A mediation without the potential for an agreeable result may only waste time and energy.

Unavailable information. Mediation scheduled before investigation or discovery is completed may need to be postponed and rescheduled if one or both parties need to obtain or exchange information to be able to evaluate all the issues in the case. Often, early mediation assists in resolving discovery disputes and helps the parties exchange needed information.

C. HOW TO MEDIATE

9.5 PREPARING FOR THE MEDIATION

Planning for mediation includes:

- Objectively evaluating the case.

- Assessing what information is needed.

- Determining what negotiated results a party wants and needs.

- Establishing realistic mediation goals.

- Assessing the availability of insurance.

- Rehearsing being nice, but not overly generous.

Objective evaluation of a case. The nature and extent of an evaluation depends upon the circumstances of the matter to be mediated. Each situation should be reviewed from the perspective of the other side to obtain a balanced understanding of the strengths and weaknesses of the situation or problem. It may be difficult to make an assessment impartially, but it is essential so that the assessment of potential solutions is not overly subjective.

Exchange of information. Parties must determine whether they have sufficient information to proceed to a mediation. Parties who do not believe they know enough about the facts or the law may be disinclined to agree to a resolution. The parties, prior to mediation, may agree to exchange information and documents. If the parties are unable to reach a mutual agreement, the parties may present their disagreement to the mediator who may be able to assist them in assessing what information they need before proceeding to mediate the merits.

Determination of needs and interests. Parties must also determine what their interests are and what they want or need through a negotiated agreement. This determination includes an assessment of what a party will minimally accept (the bottom line), initial negotiation positions (the first offer or demand), intervening positions, and common goals and interests of the parties.

Establishing realistic expectations. The determination of what a party wants must be placed in proper perspective. Parties need to approach the mediation with realistic goals. Mediated settlements typically require the parties to compromise and accept less or give more than they prefer. A party approaching mediation should be prepared to engage in a give-and-take process.

Available Insurance. The existence of insurance in mediation may dramatically influence the outcome. A party who is insured for a claim or controversy has the resources of the insurance company available. The amount of insurance may substantially affect the mediated result. It is critical for the parties and the mediator to know whether insurance exists, the amount of coverage, and the limits of the policy.

9.5.1 Assessing Factors

Lawyers preparing for mediation should consider how the mediation will proceed and what influence they want on the process. These predictions are essential to the parties obtaining a favorable settlement. Factors a party should consider include:

Questions
- What questions do I want to ask the other side?
- What questions do I want the mediator to ask the other side?

Disclosure
- What do I want to disclose to the mediator? To the other side?
- What don't I want to disclose to the mediator? To the other side?

Documents

- What documents do I want to provide the mediator? To the other side?

- What documents do I want to see from the other side?

Strengths and Weaknesses

- What are the strengths and weaknesses of my position?

- What are the strengths and weaknesses of the other side's position?

Time

- How much time do I want to spend in mediation?

- How do I want to spend that time in mediation?

Participants

- Whom do I want to speak for my client? Me? My client? Another representative?

- What authority do I want to give an agent or employee who will mediate?

Approaches

- What strategies, tactics, and techniques will I use during mediation?

- What approaches will I suggest the mediator use during mediation?

Alternatives

- What would cause me to deadlock or walk out of the mediation?

- If the mediation fails, what other dispute resolution methods are available for me to obtain what I want?

- How much will it cost me to pursue what I want through another dispute resolution method if mediation fails?

- What are my other options to get what I want?

- How can I convince the mediator I truly deserve everything and the other side less than nothing?

9.5.2 Preparation by Mediator

The mediator needs to become familiar with the situation or dispute before the mediation begins. Many mediators ask the parties to submit something confidential in writing. A party should comply with this request and may want to submit additional information. If a party has not been asked to make any written submissions the party should consider whether it is advantageous to submit some information and determine whether the mediator will accept or read what is voluntarily submitted. Some mediators may also do research on their own. A party should determine ahead of time what a mediator knows and how the mediator is prepared for the mediation.

9.6 THE MEDIATION SESSION

A mediation session may begin with a joint session with all parties and their attorneys or representatives present in the same room from the very beginning of a mediation. Or, the mediation session may begin with the parties in separate rooms. Some parties may not want to be in the same room with the other party, and the mediator may initially prefer to separate the parties.

Most mediators begin the mediation session with an explanation of the mediation process. Typically, mediators:

- Introduce themselves.
- Commend the participants for attending.
- Describe their experience as a mediator.
- Explain their role and their neutrality and impartiality.
- Describe the mediation procedure, including caucuses.
- Explain the bounds of confidentiality.
- Describe the conference room and logistics.
- Suggest some behavioral guidelines.
- Answer questions from the parties and attorneys.
- Explain the issues the mediator believes need to be addressed.

- Ask the parties and attorneys whether additional issues need to be resolved.

- Establish a cooperative atmosphere and seek a commitment from both sides to proceed.

- Ask whether anything else needs to be discussed.

- Occasionally, show videotaped replays of their most successful mediations.

9.6.1 Disclosing Mediation Information

Mediators typically permit the parties during the mediation an opportunity to tell the mediator whatever it is the parties want to disclose. The parties should consider disclosing the following information:

A favorable first impression. The parties should convey an impression to the mediator that the party is prepared and open to the possibility or probability of a mediated agreement.

Issues and nature of the situation. A mediator needs to know the issues and precise nature of the situation that exists between the parties.

Theory of the deal or case. A party should concisely explain to the mediator what the party wants and why.

A summary of the important facts. The parties should make sure the mediator knows all relevant and reliable facts.

Applicable law. The mediator may or may not need to know a party's view of the law supporting the party's positions. The party should be prepared to explain the law if it will be useful or requested.

Common interests between the parties. A primary goal of the mediator will be to focus the mediation on common interests which may bridge the gap between the parties. Parties can assist in this process by suggesting mutually held perspectives on these issues.

Documents. Significant documents that contain information ought to be shown to or provided to the mediator. Visual aids may be prepared which assist the mediator in understanding differences and similarities.

Status of the lawsuit. If a lawsuit is being mediated, the mediator needs to know the procedural aspects of the case, including the status of pleadings, discovery, and motions.

Previous negotiation efforts and discussions. The mediator may want to know what, if any, negotiation talks have transpired, or why there have been no efforts.

Goals. Some mediators may ask what a party hopes to accomplish during the mediation. An effective answer is to say: "We're open to whatever happens. We are here in an effort to reach an agreement that meets our needs."

Results. The mediator may ask at some point during the mediation what a party hopes to achieve. The party should consider what mediated result will satisfy the party's needs, and what should be disclosed to the mediator.

This and other information should be presented to the mediator in a persuasive and interesting way. The informality of the mediation process encourages parties to engage in discussions in a conversational approach. But, they shouldn't necessarily try to interject marginal humor the way we try in this book.

9.6.2   Communicating With the Other Side

A mediation session provides the parties with an opportunity to communicate with each other. A party may do so during mediation by directing statements to the other side, or may do so indirectly by asking the mediator to convey information. A party, when meeting with the mediator separately, can request that the mediator communicate information to the other side. A party may also suggest the mediator be present in the room when a party conveys information to the other side. This approach may be especially effective if the other side has refused to listen.

Equally important is what parties do not want to communicate to the other side. It usually is ineffective in the presence of the other side to make negative or derogatory comments about the other party (however tempting), or to inflame inappropriate hostile emotions that exist between the parties (however cathartic). It may be very useful to explain to the mediator, in a reasonable way, the existence of hard feelings and what underlies the feelings because the mediator may need to know about these adverse attitudes.

D. MEDIATION APPROACHES

9.7 MEDIATION TACTICS AND TECHNIQUES

Mediators may use a variety of effective tactics and techniques during mediation.

9.7.1 Assess the Case

Determine the needs, interests, and values of each party. A mediator must learn the actual needs and real interests of the parties and their values. The negotiation process may cause the parties to exaggerate their needs and hide their real interests from the other side. The mediator needs to probe to determine what they want and why they want it.

Identify issues. It is critical for the mediator to make a list of all the issues that need to be resolved. The parties are unlikely to agree unless all issues, from their perspective, have been resolved.

Probe positions. Parties will take various positions during mediation. The mediator must determine how firm or soft a party is regarding a position. Certain positions may be non-negotiable, while other positions may be very malleable.

9.7.2 Communicate With the Parties

Establish an agenda. The mediator can set an agenda for the mediation or assist the parties in establishing the issues that need to be discussed and resolved.

Caucus with the parties. Caucuses are common in many mediations. Caucuses occur when a mediator meets and talks separately with a party, outside the presence of the other party. In this private setting, a party may be more forthcoming and more open and honest about real needs and interests.

Engage in "shuttle" diplomacy. During mediations when the parties are in separate rooms or locations, the mediator may go back and forth between the parties. The mediator may obtain a demand from one party and visit the other party to explain the demand and then return to the first party with a counteroffer. This process works effectively where the parties need to or prefer to exchange concessions while reaching a compromise settlement.

Exchange information. The mediator may assist the parties in understanding what information is necessary to clarify inaccuracies. The parties may disclose to the mediator certain information which the mediator, with the permission of the parties, can communicate to the other side.

Maintain civility. The mediator can establish a productive environment for settlement by maintaining civility and order between the parties during discussions.

Encourage communication. The mediator can allow an opportunity for the parties to speak to each other or to speak privately to the mediator, encouraging full communication.

Explore feelings, hopes, and dreams. Psychological and emotional attitudes can significantly influence a party, and a mediator needs to understand, defuse, and discuss these attitudes.

Retain confidential information. The mediator can provide the parties with an opportunity to disclose confidential information, which the mediator will continue to keep confidential and only reveal to the other side if the disclosing party allows the mediator to do so.

9.7.3   Propose Alternative Resolutions

Provide a different perspective. The mediator can provide the parties with a neutral and independent perspective regarding the strengths and weaknesses of their positions, the value of their interests, and the reality of their obtaining what they want.

Suggest strategic and tactical approaches. Mediators may suggest to the parties the use of a strategy or tactic to improve the chances of settling the case. Mediators need to be cautious so that they do not appear to be taking sides by suggesting to a party what to say or do.

Explore options. One of the chief roles of mediators is to discuss with the parties various options they may or may not have considered. Mediators can brainstorm with the parties separately or together in an effort to discover and evaluate alternative solutions.

Propose an innovative remedy. Mediators may suggest specific resolutions the parties have not considered or may even have previously rejected. Mediators can explain the advantages, as well as disadvantages, of the proposed solutions.

Offer opinions regarding the issues. Mediators, on their own initiative or at the suggestion of a party, may offer their opinions about a fact, legal position or issue in a mediation. Mediators must be cautious when doing this, as their opinion may be perceived as favoring one party and damaging their neutrality.

Take a position. In some mediations, it may be appropriate or necessary for the mediator to assert a position. This does not mean that a mediator sides with one party as opposed to the other, but rather, that the mediator takes a reasonable position supported by the facts, circumstances, and law. It is important for the mediator to support the expressed position with a reasonable explanation and to avoid asserting a personal preference.

Suggest a non-binding solution. The parties may request, or the mediator may recommend, that the mediator make a non-binding decision regarding an issue, based upon the presentations of the parties. This resolution may effect the position and judgment of the parties and may help break an impasse.

Urge resolution. Mediators can urge the parties to reach an agreement by explaining to them the consequences of a failed mediation. The parties may not have fully considered the disadvantages of not reaching an accord, and the mediator can point out why a compromise resolution is in their best interests.

Seek joint gains. The mediator can seek joint gains for the parties by encouraging the parties to be creative in fashioning a result and by proposing creative ways to resolve an impasse.

Partially resolve a matter. A mediation may not resolve all the issues, but may still be a success. If the parties do not reach a complete agreement, they may be able to reach a partial accord on some issues, or narrow the issues for subsequent determination by an arbitrator or judge.

9.7.4 Continue or Conclude the Mediation

Schedule another session. The mediator can schedule another mediation session if appropriate or desired by the parties.

Memorialize the agreement. A written summary of the complete agreement should be recorded, and the mediator should make sure this occurs.

Declare an impasse. The mediator can declare an impasse if continuing mediation discussions would be fruitless. A party can also request that an impasse be declared. The mediator can suggest the parties meet again to consider some specific issues or how they should resolve their dispute by using another method, such as arbitration.

Recommend exercise. Sometimes the best thing a mediator can do is to tell one or all of the parties to take a hike. Just kidding. This is why patience and perseverance is a virtue, especially for a mediator.

9.7.5 Employ Advanced Mediation Approaches

Use additional techniques. Mediators have other techniques available. During a mediation, a deadlock or an impasse may appear imminent or actually occur. Attitudes vary among mediation professionals regarding the role of the mediator at this point in the process. It may or may not be appropriate for the mediator to become more actively involved. Some possible techniques with an explanation of philosophy follow.

Suffer/suffer. Sometimes effective mediation tactics will result in an accord satisfying everyone. But many mediations result in a resolution only after everyone has lost something important. Many parties are unwilling to reach an accord unless they perceive the other side suffers as much as they do. This "suffer/suffer" approach can be explained by the mediator so that the parties understand that each has suffered more than their fair share.

Reality therapy. A party may not understand or perceive the advantages of a proposed agreement. The mediator can meet privately with the party and provide some "reality therapy." A party who hears this message from the mediator may reassess the situation.

Emotionally charged atmosphere. In some mediations, the parties strongly dislike each other because of prior unpleasant experiences. These hostile emotions need to be acknowledged and usually dissipated before an agreement can be reached. The mediator can caucus with both sides individually and allow each side to vent their emotions in the presence of the mediator.

Bridging the Gap. Mediation may result in both sides becoming entrenched in a position and unwilling to make another offer or demand unless the other side first makes a move. At this juncture, the mediator can propose settlement terms and tell both sides that if either side rejects the mediator's proposal, an impasse will be declared, but that if both sides accept, there is a final settlement.

Simultaneous exchange of a response. Parties in some mediations respond to a proposal by a mediator only after the other side responds. If both parties take this attitude, the mediation will deadlock. One way of avoiding this problem is to have the parties submit simultaneously to the mediator a written response to the proposal made by the mediator. In this way, neither side gains any advantage by having the other side first disclose their position.

Cooling off period. Some cases require a number of mediation sessions before an agreement is reached. Instead of declaring an impasse after a mediation session, the mediator can suggest that parties have a "cooling off" period to reassess their positions and schedule another mediation session. The mediator can also suggest the parties consider some issue or do something during this time to increase the chances that the subsequent mediation session will achieve an accord.

9.8   TERMINATION OF MEDIATION

A mediation may end in a number of ways:

- The parties reach an agreement.

- One or more parties decide not to participate in the mediation any longer.

- The mediator declares an impasse and the mediation ends.

- Everyone participates in some joint celebration, or a celebration in some joint.

9.8.1   Settlement Agreement

An agreement reached by the parties during the mediation is often a binding, enforceable contract. A written agreement, even if handwritten, should be signed by the parties and attorneys before the mediation ends. If a party later fails to or refuses to abide by the terms of the contract, the other party may seek to enforce the agreement. This failure or refusal may lead to a dispute, which can also be attempted to be resolved through mediation.

It may seem that mediation may never end, but it will, as has this chapter.

*

Part Three
DISPUTE RESOLUTION PREPARATION

Chapter Ten
INVESTIGATIONS: OBTAINING INFORMATION FROM THOSE IN THE KNOW

I think I'll look over there.   I'm pretty sure that's where I'll find it.

I don't see it.   I'm going to have to ask someone about it.   Maybe they saw it or know where it is.

Whom should I ask?   I'll have to find out whom I should ask to find out what I want to know.

Maybe it's written down.   I can read fairly well, all I have to do is find it.

How will I know they are telling and giving me everything?   They may not want to talk to me.   They may want to withhold information.

I'm going to have to be as good as Paul Drake was when he discovered whatever Perry Mason needed to know.

Now how did he go about doing that?

A.   INTRODUCTION

10.1   SCOPE OF INFORMATION

This chapter concentrates primarily on the informal gathering of information from sources other than a client or opposing party.   Chapter Three dealt with obtaining information from clients.   Subsequent chapters explain how to discover information from opposing parties.

Information is available from two primary sources: people and documents.   By people, we mean humans and exclude outer space aliens (although if you make contact with them we will include them in our next edition). By documents, we mean written and recorded information appearing anywhere.

B. THE HUMAN TOUCH

10.2 PEOPLE

There are four major categories of people available who may know something useful:

- Friendly witnesses
- Neutral witnesses
- Adverse witnesses
- Experts
- Bullwinkle the Moose's Mr. Know-it-All. Okay, we only said people.

10.2.1 Friendly Witnesses

Broadly defined, a friendly witness is anyone who likes your client. These people include family (well, most of them), friends, acquaintances, and colleagues. A friendly witness is also someone who may not know your client but who supports their position. Other sources can be equally friendly and useful. Regulators of a particular business, although forbidden by law from playing favorites, may be inclined to help by providing information to people they believe are deserving of the information.

Perhaps the most useful aspect of friendly witnesses is that they will be cooperative and relatively easy to contact in seeking information. All you need to do is tell them who you represent and what you want, and they will tell you what they know or where you may find what you want. It is not always that easy, but it is a lot easier than dealing with the other types of witnesses.

10.2.2 Neutral Witnesses

A neutral witness is (obviously) someone who is (ostensibly) impartial. The major difference in dealing with neutral witnesses is the way you approach them and the manner in which you attempt to obtain information. Neutral witnesses will usually not be as cooperative, receptive, or available to provide information. You are, after all, asking them for a favor for a total stranger (your client).

10.2.3 Adverse Witnesses

An adverse witness dislikes your client, wants your client to lose something, or both. The most obvious problem with this type of witness is that the witness will not talk or cooperate with you. You know you can always subpoena them (as you can with any other witness including a neutral or friendly witness) to talk with you or bring documents to a deposition. But it may be to your client's advantage for you to contact them to obtain information informally.

There will be some adverse witnesses you will not be able to informally contact. An adverse party represented by an attorney cannot be contacted directly except through their lawyer. Adverse witnesses who are agents or employees of a party or who may be closely affiliated with the party can also not be contacted without permission of opposing counsel. To do so would violate the rules of professional conduct which prohibit you from making such ex parte contacts.

10.2.4 Experts

You may need an expert to help you interpret or create information or provide you with an opinion. You may need an expert for a transaction (a tax accountant), and you may need an expert for litigation (a psychiatrist, but not for yourself). You can contact experts to determine their availability, interest, and fees. Experts usually expect to be paid by the hour or a flat fee, plus expenses, often with a retainer.

The most effective way to locate an expert is through referrals from other counsel, clients, professionals or associations, or other experts. It is wise to research experts before contacting them to determine their experience, reputation, and special knowledge. You can obtain this information from your referral source, periodicals, media information, and a paper trail of their publications. You also want to consider (when you contact and interview them) their cooperativeness, working style, punctuality, personality, and cost. There is no substitute for a reasonable, affordable expert who works well with others.

After you retain experts, you can meet with them or provide them the information they need to be of assistance. If you are involved in a transaction, you will need to tell them what they need to know. If you are involved in litigation, what you tell your expert may depend upon what role they will play in litigation. See Section 12.5.

10.3 WITNESS COOPERATION

You can increase the cooperation of a witness by following certain interviewing approaches:

Be kind. Listen to some John Denver music if necessary to get into the mood.

Select a convenient time and place for the witness. Make it as convenient as possible for the neutral witness to provide information. Make things as easy as possible by going to them instead of asking them to come to your office, sending someone to help search for materials or copy documents, agree to meet after business hours or on weekends, and reimburse them for reasonable expenses.

Be punctual and brief. You should avoid wasting their time and use as little of it as necessary.

Make them feel good about cooperating. Unless you are a Hobbes fanatic, approach witnesses as if they were good people who are willing to help. They usually will if they feel they are doing something beneficial for someone else, their job, the public good, or themselves. So tell them how talking with you benefits your client, how it is part of their job responsibility, how it helps promote societal interests, or how it benefits them. For example, a neutral witness may have a self interest which they may not be initially aware. An uncooperative neutral witness may provide evidence in litigation regarding artwork after being advised that an adverse result could cast doubt on the authenticity of the witness' own valuable art collection.

Act respectfully. A brusque, haughty demeanor is not appropriate. Neither is begging, as this tends to cause the witness to pity the groveling lawyer.

Remain courteous while being persistent. Being impolite and rude to a reluctant witness will immediately accelerate the end of the interview.

Empathize with the witness. Identify with appropriate attitudes and positions and listen approvingly.

Personalize the client. Describe your client as an individual who needs help and the assistance of the witness.

Rely on altruism. A polite appeal to altruism may go a long way. Most humans have a bit of it, no matter what neoclassical economists may say. For example, telling a witness that an injured client has only limited insurance and needs to prevail to obtain full compensation may help.

Consider who is present. The presence of someone else besides the witness may make it more difficult for the witness to testify accurately and without unnecessary influence. Or, they may be more willing to talk if someone else is present.

Ask why they refuse to cooperate. This information will help you understand their position.

Provide them with a reason to talk to you. A reasonable explanation by you which responds to their refusal to cooperate may give you what they know.

10.4   DIFFICULT WITNESSES

You should not shirk from pursuing the difficult witness. You are unlikely to convince the witness to switch sides or become pals, and attempting to do so may further alienate the witness. You may, however, be able effectively to use additional approaches to gain information:

Appeal to their natural inclination to want to tell the truth. Say: "I understand you don't want to talk to me, but you do want us to know what really happened, don't you?"

Let them persuade you of the correctness of the opposing position. Say: "Tell me what you know and my client may not pursue this matter."

Let the witness rant and rave. Encourage them to tell you what happened and disclose their biases and prejudices. Say: "I need to know all the bad things about my client. What do you know?"

Appeal to their self interest. Say: "You may want to talk to me if you knew what some people have said about you. I heard you were a ... just the nicest person in the entire county."

Focus on their involvement. Say: "You may want to tell me some things that directly involve you. Let me ask you a few questions to clarify your involvement."

Appropriately threaten them. Explain they will have to talk to you when you subpoena them to a deposition. Further explain that the timing and location may then be an inconvenience for them.

10.5 WITNESS PAYMENTS

The general rules are these:

- The only expenses that may be reimbursed for a lay witness are reasonable costs for travel and compensation for loss of time.

- A lay witness cannot or should not be paid for giving information or for testifying.

- Expert witnesses may be paid for their professional services.

- Some witnesses may expect to be reimbursed for their personal time spent being interviewed, such as individuals who are often eye witnesses (e.g. police).

- You cannot buy a story from a witness, unless you have your own television show.

C. THE STUFF

10.6 DOCUMENTS

What you need to know may exist in some written or recorded form. How to uncover this information depends upon its type, source, and format.

10.6.1 Types

There are two basic types of information: stuff another party has created and other stuff about relevant issues. The former includes specific information someone involved in the case has written or developed, for example, the proverbial "hot document" which reveals damaging information. The latter involves general information about a matter related to the case, such as an article written about a party, statistics gathered about a particular field, or data publicized by a specific industry.

10.6.2 Sources

The two primary document sources are private and public information. Private information may only be obtained with the consent of the holder of the information or through a subpoena. For example, a business may only be willing to reveal information it has because it wants to or because a court orders it to. A private corporation may provide copies of bills and invoices only to individuals involved in the transaction. A bank may not reveal any of its records without a subpoena. On the other hand, public information should be readily available on request. For example, you can take a bus to the library to research information, you can stay at home and use a computer and a modem to search on-line for data, or you can contact a governmental agency for information. The Freedom of Information Act and comparable state statutes are powerful tools for dislodging public information.

Public information may have a high degree of credibility because it is generated by disinterested persons made for some purpose usually unrelated to your case. Although some public records are poorly conceptualized (they give you every imaginable statistic but not the really useful information), organized (they have the information but it is hard to decipher), or kept (the required record is misplaced), many are useful and easily accessible. Public information can be cheaper than seeking information from resistant witnesses and opponents. Public information can also be used as a check on the degree to which counsel is receiving complete and correct information from witnesses and opponents.

10.6.3 Format

The availability of documentary information may depend upon its format. It may appear in written form in an article or book. It may be retained as a separate piece of information or as part of a file or report. It may exist in bits in a computer system. It may be a recording on a tape or CD–ROM. On-line services provide a wealth of information. News service databases provide sources and information. Internet and other computer accessed sources provide databases, secrets of the world, and opinions from outside our known galaxy.

10.7 THINGS

Things are where you find them. If they are commercially available, you can buy one. If they are public property, you can view them. If they are on private property, you will need the consent of the owner to see them. With some things, you may need the original, if it is still available. You may want to inspect it or test it. With other things, a duplication or similar model will suffice.

D. The How

10.8 ASK. LOOK. DEMAND.

What you need often involves contacting a person. If you want what someone knows, you obviously have to talk to them. If you want a document or thing you may need the cooperation of someone who has it. To get what you want, you can:

- Ask for what you want
- Look for what you want
- Demand what you want

10.8.1 Asking

The medieval knight Parzifal (a.k.a. Percival) possessed the ability to liberate an anguished knight (and by allegorical implication, the forces of righteousness) by asking a question about the knight's plight. Parzifal needed hundreds of pages to get to the moment of magical inquiry. Lawyers, on the other hand, can start asking questions immediately of everyone connected with the matter who is willing to talk. When involved in a transaction, the lawyer can ask about other prospective parties, the goals of the deal, the client's situation, previous similar dealings, or standard practices in the industry. When engaged in dispute resolution, the lawyer can ask questions of persons with knowledge of the dispute. This path to understanding relationships and disputes can include asking follow-up questions of other persons. Sometimes this is the only way to learn as the participants may know things that were never recorded in any other medium. Sometimes, further inquiries may reveal the existence of documents and things.

10.8.2 Looking

The Biblical adage "seek and you shall find" is good, practical advice for practice. Whether counsel is reconstructing an event giving rise to a dispute or attempting to determine whether Purpleacre is really worth the multi-million dollar price tag, there may be no substitute for simply digging around. Where possible, counsel or an assistant should view the property in question, visit sites of events, review physical material, and study other relevant things.

Often, looking can be done informally because the material to be examined is in plain view or available to the public. Sometimes, special arrangements may need to be made (e.g. a tour of a plant subject to possible sale). With voluntary transactions other parties will be inclined to cooperate in order to facilitate a legal project. Other times, particularly in disputes, looking is not as easy as a simple walk-by but will require the consent of the other side and perhaps the instigation of a formal request procedure.

10.8.3 Demanding

If information is not forthcoming voluntarily, a lawyer can always demand the information. In transactional work, the demand may prompt the other side to cooperate if it is in their best interest because otherwise the deal may not be completed. In disputes, the threat of a demand without serving formal documents may be sufficient to gain cooperation. If not, discovery methods may obtain information from a party or a subpoena duces tecum may obtain the information from a third party. See Section 14.11. Information in government hands may be demanded pursuant to the Freedom of Information Act or similar state statutes. See Section 14.12.

10.9 THE HOW, THE WHEN, THE WHERE, THE WHO

Just as not all legal precedent is created equal, not all prospective information is created equal. Some information is more germane to determining legal rights or responsibilities. Similarly, all sources are not created equal. Some are more important because they are more likely to possess relevant information.

10.9.1 The How

Face to face interviews obviously allow the interviewer to observe the witness and develop a more personal relationship with them. Telephone interviews can be much more economical and still provide sufficiently useful information.

10.9.2 The When

Effective investigators generally direct their initial and subsequent resources in descending order of importance. The most valuable information and sources should be pursued immediately both to ensure obtaining accurate information (e.g., before prospective opponents contact the source and create interference) and to ensure the information is not eroded in some way. Information and sources should also be preserved before something expected or unexpected happens. A key witness may later be unavailable and should be talked to quickly. An important witness may die and valuable information unless preserved by documents or admissible hearsay may also die with the witness. Probing for some information may have to wait until it is available or until a witness returns to reality (e.g. the consulting engineer who is trekking in Nepal until the snow flies).

10.9.3 The Where

The best location for an investigation depends upon the circumstances. A witness who is favorable and is willing to talk may be willing to come to the lawyer's office for an interview. A lawyer will usually need to go see a neutral or adverse witness. If a witness will be referring to documents and other things that are best illustrated on site, that location will be preferable. Sometimes a neutral interview site is required for purposes of accommodating schedules or avoiding attention. A witness may want to be helpful but may not want to be seen. Usually interviews should be conducted in an accommodating location, but sometimes interviews should be conducted in an intimidating atmosphere. It all depends on the witness, the allegiance of the witness, the nature of the information sought, and related factors.

10.9.4   The Who

While we have focused on the lawyer as being the person obtaining the information, it is often more productive and less costly for others to be information gatherers. An experienced investigator, retained independently or employed by the law firm, can often be more effective. This investigator may be more available, knowledgeable, and better equipped to obtain the information, and may also do a significantly better job than an attorney because some investigations require the gathering of physical, technical, and scientific information. Experienced investigators may also be better able to interview witnesses and more efficiently record stories and testimony.

Other people besides the primary lawyers may be less expensive. Investigators who charge a lower hourly or flat fee or paralegals or associates in a firm who have low hourly fees may be more economical. Yes, there are people out there who are sometimes better than we are and who work for less.

Another consideration involving the who (not the band, nor Dr. Seuss) relates to the possible impact on the use of the information sought. If an attorney interviews a witness or negotiates with a prospective defendant, these conversations may become part of a dispute. If this occurs, the lawyer may be disqualified from continuing to provide representation if the lawyer is also to be a witness about the point in contention. To avoid this prospect, lawyers should either avoid these sorts of interviews or contacts entirely or be accompanied by a non-lawyer. If testimonial conflicts later ensue, the non-lawyer can provide the needed testimony without necessarily disqualifying the lawyer.

10.10 INTERVIEW APPROACHES

Three common interviewing techniques are:

- Conducting a narrative
- Asking specific questions
- Asking cross-examination questions

These techniques may be and usually are mixed during any one interview. Your goal is to achieve completion, clarity, and closure. A narrative approach has the witness relate in story form what the witness knows. Specific questions clarify information, add details, and elicit new information. Cross-examination questions pursue evasive answers, resolve conflicting information, test the perception of the witness, and search for impeachment. These approaches are identical or similar to interviewing approaches used in client interviews and depositions, discussed in Chapters Three and Thirteen. Suggestions contained in these chapters relating to clients and deponents also apply to the questioning of witnesses.

10.10.1 Interview Techniques

Investigators may assist a witness in accurately remembering and correctly reciting information. Or, investigators may attempt to influence responses a witness gives during an interview. These approaches recognize that witnesses may not have seen or heard everything, may have forgotten some things, or may be mistaken regarding their perceptions. Techniques that some investigators employ to influence witnesses include:

Word choice. The selection of certain words may create a more helpful and persuasive witness story and statement. The suggestion or inclusion of adjectives and impact words may strengthen a witness' version. For example, adding "very" to modify the word fast will make an obvious difference, and substituting "screamed" for "said" may also make a difference.

Leading questions. Questions which suggest an answer may have the witness agreeing with the suggested answer.

Filling in details. An interviewer may tell the witness what happened so the witness will include that information in a story they may otherwise have forgotten.

Other versions. An investigator may tell the witness what other witnesses have said to influence the interviewee. For example, an investigator may say: "Two other witnesses have told me the light was green, what color did you see?"

Disagreeing with the answers. The interviewer may explain why what a witness has said may be inaccurate, implausible, or mistaken in an attempt to change the mind of the witness.

Composing a story. After an interview, the investigator may draft a witness statement and compose it in as favorable a light as possible for a client.

These techniques must be done carefully to avoid unfairly influencing the witness. It sometimes is a fine line between what is appropriate and what may be unethical or illegal. If in doubt, the investigator must avoid improper techniques.

10.10.2   Advising Witnesses

An attorney cannot provide legal advice to a witness unless the attorney represents the witness. The most tempting advice to give a witness is not to talk to anyone else about a situation. But it is unethical and a tactical error to tell a witness to refuse to talk. It is improper and a conflict of interest for an attorney to provide legal advice to a non-client witness. It is also a tactical mistake to create an impression that the investigator has something to hide and has to rely on withholding information in an attempt to gain an advantage.

A lawyer may properly and carefully, without providing legal advice, explain the consequences to a witness of talking or not talking to the other side. A lawyer cannot suggest or tell a witness what to do and should expressly tell the witness this. A lawyer may provide general information to witnesses informing them about their rights, and witnesses may rely upon this explanation in making their own independent decision.

10.11   RECORDING THE INTERVIEW

An investigator needs to decide before, during, or after an interview whether the information should be recorded. It may be unnecessary to record information obtained from a friendly witness who will always be available. It may be necessary to record information from a neutral or adverse witness who may be unavailable or who may later change their story. Three common ways to record information are:

- A file memo

- A witness statement

- A contemporaneous recording

10.11.1   File Memo

The file memo may contain several parts:

- A summary of the information obtained.

- A description of the demeanor and credibility of the witness and the importance and implication of the information.

- Additional relevant comments produced in the interview.

The lawyer investigator should be involved in the drafting of these memos and their content and comprehensiveness. File memos are usually not discoverable because they contain private information in transactions or constitute work product. Care needs to be taken in drafting a file memo to determine whether all or part of the memo may be later discoverable. See section 12.4.2.

10.11.2   Witness Statements

Witness statements may include the following components:

- The identity of the witness, including name and address.

- Statements in the first person, with the statement written as if the witness was telling the story.

- Using the witnesses' own language and expressions to reflect their story.

- Clear and understandable language which is not ambiguous or confusing.

- Information which is sufficiently complete to reflect what the witness knows.

- Selective information which supports the story most helpful to a client.

- A concluding statement that the witness has read and understands the statement and that the statement is true and complete.

- A wax seal bearing a Latin inscription with an interlinear translation.

Other considerations affecting the content of the statement include:

Timing. A witness statement may be composed during or after an interview. Completing the statement in the presence of the interviewee is the most efficient and economic procedure. Completing the statement later requires the investigator to meet with the witness again and may permit some event in the interim to cause a witness to change a story.

Format. Witness statements are typically handwritten or printed documents. The investigator who drafts the statement is better able to control the structure, the words used, and facts included. A witness statement may also be composed as a sworn affidavit which may influence the witness to be sure to tell the truth and to increase the impeachment value of the statement.

Review. A witness must read a statement for accuracy and completeness and to correct any mistakes. This avoids later efforts by the witness to recant the story and reduces a claim against the investigator for unfairly influencing the witness.

Adopting the statement (but not the witness). It is usually best for a witness to sign a statement, and they may need to initial each page in a multi-page statement. Alternatives if the witness refuses to sign a statement are to have the witness initial the statement or to have the investigator read the statement to the witness with the witness signing a statement that it is accurate as read.

10.12 RECORDING THE STATEMENT

Recording the interview may be preferable to composing a file memo or a witness statement. The two most common forms of recording are an electronic recording and a court reporter statement. Electronic recording may be made by a tape recorder or by a video camera. A court reporter statement is a transcript prepared by a reporter who accompanies an investigator and who contemporaneously records the interview.

In most jurisdictions it is permissible to electronically record a face to face interview without the knowledge or consent of the interviewee (sort of like Candid Camera). It is permissible in all states to electronically record a face to face or telephone interview if both the interviewer and interviewee consent. It is permissible in most states to record a telephone interview as long as one party consents.

A recorded interview has the advantage of preserving the exact words of a witness and the complete story. An audio recording captures the voice inflections and sounds of the witness. A video recording reproduces everything that is said and done. These electronic devices may make the witness uncomfortable causing them to decline an interview or withhold some information.

10.13 WRITING A SCREENPLAY

After you complete a particularly scintillating interview in a case, you may want to start writing a screenplay. But wait until the case is over—and you win.

Chapter Eleven
ASSERTING CLAIMS AND DEFENSES: THE RIGHT WAY

I'm right and you're wrong.

No, you're wrong and I'm right.

No I'm not.

Yes you are.

You're just alleging I'm wrong.

And you're just alleging you're right.

You can never admit you're at fault.

And you can never accept that you're at fault.

Let's have someone else resolve this.

We finally agree on something.

How do we go about doing that?

A. INTRODUCTION

Sometimes the best thing to do in a dispute is to start a lawsuit, initiate an arbitration proceeding, or file an administrative petition. Sometimes the best potential result for a client is to have the dispute resolved by an impartial judge, jury, arbitrator, or administrative judge. Sometimes the best thing to do for you is to litigate or arbitrate. It will make you feel like a real lawyer. Just kidding again.

Planning to start something requires an analysis of the issues discussed in Chapter Six. This chapter covers the actual process of starting something and responding to what is started. There are basically six major parts to this process:

• Ascertaining the Right Jurisdiction

- Selecting the Right Forum for the Right reason

- Complaining the Right Way

- Drafting the Right papers

- Responding with the Right Defenses and Motions

- Reveling in Being Right

It's important to do the right thing because the wrong thing may lose the case for your client and reveal your deficiencies, which is surely the wrong way to practice.

11.1 ASSERTING THE RIGHT JURISDICTION

There are two basic types of jurisdiction, both of which must be present in a case: personal jurisdiction and subject matter jurisdiction.

11.1.1 Personal Jurisdiction

A forum must have jurisdiction over the defendant or respondent. The forum usually has personal jurisdiction if:

- The defendant resides within the jurisdiction.

- The defendant is incorporated, has a place of business, does business within the forum, or is licensed by the forum.

- A defendant has substantial or significant contacts with the jurisdiction.

- The respondent has expressly consented to jurisdiction, e.g., a party agrees to arbitration.

- The defendant has impliedly consented to jurisdiction, e.g., the defendant owns property within the state.

- A long arm statute provides jurisdiction over a non-resident defendant who has a single or multiple contacts with the state, e.g., someone who commits a tort or executes a contract within the jurisdiction.

- A statute imposes jurisdiction over the respondent, e.g., an employer will be subject to a workers compensation claim for employees who work in a state.

- A defendant voluntarily appears in the state and is personally served with a lawsuit.

The concept of personal jurisdiction is that no forum has the power or right to force someone to be a defendant or respondent unless it is fair to do so. The defense of lack of personal jurisdiction is usually not waivable, so even if it is not raised during the case the party can later raise it when the judgment or award is trying to be enforced. So if you can't be absolutely sure that personal jurisdiction exists, be reasonably sure before you seek relief in a specific forum.

11.1.2   Subject Matter Jurisdiction

Subject matter jurisdiction is the power of a forum to hear and decide the dispute. Courts derive this authority from constitutional provisions and legislative enactments. Arbitrators derive this authority from the arbitration agreement and the applicable law. Administrative judges draw this power from statutes and regulations.

State courts are courts of general jurisdiction and can hear and decide most disputes. State courts often specialize according to the subject matter of a dispute (e.g., family court, probate court, housing court) or the amount in dispute (e.g., small claims). A case needs to be brought in the proper division for that court to have jurisdiction.

Federal courts are courts of limited jurisdiction and will entertain (there is an interesting concept) certain lawsuits. Three types of federal jurisdiction are:

- Federal law jurisdiction, which are specific types of cases required to be brought in federal court, such as patent cases.

- Federal question cases, which occur when a claim arises under the federal constitution, national treaties, or federal statutes.

- Diversity jurisdiction which exists when all the plaintiffs and all the defendants are citizens (which generally means domiciled) in different states and the amount of controversy involves more than $50,000.

Most foreign countries do not divide their courts into federal and state systems. They do have specialized judicial divisions some of which have general jurisdiction and some which have limited jurisdiction. If your legal atlas is not current, a litigator practicing in that foreign country will know about proper jurisdiction.

B. SELECTING THE RIGHT FORUM FOR THE RIGHT REASON

11.2 HOW TO SELECT A JURISDICTION

You may have a choice in selecting a jurisdiction. Differences among available judicial forums may be significant and should be considered:

Judicial appointment system. Federal judges are appointed for life; some state court judges are elected.

Civil procedure rules. Discovery and motion practice may be more advantageous or disadvantageous depending on the jurisdiction. Federal discovery rules may be more liberal than some state procedural rules.

The decision maker. Federal and state courts allow jury trials in similar cases, but the pool of available jurors may differ significantly, with federal districts often drawing from a larger geographic area.

Rules of evidence. Some jurisdictions have strict hearsay rules while other courts may more readily permit hearsay.

11.3 WHERE CAN RELIEF BE OBTAINED?

Venue determines the specific location where the hearing or trial is conducted. In litigation, the city where a trial is held is usually where the defendant resides, where the cause of action arose, where the defendant is doing business or has an office, or where the plaintiff resides. Similarly in administrative proceedings, venue is where the defendant is or where the claim arose. In arbitration, the place of the arbitration hearing is determined by the written agreement between the parties (e.g., the arbitration shall take place in Monte Carlo) or the rules of the arbitration organization (e.g., the place where the respondent signed the arbitration agreement).

C. COMPLAINING THE RIGHT WAY
11.4 HOW TO BRING A LITIGATION CLAIM

A complaint to initiate a lawsuit usually requires the plaintiff to put the defendant on notice of the facts, the claims, and the relief sought. Notice we said notice. Federal courts and most state courts subscribe to the theory of "notice pleading." So long as a complaint generally notifies a defendant of the nature of the allegations, this minimal information is usually enough to make the complaint acceptable and to defeat a motion to dismiss by the defendant.

Federal court rules specifically require the content of a complaint to include a short and plain statement of facts, a legal claim, and a statement of the relief sought. The facts can be stated as a summary conclusion; the legal claim must reflect a recognized cause of action; and the relief sought can be generally stated. The Appendix of Forms to the Federal Rules of Civil Procedure include examples of complaints that are very short and sweet. These forms reflect the approach that "the less said the better" or "if it doesn't help you, it hurts you" method of pleading. Discovery and motions are then used to uncover the bases of the complaint and to challenge allegations and causes of action. In practice, many lawyers prefer to draft more detailed complaints to present a stronger case, withstand dismissal motions, and better define the scope of discovery. Statements made in a complaint are usually deemed judicial admissions and bind the plaintiff to those statements.

State court rules vary the level of detail required. Approximately half the states follow the federal rules, and the remaining states typically require more factual detail and a more explicit exposition of the legal right to relief. This usually involves pleading more facts and the elements of the cause of action. For example, an auto accident complaint in the state courts would allege that defendant owed plaintiff a duty of careful driving, that defendant breached this duty through speeding and inattentiveness, and that as a result plaintiff suffered specific damages. A federal complaint, by contrast, would be sufficient if plaintiff alleged that defendant negligently caused the plaintiff's injuries and resultant damages.

11.5 WHAT ARE THE COMPONENTS OF A COMPLAINT?

There are four major parts of a complaint:

- The caption
- The contents
- The request for relief
- The signature

11.5.1 Caption

The caption includes the name of the court, the applicable division within a district, the names (and addresses in some jurisdictions) of the parties, the civil action number of the case, the word complaint, and any labeling required by the rules (e.g., contract case). Local custom often dictates the arrangements of these various parts. You should review local pleadings so that it will look like you know what you are doing.

11.5.2 Contents

The contents contain the legal and factual information discussed in the previous section. The averments of the complaint should be set forth in separate paragraphs, with each paragraph limited in so far as possible to a single set of circumstances. Each paragraph should be numbered, with Arabic numerals preferred. Exhibits may be attached to the complaint and adopted by reference in an allegation. Multiple causes of action may be stated as separate counts with preceding paragraphs incorporated by reference.

There are decisions to be made regarding the number of causes of actions to bring. The "kitchen sink" approach is to include everything that reasonably fits in the complaint. The selective approach suggests only strong claims be made. The answer to which approach to use depends upon the circumstances. There must always be a good faith basis supported by the facts and law to bring a claim. Some causes of action may be unavailable against certain defendants. Some claims should be stated in the alternative in hopes of recovering money. For example, many defendants have liability insurance which may not cover a policy holder's intentionally caused injuries. A complaint that includes negligent causes of action in addition to intentional claims may increase the opportunity to recover some money. This alternative type of pleading is permitted in almost all jurisdictions and forums.

A well drafted complaint usually includes the following:

- A description of the parties.

- A summary of relevant events.

- A specific reference to a legal cause of action (e.g., statutory cite).

- A statement of the injury suffered or damages sought.

- A statement of jurisdiction (required in federal court complaints).

- Averments of specialized matter when required, e.g. actions for fraud.

- A statement of relief.

- A photograph of the drafter.

A complaint may look something like this:

STATE OF MITCHELL

COUNTY OF SUMMIT

IN DISTRICT COURT

Northstar Oil Company,

    Plaintiff

                                        COMPLAINT

    v.

                                        Civil Action No. _____
Southstar Oil Corporation,

                                        Jury Trial Demanded

    Defendant

For its Complaint, Plaintiff Northstar Oil Company ("Northstar") states:

1. Northstar is a corporation organized under the laws of Mitchell with its principal place of business in Summit, Mitchell.

---

2. Defendant Southstar Oil Corporation ("Southstar") is a corporation organized under the laws of Grand, with its principal place of business in Lexington, Grand.

3. On January 1, 1995, Southstar offered to sell Plaintiff fuel oil at ten dollars ($10.00) per barrel.

4. On January 2, 1995, Northstar accepted Southstar's offer and ordered 30,000 barrels of fuel oil at the $10.00 per barrel price.

5. Southstar failed to deliver fuel and in a letter dated January 10, 1995, informed Northstar that it would not perform the contract.

6. As a result of Southstar's failure to deliver, Northstar was forced to purchase 30,000 barrels of fuel oil at $15.00 per barrel.

7. As a result of Southstar's breach of its agreement with Northstar, Plaintiff Northstar has suffered damages of one hundred fifty thousand dollars ($150,000.00).

WHEREFORE, Plaintiff Northstar requests Judgment as follows:

1. Judgment in favor of Plaintiff Northstar and against Defendant Southstar in the amount of one hundred fifty thousand dollars ($150,000.00) plus interest and costs to the extent recoverable by law.

2. Such other relief as the interests of justice may require.

Dated: January 26, 1996.

Cara Commercial
Lassez & Faire
123 Commodity Place
Commercetown, New York
11111
(123) 999–9999

Counsel for Plaintiff
Northstar Oil Company

This same complaint reduced to its bare minimum might look like this:

During January 1996, Defendant breached a contract with Plaintiff to sell 30,000 barrels of oil at $10.00 a barrel, causing plaintiff damages of in excess of $50,000.

11.5.3   Request for Relief

We already told you something about this in Section 6.4. Remember? If not, go back five chapters.

11.5.4   Signature

The attorney representing the plaintiff must sign the complaint, include an address, telephone number, and an attorney registration number. This signature in federal court and most state jurisdictions constitutes a certification that counsel has read the pleading, that there are facts and law to support that allegations, and that the pleading is not interposed for harassment or delay. Sanctions for violation of this signature may be available under Federal Rule 11 or similar state rules. You should not draft and serve a pleading unless you are reasonably sure that such a claim is valid. This will require you to make a reasonable investigation to support your client's position and to conduct reasonable legal research to determine whether such a cause of action exists in the jurisdiction. In other words, you cannot make things up, nor think about making things up.

11.6   HOW TO BRING AN ARBITRATION CLAIM

The document initiating an arbitration proceeding is usually called a claim and not a complaint. There are two types of arbitration claim forms, the short one and the detailed one. The rules of the arbitration organization specify which is required. The short version may be submitted by completing a form available from the arbitration organization. The detailed arbitration claim may explain (surprise!) the details of the dispute, the supporting facts and law, and the specific relief sought. The advantages of the short form are that it is quick and efficient. The advantages of the longer form are that it requires the claimant to prepare a case, it more thoroughly advises the respondent of the details of the claim, and it reduces the assertion of frivolous claims.

11.7 HOW TO INITIATE AN ADMINISTRATIVE CASE

The initiation of a proceeding in administrative cases is usually called a petition, although it may also be called a complaint or a claim. The statutory provision or rules of the administrative agency determine what is required. The petition may be short or lengthy, or may be a form document which the petitioner completes.

11.8 IS THAT ALL THERE IS?

Pleadings are important not only for their formal aspects but also because they must be submitted with a clear eye to counsel's strategic and tactical objectives. For example, a complaint not only initiates a lawsuit and (hopefully) beats the statute of limitations, it also defines what is at issue in a lawsuit. Consequently, it also defines what is relevant in a case for purposes of disclosure and discovery. In addition, the allegations of the complaint may foreclose or invite certain claims, defenses, and responses. Similarly the complaint also determines the forum which can affect other aspects of litigation. This analysis applies also to arbitration and administrative proceedings. Whatever happens in the beginning of a case has an influence on the end of a case, and sometimes is outcome determinative (sound familiar)?

D. DRAFTING THE RIGHT PAPERS
11.9 HOW TO DRAFT

Open a window, follow another car extremely closely, or own a sports team. Struck out? Then, when drafting a complaint, claim, or petition, consider the following drafting techniques:

Clarity. Pleadings should, somewhat ironically, avoid legalese. Plain, simple language is usually preferred to legal jargon, such as: on or about, at all times material and relevant, hereinafter, and aforesaid.

Brevity. Whether the pleading is short or detailed, conciseness should be the goal. Say what you mean, and nothing more.

Documents. Pleadings can and should be supported by relevant, attached documents. An affixed document can generally be incorporated in the complaint by reference to avoid having to repeat the contents of the document in the pleading.

Structure. Pleadings should be structured so that they are easily understandable. Pleadings which contain multiple causes of actions should be structured with headings such as: "First cause of action" or "Second claim for relief." Specific items of relief can be structured in a list rather than in a one sentence conclusory statement.

Realistic request for relief. Demands for billions of dollars or for an order requiring defendant to read this book do little to enhance a plaintiff's case. Grossly inflated claims have little utility and may be counter-productive. Some judicial jurisdictions prohibit a plaintiff from stating a specific amount of relief and require them to include in the ad damnum clause a statement such as "in excess of $50,000." The request for money damages in arbitration claims may be pragmatically limited because the amount of the filing fee depends upon the amount of damages requested. Small claims may have a filing fee of $100; a million dollar claim may have a filing fee of $10,000. The relief sought in an administrative petition may be specifically limited by statute or rule.

Reviewing the complaint. After drafting a proposed complaint, claim, or petition it is useful to review to see if it is understandable and to attempt to answer it as if you were the opposing party. This approach usually reveals deficiencies which may be alleviated with proper redrafting, unless you are perfect, and then you are ready to become an appellate judge.

E. RESPONDING WITH THE RIGHT DEFENSES AND MOTIONS

11.10 HOW TO RESPOND

In litigation, a defendant serves an answer. In arbitration and administrative proceedings, a respondent usually serves a response. The contents of this answer or response usually consist of admissions and denials and affirmative defenses.

11.10.1 Admissions and Denials

A party must respond to each of the numbered paragraphs by: admitting the numbered allegation, denying it entirely, admitting or denying it in part, or stating that the defendant/respondent is without knowledge or information sufficient to form a belief about the truth or falsity of the averment. In other words, you have to admit what is true, deny what is untrue, or state that you cannot admit or deny because you do not know. It does all begin with a search for the truth.

11.10.2 Affirmative Defenses

An affirmative defense may need to be explicitly stated to provide notice to the plaintiff/claimant about a defense that exists. An affirmative defense alleges that the defendant/respondent is not legally liable. Examples of affirmative defenses include statute of limitations, statute of frauds, accord and satisfaction, contributory negligence, and fraud. If an affirmative defense is not pleaded, it may not be used as a defense. If in doubt, assert the defense so everyone knows your position, including yourself.

11.10.3 Counterclaims

An answer may also include counterclaims, which are claims made by the defendant/respondent against the plaintiff/claimant. A compulsory counterclaim arises out of the same transaction or occurrence that is the subject matter of the complaint and must be asserted or it is barred from a subsequent case. A permissive counterclaim is one involving any dispute between the plaintiff/claimant and the defendant/respondent with the judge/arbitrator having discretion to refuse to hear the counterclaim because it is too remote from the main action. Prior considerations described in drafting a complaint apply to the drafting of a counterclaim.

11.10.4 Defensive Motions

A defendant/respondent may alternatively respond with a motion, instead of an answer. The motion attacks the pleadings and seeks to dismiss all or part of the complaint. Federal Rule 12 and similar state rules list available grounds for dismissal motions. Section 11.11 explains the purpose and usefulness of these motions. It is critical to remember that these grounds for dismissal need to appear in either the answer or a motion to avoid a party waiving rights to dismiss a pleading on these grounds. Otherwise, a party may unwittingly wave bye-bye to valid defenses. Now, there's a curious image.

11.10.5 Other Claims and Defense

Other claims and defenses may be brought by a party including:

Cross-claims. Cross-claims are claims between co-parties and differ from counterclaims which involve parties on opposite sides of a case. A plaintiff may bring a cross-claim against another plaintiff; a defendant may bring a cross-claim against another defendant.

Third party claims. A defendant may bring in another party as a third party defendant in limited situations. In litigation, a defendant may file a claim against a third party who is vicariously liable to the defendant if the defendant is liable to the plaintiff. A third party claim states that if the defendant is found liable, the third party defendant should indemnify the original defendant because of the third party defendant's legal wrongs. This process is known as impleader. The third party defendant answers the third party complaint just as a defendant answers a complaint. In arbitration, a respondent may be able to bring a claim against a party who has also signed an arbitration agreement to arbitrate the dispute. In administrative proceedings, a respondent may be able to bring in a third party with the permission of the administrative judge.

Reply. Counterclaims must be responded to by the plaintiff claimant. The technical term for this response is a "reply," which is why we included it in this subsection. Smart, huh?

Amending pleadings. Any of the pleadings discussed above can be amended. Amendments are usually allowed with the consent of all the parties or by leave of the judge or arbitrator if the amendment is timely, promotes fairness, and does not prejudice other parties. The applicable rules may establish deadlines for the bringing of an amendment. The latest deadline is usually a reasonable time before a trial or a date after which a party becomes unduly prejudiced. Fairness is promoted if justice will be done by an amendment and injustice prevented. Prejudice suffered by the adverse party may be sufficient grounds to deny the amendment.

Related procedures. There are other procedures involving the addition of claims and parties. Joinder rules provide standards for the inclusion of new parties and causes of action. Other rules regarding severance and separation provide ways for causes of action and parties to be removed from a case and actions tried independently. Intervention is the request by someone who is not a party to become a party in a case because of a specific interest in a case. We leave the details of these proceedings to Civil Procedure where they can be fully appreciated.

11.11 ASSERTING THE RIGHT MOTION

Proceeding with and defending a case often involves the use of motions to get some things done. Attorneys may or should bring the following motions when they answer any of the following questions affirmatively (rule references are to the Federal Rules of Civil Procedure):

11.11.1 Motion to Dismiss

Do I want all or part of a case to be over? If yes, a primary motion that may be brought is a Rule 12 Motion to Dismiss. The grounds for this motion seek to dismiss a complaint because:

Service of the complaint is improper. Service may be wrong because the summons is inadequate or, more commonly, the service of process defective. The most common defects are that the service did not comply with the required service rules (e.g., required personal service was not made) or the wrong person was served (e.g., an employee not able or authorized to receive service was served).

There is no personal or subject matter jurisdiction. Section 11.1 explained the need to get both personal and subject matter jurisdiction correct. This motion tests the existence of valid jurisdiction.

The pleading is deficient. The complaint may be deficient because it does not include required information (See Section 11.5) or because it does not include enough specificity required with certain claims (e.g., fraud and others listed in Rule 8).

The claim or defense is legally inadequate. A complaint which fails to state a claim upon which relief can be granted can be dismissed pursuant to Rule 12(b)(6). A complaint must be based upon a legally cognizable cause of action. If the jurisdiction does not recognize the asserted claim (e.g., recall Harry's claim for a broken heart), this motion will cause the complaint to be dismissed.

Procedurally, in considering whether to grant or deny a Rule 12 motion, the judge or arbitrator can only review the pleadings. If matters outside the pleadings need to be considered, the proper motion to be brought is the following motion.

11.11.2 Motion for Summary Judgment

Do I want all or part of this case to be really over? The grounds for a Rule 56 motion are that no genuine issue of disputed material facts exist and that the movant is entitled to a judgment as a matter of law. This motion permits a judge to review the undisputed material facts of a case and determine which party should prevail. Because there are no disputed material facts, there is no need for a trial and the judge can apply the law to the facts and decide the case summarily. This motion needs to be supported by affidavits or discovery responses which establish the facts and the absence of any material dispute. This motion may be brought at anytime but is typically brought after facts have been disclosed or discovery completed. Rule 56 explains the procedures to be followed in successfully bringing and defending this motion. Strategic and tactical decisions about whether, why, and when to assert this motion are left to other texts and courses. See Section 11.11.6.

11.11.3 Other Motions

Do I want to change, add, or delete some issues or parties? A motion to amend or supplement a pleading permits changes to be made pursuant to Rule 15. A motion to include or exclude issues (allowed by Rule 20) or parties (allowed by Rule 14 and 22) may also be brought to change the shape and scope of a case.

Do I want to do something procedurally the other side does not want me to do? If you want to obtain more time to do something or delay something from happening, you can bring a motion under an applicable rule.

Do I need something from the other side or want to have them sanctioned? The most common situations involve discovery disputes. If the other side does not comply with your proper discovery request you can move to require them to respond or seek sanctions for their refusal pursuant to Rule 37.

Do I need some immediate relief? Your client may need urgent injunctive relief, and you can bring a Rule 65 motion; or your client may need to seek relief from a default judgment, and you can bring a Rule 60 motion to vacate that judgement.

There are other reasons to bring motions. There are about as many reasons as there are needs lawyers have in a case for some form of relief. If you need something, you can probably find a rule, statute, or court decision permitting a motion to be brought seeking the needed relief. Whether you get it or not, of course, depends upon whether the judge thinks you are right and deserving of it.

11.11.4 Reasons Not to Bring a Motion

There are also reasons not to bring motions. You don't want to bring a motion if you don't want to:

Ask for something you don't really need or want.

Ask for something you can't get.

Bring a motion you have no support for.

Bring a motion primarily to get back at the other side.

Unnecessarily bother a judge or arbitrator.

Appear to be a whining, desperate lawyer, unless you already are.

11.11.5 Motion Documents

The bringing of a motion ordinarily requires the submission of supporting documents including a written motion, a notice for the hearing of the motion, an affidavit(s), a memorandum of law, and a proposed order. The motion hearing ordinarily requires the preparation and presentation of an oral argument, although some motions may be decided without oral argument.

11.11.6 More on Motion Practice

If you want to know more about motion practice and are lonely, you may refer to Roger Haydock, David Herr, and Jeffrey Stempel, *Fundamentals of Pretrial Litigation* (West, 3rd Ed. 1994). If you are just lonely, you can read the next chapter.

Chapter Twelve
DISCLOSURE AND DISCOVERY: WHAT DO YOU KNOW?

Shh! They won't find out.
Of course they will. They should.
Not so loud. We can keep it quiet.
We should tell them.
Huh?
Because it's only right and fair, and justice should not be a game.
You want to disclose stuff to them?
Sure. Well, we'll want to discover stuff from them.
Sure. What can we discover?
Whatever is discoverable.
What's that?

A. INTRODUCTION

What and when information needs to be disclosed depends upon the type of transaction or case. Transactional work usually involves the disclosure of information during the drafting and negotiating segments of the transaction. Chapter Ten discusses disclosure of information during these events. Dispute resolution work involves the disclosure and discovery of information during the pendency of the dispute. Information exchange permits lawyers to know as much about a case as they need to know and allows them to review and probe the good, the bad, and the ugly in order to evaluate a transaction or case.

12.1 PURPOSES OF DISCLOSURE AND DISCOVERY

Disclosure and discovery—what we call discovery—serve many functions in a dispute resolution proceeding, including the exchange of relevant information explaining a party's claim or defense and supporting information. This information exchange:

- Promotes negotiated settlements.
- Explores the other side's case to understand their positions.
- Equalizes resources on both sides without allowing one side to take undue advantage of the other.
- Obtains information to support or oppose a motion, such as for summary judgment.
- Provides information for a hearing or trial.
- Fosters a final decision based on shared information.
- Gives us something to do on weekends.

Disclosure is the providing of information by one party to another voluntarily or based on the rules of the forum. Discovery is a process of one side asking for information and the other side responding to these discovery requests. Disclosure rules require a party to disclose information without the need for a request from the other side. Discovery rules allow a party to search for information and obtain data the other side may not want to disclose. Federal Rule of Civil Procedure 26 and similar state rules govern the scope of disclosure and discovery.

12.1.1 Early Disclosure

Disputants may voluntarily disclose information to each other before the formal initiation of a proceeding or during its pendency. Information may be disclosed before a claim is filed in an effort to resolve the dispute quickly. Information that supports a party's position may be disclosed along with information that weakens or rebuts an opposing party's position. This information can be disclosed by:

- Providing fact summaries.
- Disclosing original documents or providing the other side with copies of originals.
- Submitting a draft of a complaint to the other side, called a courtesy complaint.

- Preparing a settlement brochure and other documents to encourage a negotiated result.
- Sending Hallmark happy disclosure cards.

12.1.2 Disclosure During a Proceeding

Arbitration, administrative, and judicial forums may require the disclosure of certain information when initiating a proceeding.

Arbitration. A detailed arbitration claim by its nature includes detailed information and documents which support the claim. The procedural rules of the arbitration organization may require the following specific information and documents:

- The claim setting forth in plain language the nature of the dispute, the specific grounds supporting a claim, the amount of any money requested, the computation of the money sought and the reasons for the various amounts requested, other relief sought, and any other relevant and reliable information supporting the claim.
- A legible, authentic copy of the arbitration agreement signed by the parties.
- A legible, authentic copy of any documents supporting the claim.
- An affidavit establishing the authenticity of the arbitration agreement and supporting documents.

The purpose of this detailed information is to provide the responding party with all information supporting a claim so they understand the claim and are better able to respond and engage in settlement discussions. Similarly, the party responding to the claim must usually include specific detailed information and documents, so that all parties to the arbitration understand each other's positions.

Administrative proceedings. The type of administrative proceeding determines the extent of required initial disclosures. Some administrative proceedings are initiated by the completion of a form which includes very little information about a claim. Other administrative proceedings are initiated by a petition which include very detailed and specific information and supporting documents. The applicable statute or rules determine the scope of this disclosed information.

Litigation. The initiation of a lawsuit may include the disclosure of very little information or significant information. Most state court jurisdictions require only notice pleading in drafting a complaint, as explained in Section 11.4. The information disclosed is very cursory and need not be supported by documents. Most federal and a growing number of state court jurisdictions require the disclosure of specific information in addition to the pleadings filed.

Federal Rule 26, in operation in most federal cases, requires initial disclosures of the following specific information relevant to disputed facts alleged with particularity in the pleadings: the identity (name, address, and telephone number) of each person likely to have relevant information, a brief summary of what witnesses know, and a copy of or description of relevant documents and tangible things. Rule 26 also requires a party seeking damages to disclose the computation of the damages and all documents supporting the computation. Further, this Federal Rule requires a disclosing party to provide any insurance agreement which may satisfy part or all of a judgment. Federal Rule 26 also requires the disclosure of information later in a case regarding experts and expert testimony and evidence to be offered at trial.

The parties are obligated under the federal rules to meet and discuss issues that may arise surrounding the scope of these disclosures. These discussions provide both sides with a better understanding of each other's case and help promote early settlement. A defendant has the same disclosure obligations as a plaintiff.

12.2   METHODS OF DISCOVERY

There are five major discovery methods a party may use to request information:

Depositions (Federal Rules 28, 30, 32). Depositions require deponents to testify to what they know. A deponent answers questions under oath asked by a deposing attorney, with other attorneys in attendance. The questions and answers are recorded and may later be transcribed.

Production of documents (Federal Rule 34). One party may require another party to provide documents and tangible things for inspection or copying or to permit entry onto land or access to other property for inspection, testing, or sampling. A party may be able to obtain the same access to documents, things, and land from a non-party through a subpoena duces tecum (Federal Rule 45).

Interrogatories (Federal Rule 33). Written interrogatories are written questions submitted to a party to be answered in writing under oath. This device can be useful in obtaining information involving specific factual data, expert witnesses, and the existence of information.

Request for admissions (Federal Rule 36). Responses to requests for admission help determine the truth of specific matters and the genuineness of documents. This device primarily resolves or identifies disputed issues for trial and may also discover useful information.

Physical or mental examinations (Federal Rule 35). A party may be able to obtain a physical or mental examination of another party if the condition of that person is in controversy and if there exists good cause for an examination. These types of examinations usually occur in personal injury litigation.

Captain Bond's magic decoder ring. Actually, this is only available in secret cases no one ever knows about.

These discovery methods are discussed in greater detail in Chapters 13 and 14.

12.2.1 Availability of Discovery Methods

Litigation. These five methods are generally available in judicial disputes. Federal Rules of Civil Procedure 26 through 37 and similar state rules authorize and govern these devices. The availability of liberal discovery permitting extensive searches for information and requiring the exchange of lots of information is a reason why parties choose litigation to resolve certain types of disputes.

Arbitration. The extent of available discovery in arbitration depends upon the rules of the arbitration organization and the agreement of the parties. Arbitration organization rules typically limit discovery. Arbitration rules ordinarily allow requests for the production and exchange of relevant documents and things. The rules may only permit the use of depositions for key witnesses or at the discretion of the arbitrator. There often is no need for interrogatories and request for admissions in arbitrations because the parties are initially required to disclose this type of information. Parties in arbitration may, however, agree to use any discovery device to obtain information.

Administrative proceedings. The extent of discovery in administrative proceedings varies depending on the type of proceeding. All five discovery devices may be available, or parties may only be able to demand the production of documents and written information. The rules and statutes of the administrative proceeding determine the availability of discovery. Informal administrative proceedings usually allow limited discovery, and formal administrative proceedings may allow full discovery.

B.   SCOPE OF DISCOVERY
12.3   RELEVANT INFORMATION AND DOCUMENTS

The primary scope of discovery is relevancy. Information that is relevant or likely to be relevant in a case is usually discoverable. The general rule is that the extent of relevancy in litigation is broad and liberal and in arbitration and administrative proceedings more restrictive. In litigation, parties may obtain oral and written information regarding any matter relevant to the subject matter, claim, or defense involved. Relevancy in litigation encompasses any information that bears on or could bear on any existing or potential issue in a case or that could reasonably be calculated to lead to the discovery of other information or evidence. See Federal Rule 26 (b)(1). This broad definition includes facts, opinions, contention, conclusions, and written data.

The litigation standard of relevancy is not limited by the evidentiary standard of relevancy. It is much broader in scope and encompasses any information that relates to the case regardless of its admissibility at trial. It includes information exclusively within the knowledge or possession of the other side and information already known to the discovering party, as well as data equally available to the parties. These standards have been liberally interpreted by federal and state courts creating a very broad scope of discoverable information. A primary reason why discovery is so broad in litigation is because the pleadings are so skeletal that the parties need discovery to learn about the other side's case.

12.3.1 Litigation

Trial practice has evolved the following general approaches to discovery:

Ask for everything you want to discover, whether you firmly believe it to be discoverable or not. The broad discovery standards result in wide divergence of opinions regarding the discoverability of various types of information. What one lawyer or judge thinks not to be discoverable, another attorney or judge believes is always discoverable. Ask and you may receive.

Ask only for information you have the time and finances to pursue. The theoretical scope of relevant discovery will be limited by your client's resources and your strategies. There will be financial restrictions on the number of depositions or interrogatories available, and you will need to use reasonable discretion in discovering information.

Ask for information you intend to obtain through a court order, if your request is refused by the opponent. If an opposing party refuses to provide information, you can seek a court order requiring them to produce the requested information. Judges favor liberal discovery. Reported opinions allowing discovery outnumber cases prohibiting discovery, and judges are more willing to grant a party discovery who takes the time and effort to obtain a court order. Judges will also balance the competing interests of parties in deciding whether to order the disclosure of specific information. The interest of one party may outweigh the discovery interest of another party, especially when the use of the discoverable information is questionable or marginally relevant.

Ask, if you have seen it done in soap opera litigation cases. It could be controlling precedent.

12.3.2 Arbitration Proceedings

The standard and practice of discovery in arbitration is usually more limited and restricted than litigation. Arbitration relevancy typically refers to matters directly relevant to the issues in the case and not to potential information likely to lead to new issues. This narrower standard of relevancy reflects the practice of arbitration. Arbitration proceedings require parties to disclose more and allow them to discover less. Arbitration practice encourages parties voluntarily to exchange information without the need for requests and schedules hearings much more quickly than courts allowing less time for discovery methods.

12.3.3 Administrative Proceedings

The standard of relevancy in administrative proceedings once again depends upon the type of administrative proceeding and applicable rules and statutes. All five discovery devices may be available, reflecting the litigation process. Or discovery may be much more limited, reflecting the arbitration approach.

12.4 DISCOVERY RESTRICTIONS

All discovery requests regardless of the forum—judicial, arbitration, or administrative—have restrictions placed on their scope. The three major restricted areas are:

- Privileges
- Work product, including trial and case preparation materials
- Attorney mental impressions

12.4.1 Privileges

The general rule is that privileged matters are non-discoverable. The law has established specific privileges that allow the parties to withhold information in certain circumstances. What is and what is not privileged for discovery purposes is defined by constitutional provisions, statutes, common law, evidentiary rules, and judicial opinions. Common privileges which allow a party to refuse to provide information in discovery include: the attorney/client privilege, marital spousal privilege, business privileges, physician/patient privilege, government privileges, and the fifth amendment privilege. Other privileges which may exist, such as clergy, parent/child, political vote, reporter, and law school exam privileges, depend upon the law of the applicable jurisdiction.

In determining whether an existing privilege should restrict discovery requests, courts apply balancing tests which include the following factors:

The scope of the invasion of privacy. The broader the breach of confidentiality sought by discovery, the less likely discovery will be permitted.

The needs of the party for the information. The more essential the information is, the more likely it will be obtainable.

The availability of the information. If there is no other way a party may obtain critical information, the balance may swing in favor of discovery.

The status of the person claiming the privilege. If a claimant is a party, it is more likely discovery will be allowed.

The specific kind of privacy invaded. The more critical or essential the right protected by the privilege is, the less likely it will be revealed.

The interests of society. If the greater interests of society are better served by disclosure, it will more often be allowed.

Undeserved privileges. If the opposing attorney's life has been nothing but a series of undeserved privileges, then anything goes.

12.4.2 Work Product (Trial and Case Preparation Materials)

Work product is the work that parties prepare or complete in anticipation of a trial or hearing. See Federal Rule 26 (b)(3). Discovery is not allowed to obtain the work product or written trial or case preparation materials of an opponent. This information is protected because it would be unfair for one party to obtain this information and because attorneys should be encouraged to prepare a case thoroughly without concern of having to turn over their work to an opponent.

Four primary factors determine the practical application of work product restrictions:

Who assembled the materials? Materials prepared by or with the involvement or assistance of an attorney are usually protected.

When were the materials gathered? Materials gathered or created immediately before an action or during its pendency will ordinarily be protected. Materials existing before a claim exists or before a proceeding begins will often not be protected.

Why were the materials prepared? If the materials were prepared primarily as trial or hearing preparation materials, they will be protected. If the materials were assembled because of governmental or public law requirements or in the ordinary course of business, they will not be protected. For example, if an attorney in investigating a case prepares written materials containing a mix of facts, legal opinions, and the law, these materials would be protected. If written materials are routine business reports or reports prepared pursuant to government regulations, they would be discoverable.

Is the document a witness statement? Discoverable documents include certain types of witness statements, defined as a written statement signed by a witness or an electronic recording of a witness interview. These types of documents and tangible things are routinely discoverable. A party can obtain a written statement that the party made which is in the possession of the other side, and a witness can obtain a copy of a statement the witness made from any party. Non-witness statements are ordinarily non-discoverable. For example, notes made by an investigator during a witness interview about a disputed incident that is not signed or approved by the witness is usually considered work product and not discoverable.

Work product and trial and hearing preparation materials are not absolutely protected. A party may obtain these materials from an opposing party if they can make a showing of substantial need and undue hardship. Substantial need is demonstrated by showing that the materials are critically important to a case, and undue hardship is established by showing that the substantial equivalent cannot be obtained reasonably from any other source. Judges, arbitrators, and administrative judges are very reluctant to permit the discovery of work product and trial preparation materials, and consequently, they are seldom discoverable, unless you can provide a treasure map with them.

12.4.3 Attorney Mental Processes

Attorney mental impressions, conclusions, opinions, legal theories, strategies, or tactics concerning a case are protected from discovery. See Federal Rule 26 (b)(3). This protection prohibits one party from inquiring into the thoughts, ideas, and approaches of another party. Our judicial, arbitration, and administrative law systems permit attorneys to say or write their theories, opinions, conclusions, and impressions about a case free from concern that this information will be discovered. This information is absolutely protected. Isn't it nice they think we are going to have at least one idea worth protecting?

12.5 DISCLOSURE AND DISCOVERY OF EXPERT INFORMATION

Experts are an essential part of many court, arbitration, and administrative cases. An expert can provide information about medical, scientific, psychological, engineering, economic, and technical matters. Experts include medical doctors, scientists, psychologists, engineers, economists, and anyone who has specialized information helpful to an attorney, party, and decision maker. Experts assist lawyers in preparing a case and testify at hearings and trials.

The disclosure and discovery of expert information depends upon the use an attorney makes of an expert during a case. See Federal Rule 26 (b)(4). Advocates typically employ experts as trial or hearing experts, specially retained or employee experts, and informally consulted experts.

12.5.1   Trial and Hearing Experts

A trial or hearing expert is an individual who will testify during the case or who is identified by a party as likely to testify. A party must disclose the identities of these experts and their experience, opinions, bases of opinions, and any written reports they have prepared for the case. Many cases involve the "battle of the experts" and parties have a right to know which experts will testify and what they will say. The opposing party can obtain this information through interrogatories, document production requests, and depositions.

12.5.2   Retained or Employee Experts

This type of expert is an individual who is specially retained for a case or is an employee by a party involved with the case. It is common for an attorney to retain an expert to assist in investigating or preparing a case but who will not testify at trial. It is also common that a corporation may make available experts who are in their employ to assist its attorney. The general rule is that information about this type of expert is not discoverable. Some jurisdictions permit discovery about the existence of these experts and what they know only in exceptional circumstances.

12.5.3   Informally Consulted Experts

This type of expert is one who has been approached by a party for some information or an initial opinion but who will not testify at trial and who has not been specially retained and is not an employee of the party. The general rule is that nothing is discoverable from or about an informally consulted expert. An attorney may search for an expert who has a favorable opinion without a concern for having to reveal this information. An expert who is initially contacted may later be specially retained or be designated as a trial expert and the previously described disclosure and discovery rules would apply in those situations.

12.5.4   Inexpensive Experts

An oxymoron.

12.6 SUPPLEMENTAL DISCLOSURE AND DISCOVERY

A party is usually under a continuing duty to supplement disclosures and discovery responses. See Federal Rule 26(e). This duty extends to all forums. A party is usually required to supplement previously revealed information that is incomplete or incorrect in some material respect. A party typically has to disclose this new information within a reasonable time after learning about it or at some appropriate stage of the proceeding. If a party does not supplement or is not obligated to supplement information, a discovering party can request a supplementation through interrogatories or a request for production of additional documents.

C. PLANNING

12.7 DISCLOSURE AND DISCOVERY PLANNING

It is axiomatic that advocates need to plan for the disclosure and discovery of information. The rules of the forum will determine applicable disclosure requirements and allowable discovery requests. A litigator planning a disclosure/discovery plan should consider the following issues:

INFORMATION: THE WHAT

Types/Sources of Information	What Must I Disclose	What Must The Other Side Disclose
Witnesses		
Documents		
Insurance		
Claims		
Remedies		
Damages		
Defenses		

METHODS: THE HOW

Type/Sources of Information	Depositions	Production of Documents	Interrogatories	Request For Admissions	Physical/Mental Examinations	Other
Witnesses						
Documents						
Insurance						
Claims						
Remedies						
Damages						
Defenses						

Disclosure and discovery plans can and, in many cases, must be developed in other ways. Advocates may meet voluntarily or meet pursuant to a court rule or order. Yes, we may be forced to talk with someone who graduated with a higher, or lower, class rank. Cases involving little or limited discovery, including arbitration and administrative cases, may not need or require this extent of planning. Litigation cases involving significant discovery will usually involve this level of preparation. Court rules may require the attorneys to meet on their own to agree on a discovery plan, or may require the attorneys to attend a discovery plan conference with a judge who will issue a discovery scheduling order, or both procedures may be used. See Section 12.9.

12.8 DISCLOSURE AND DISCOVERY BY AGREEMENT

A substantial amount of information is exchanged by agreement of the attorneys. Federal Rule 29 and similar state rules encourage such oral and written agreements. For example, attorneys may agree to schedule more depositions than provided by a rule, to exchange documents without formal requests, or to answer more interrogatories than allowed.

Attorneys may agree to certain procedures by a written stipulation which contains the agreement and is signed by the parties or the attorneys. Stipulations may be formalized in a written agreement or be contained in a confirming letter from one attorney to another. A sample stipulation may read: [Plaintiff] and [Defendant] stipulate that (explain agreement) (signatures). It's as simple as that. A court may issue an order upon the filing of a stipulation without any notice or hearing.

12.9 DISCOVERY PLAN AND ORDER

Federal Rule 26(f) requires parties to confer and develop a discovery plan. This plan is to contain a mutual agreement by the parties or their separate, different views concerning: what disclosures will be made, the timing and scope of these disclosures, what discovery requests will be served, when responses will be due, when discovery should be completed, what changes will be made in any of the applicable discovery rules, what additional pleadings may be served, and what motions may be brought.

The report may contain legitimate disagreements the parties have or alternative suggestions to the court regarding a plan. An agreed upon plan may be submitted to the court and become the basis for a scheduling order issued by the court. If the parties have disagreements or if the court rules do not require the parties meet and prepare a plan, a discovery conference can be scheduled with the judge to discuss these issues after which an order will be issued. In some jurisdictions, these conferences are known as pretrial conferences. As the case approaches to trial, changes may be made by agreement of the parties or by the court in the discovery scheduling order or the final pretrial order. It sometimes sounds like a military operation, doesn't it?

12.10 DISCLOSURE/DISCOVERY ORDERS

Parties may seek an order from a judge, arbitrator or administrative judge regarding disclosure and discovery. There are two basic types of orders. One is a *protective order* seeking to limit discovery or protect a party from unnecessary discovery, initiated by a motion or request for such an order. The second is an *order enforcing a discovery request* and requiring a party to provide information, also initiated by a motion to compel discovery or for sanctions.

12.10.1 Protective Orders

A party faced with a disclosure or discovery problems may seek a protective order requesting any of the following relief (Federal Rule 26 (c)):

- Discovery not proceed: e.g., because it is not authorized by rule or is untimely.

- Discovery be permitted on specific conditions: e.g., documents be disclosed before the taking of a deposition or a deposition be limited in time or scope.

- The scope of discovery be limited: e.g., prohibiting the disclosure of irrelevant or privileged information or attorney mental impressions.

- Selected individuals not have access to revealed information: e.g., only attorneys or named representatives of a party have access to confidential information.

- Trade secret or other confidential information be sealed and not made public: e.g., the disclosure of such information may place a party at a significant disadvantage with competitors.

- Discovery requests or responses be exchanged simultaneously: e.g., to avoid parties from being influenced by what they request or exchange.

- For any other reason which justice requires: e.g., whatever you as an advocate can justify without shouting too much.

- Your employment rejection letters. Certain things are sacred.

Protective orders will more likely be granted if the harm caused by the disclosure is not substantial or serious, the request for the relief is narrow and appropriate, and there is no alternative way of protecting the interests of the parties. Protective orders may also be modified after being initially granted depending upon the type of information disclosed and the circumstances of the particular case.

12.10.2 Enforcement Orders

Parties may disagree about what is to be disclosed or discovered. Legitimate attempts to obtain information may be met with unsatisfactory responses or objections, or even silence, insults, or threats. A party can enforce its disclosure and discovery rights in two primary ways. First, a party can attempt to resolve the dispute with the opposing party through discussions and negotiations. A party may revise a discovery request to satisfy the concerns of the other side. The responding party may be willing to disclose most but not all of the requested information. These informal efforts of enforcement should first be made before attempting the second enforcement method: a court order.

Federal Rule 37 and similar state rules provide methods for obtaining judicial assistance in enforcing disclosure and discovery rights. The typical relief is for a court order requiring the other side to respond to the discovery requests or to complete incomplete disclosures: for example, to appear for a deposition, to answer all interrogatories, or to provide relevant documents. A party may also seek the award of attorney's fees and other expenses if the motion is granted, and the court may impose these costs on the non-responsive party if the reasons for being recalcitrant are unreasonable. Yes, you can be recalcitrant, though reasonable.

Federal and state rules also provide for other sanctions that may be imposed for failure to comply with a discovery request and with an order for discovery, such as:

- Discovery the offending party wants may be restricted.
- Fees and costs may be awarded against the offending party.
- Facts may be deemed established against the party.
- Evidence may be barred in a hearing or trial.
- Pleadings may be stricken, eliminating a party's claim or defense.
- Part or all of case may be dismissed or a default judgment entered (only in egregious situations).
- A party may be found in contempt (in even more egregious situations).
- The lawyer's ads may be pulled from prime time cable.

Chapter Thirteen
DEPOSITIONS: GETTING TO KNOW YOU

Q: Why did you do it?

A: Do what?

Q: What you did.

A: Did I do it?

Q: I'm asking the questions.

A: Why?

Q: Because that's my job.

A: What is?

Q: To get information from you.

A: But why?

Q: Why what?

A: Why did you do it?

Q: Do what?

A: Go to law school?

Q: To learn how to do this.

A: Maybe you're not ready to do this yet.

Q: I'm a quick study.

A. THE WHY

13.1 WHY SHOULD I TAKE A DEPOSITION?

You should take depositions to:

- Determine what a deponent knows and does not know.

- Obtain information through prepared and spontaneous follow-up questions.

- Assess the demeanor and credibility of a witness.

- Probe for weaknesses in a case or confront a deponent with damaging information.

- Obtain admissions or impeachment evidence.

- Obtain information in support of or in opposition to a motion.

- Preserve direct examination testimony from a witness who will be unavailable for a hearing or trial.

That's why. Federal Rules 28, 30, and 32 and similar state rules govern depositions.

B. THE HOW

13.2 WHO SHOULD I DEPOSE?

It's: "Whom should I depose?" You should depose whoever has information that can help you with the purposes described in the previous paragraph. Is it whoever? You can depose any party or any witness. Usually depositions are taken of adverse parties, their agents and employees, and witnesses who are unwilling to talk with you. You may also take a deposition to preserve testimony of a favorable witness who will be unavailable to testify at trial.

13.3 WHEN CAN OR SHOULD I DEPOSE?

You can ordinarily schedule depositions shortly after a case has begun. See Federal Rule 26. You may depose after pleadings have been served or the discovery plan has been established, depending upon the rules of the forum. You may also schedule a deposition earlier if you have good reason and can convince a judge of your urgent need.

You should depose when you are prepared to depose and when it is strategically best to do so. You may want to take a deposition of an adverse party as soon as possible. You may want to delay a deposition until after you have reviewed documents. If there are a number of important witnesses to be deposed, you may want to schedule them in a specific sequence. Ask yourself: Am I prepared to take this deposition, or should I wait until I obtain some other information? Or would I rather spend the day spell checking another legal memo?

13.4 HOW OFTEN CAN I DEPOSE?

You can usually depose a person only once, unless the initial deposition has been continued or good reason exists for a second deposition. Some jurisdictions place limits on the total number of depositions to be taken in a case. Federal Rule 30(a)(2) limits the number of depositions to ten and permits more to be taken only if a judge or the opposing party approves. State court jurisdictions may limit the number of depositions from three to ten, with court or party approval needed to take more depositions. You should take the number of depositions necessary to obtain the information you need. No more. No less.

13.5 WHERE SHOULD I DEPOSE?

You can specify the location of the deposition, within reason. See Federal Rule 30 (b)(1). Plaintiffs can be required to attend depositions in the district or county where the action is pending. Defendants may be deposed where they do business or have their residence. Attorneys usually will mutually agree to a place, often a warm place in the winter, and a cool place in the summer.

Depositions can be held in your office, the court reporter's office, the opposing attorney's office, the deponent's office, in a court house, or on the beach depending upon the weather. Holding a deposition in your office is convenient. Holding a deposition in the office of the deponent may make it more convenient for you to inspect and copy documents in the possession of the deponent. Holding it on the beach is appropriate if there is a lifeguard nearby.

13.6 HOW LONG CAN I DEPOSE?

A deposition lasts for as long as it reasonably takes to obtain the information and complete the deposition. Many depositions take a few hours, some take a day or more, and others take only an hour. The parties may agree or the rules of some jurisdictions may limit the number of hours of a deposition. Modern depositions have increasingly expanded in length with examining attorneys asking tangential, relevant questions and opposing lawyers slowing down the deposition by objections and unnecessary breaks. An attorney facing an unnecessarily lengthy deposition may seek a court order establishing a time limit or controlling the opposing attorney. Sanctions, including reasonable costs and attorney fees, may be imposed upon any person responsible for impeding or delaying a deposition. So be punctual and professional, all the time.

13.7 HOW DO I NOTICE A DEPOSITION?

You notice a deposition of a party by serving the deponent and all attorneys by mail with a deposition notice which states the date, time, and location of the deposition:

Please take notice that the deposition of _____ will be taken by oral examination pursuant to the _____ Rules of Civil Procedure before (name of court reporter) at (location) on (date) at (time). The method of recording this type of deposition will be [specify: stenographic/audio recording/videotape]. The deposition will continue until completed. You may appear and examine the witness.

That's it. See Federal Rule 30(b). If you want the deponent to bring documents and records, you may serve on the party a request for production of documents. This request directs the deponent to bring the documents to the deposition for inspection and copying. It is ordinarily a better idea to obtain these documents before the deposition so you can review them and be better prepared.

You take the deposition from a non-party by personally serving them with a subpoena stating the time, date, location of the deposition, along with a check for the witness fee established by statute or rule. Federal Rules 30 and 45. It's only fair you pay their fare. If you want the deponent to bring documents, you must also serve them with a subpoena duces tecum identifying the documents to be brought. Some jurisdictions require that before you can compel a non-party to produce documents you must make arrangements to compensate them for the time it takes to compile and produce the documents.

13.8   WHEN SHOULD I SCHEDULE THE DEPOSITION?

Depositions can be scheduled anytime during regular business hours, and at other hours for very good reasons. Brief recesses are permitted for rest and recuperation. Adjournments may be necessary if the deponent needs time to search for more information or if some other reason exists. You should discuss deposition format and the timing of breaks and lunch with the other attorney, but not necessarily over lunch.

13.9   WHO IS PRESENT AT A DEPOSITION?

They are usually the following people:

The deponent. All persons who have information relevant to the case may be deposed. This includes parties, witnesses, and experts who will testify at trial. In some cases, you may not know exactly whom you want to depose, and court rules permit you to describe the information you seek and require the opposing party to produce someone who can provide that information.

Attorneys. Present are the attorney taking the depositions, the attorney representing the deponent, and other attorneys representing other parties. We're everywhere. All parties in the case have a right to have their respective attorneys present, even though those attorneys may not represent the deponent. The deponent, whether a party or non-party witness, has a right to have an attorney present. Everyone should have one of us.

The person who administers the oath and who records the testimony. The person who records the deposition is usually an independent court reporter hired by the deposing attorney. This person administers the oath and records the deposition. This person can also have an assistant present, for instance, to operate a tape recorder or video camera. See Federal Rules 28(a) and (c).

Parties. All parties have a right to attend all depositions. Individual parties can attend; a corporate party may have a representative appear. It is a common practice for parties not to attend depositions, except their own. If there are good reasons to have them attend, however, they should be there. For example, their presence may help them prepare for their own deposition or may assist in obtaining complete and accurate testimony from the deponent. It is possible, although highly unusual, to obtain a court order excluding a party. You need better than a very good reason.

Witnesses. The federal rules and similar state rules allow witnesses and potential deponents to attend depositions, unless they are excluded by agreement of all the parties or by a court order. It is not a common practice for witnesses to attend depositions. There may be a good reason for them to attend. For example, they may learn more about the case or what another witness knows. Some jurisdictions allow the exclusion of witnesses at the request of one party. In these jurisdictions, a court order can be obtained permitting a witness to attend another's deposition.

Third persons. Can third persons (interested persons, reporters, or just plain members of the public) attend the deposition? Is the deposition a public hearing? Can tickets be sold? The rules of the jurisdiction determine these answers. Usually, third persons have no need or interest in attending a deposition. If they want to appear, and one or more of the parties excludes them, they will need to seek a court order and convince the judge they should attend.

13.10 DO I HAVE TO ATTEND?

If a deposing attorney fails to appear at a scheduled deposition, expenses may be assessed and additional sanctions may be imposed. Be sure to show up, or increase your law firm credit line.

13.11 HOW IS THE DEPOSITION RECORDED?

The party who notices the deposition chooses the method of recording. The three most common methods are: stenographic (a reporter uses a machine or computer), audio tape recording, and a video recording. See Federal Rule 30. An audio or video recorded deposition may be supplemented by a stenographic record. This stenographic recording is usually the most convenient and least expensive, because it is easier to prepare a transcript. Audio recordings are handy if no transcript is required or to supplement the stenographic method. Video recordings are becoming more popular as the equipment and its use become more commonplace. The rules of the jurisdiction typically have specific procedures to be observed when taking video or audio recordings; for example, everything must appear on the tape, and the deposition must be indexed by a time generator or another method.

Depositions may also be taken by telephone and remote electronic means. See Federal Rule 30(b)(7). Telephone depositions take place as conference calls, and satellite or cable transmission may be used with video monitors. These methods permit the deposition participants to be in different cities making travel unnecessary. Documents and written information may be exchanged through fax or e-mail transmissions. A disadvantage to these methods is that it may be more difficult to assess the demeanor and credibility of the deponent. Holographic depositions are still a few years away.

13.12   WHEN IS A TRANSCRIPT NEEDED?

Depositions are transcribed to provide the parties with a printed version of the deposition testimony. See Federal Rule 32(c). Transcripts help in reviewing what a witness said, in supporting a motion, and in preparing for trial. They also make elegant living room end table reading.

13.13   HOW MUCH DO DEPOSITIONS COST?

Deposition costs (excluding the fees for the lawyers) include the hourly fee for the court reporter, the cost of any audio or video equipment, and the cost of transcribing the deposition (if done). Whatever the total is, your client may think it is too much, and there are ways to reduce the cost. If no transcript is necessary, costs are substantially reduced. In many jurisdictions, the parties may agree not to have a court reporter present but to record the deposition by audio or video recording themselves. There are also ways to increase the cost of a deposition. It will be more costly—though, also more exciting—to travel to out of the way exotic resorts to take depositions.

C.   THE PLANNING
13.14   DEPOSITION PREPARATION

You should prepare well. You know from your first law school exam that you had to prepare thoroughly for questions and the answers in order to do well. So also with a deposition.

Preparation of a case requires familiarity with sources of factual information, legal claims and defenses, and overall discovery strategies. You need to be familiar with the subject matter of the deposition and what the deponent knows. If the deponent is an eye witness to an accident, you should be familiar with the location, site, and other matters relating to the accident. If the deponent is an expert engineer, then you need to be versed in whatever specialized engineering areas the deposition will cover.

Thorough preparation also requires a determination of the purpose or purposes of the deposition. Why are you taking this deposition? Do you want to obtain information, search for documents, obtain admissions, or do all those things? Or do you just like small get-togethers?

The rules of evidence applicable to the ultimate hearing or trial should not unduly influence your preparation for the deposition. You should seek everything the witness knows, from whatever source, whether hearsay or documentary. Sometimes it's best to forget the rules of evidence completely (easier for some of us than others) and probe for the best and the worst of what the witness knows (unless you are taking the deposition to preserve testimony).

You will need to prepare a written outline and questions. Make a list of what you want to know and the areas you want to explore. Organize the outline in some logical, chronological, or associational (by issues, claims, defenses) sequence. After you make and organize your outline, check it twice to make sure it is complete. You will need to or may prefer to write out questions. How many questions depends upon your level of experience and confidence and the goals of the deposition. The less experience you have the more written preparation you need. If you are seeking vital admissions or detailed foundation, written questions may help you obtain this information during the deposition. Too many questions may reduce your flexibility during the deposition or make you sound like a Double Jeopardy contestant. Too few questions may make it difficult for you to be thorough during the deposition. Organizing your notes and questions in a folder or a three ring binder may be of great assistance and may make it appear like you know what you are doing, which can be a morale booster.

A deposition taken to preserve the testimony of a witness for a later use at a hearing or trial needs to be especially carefully prepared. You will need to prepare specific direct or cross-examination questions which will be admitted as evidence at the hearing or trial. Your preparation for this type of deposition will be similar to your preparation for the hearing or trial. If the deposition is stenographically recorded, the written transcript of the deponent will be read to or by the fact finder. If the deposition is electronically recorded, the fact finder can see or hear the testimony.

D. THE TAKING

13.15 HOW IS THE DEPOSITION ROOM ARRANGED?

The typical deposition room is a conference room with a large table. The opposing attorney sits across from or at an angle to the deponent. The deponent's attorney sits next to the deponent. The court reporter is in a position to see and hear the attorneys and the deponent. Other attorneys sit around or near the table. If the deposition is videotaped, the camera will be placed to focus primarily on the deponent. Some attorneys prefer to bring family pictures to hang on the walls to make themselves feel at home.

13.16 HOW DOES THE DEPOSITION BEGIN?

The attorneys provide the court reporter with their cards (e.g., Go Fish), and the names of the deponent and other attendees. There may be some discussion about who will sit where, if there is a disagreement. The court reporter notes the caption of the case, the appearances of attorneys, and the persons present, and administers an oath or affirmation to the deponent.

13.17 HOW DO I BEGIN THE DEPOSITION?

You may begin by discussing procedural matters with the other attorney, by providing the deponent with some directions or by asking questions of the deponent.

Procedures. You should make sure that the record contains the information previously discussed and that the oath or affirmation has been properly administered. You or the other attorney may suggest some stipulations. Whatever stipulations are made should be specific and understood by all. It is unwise to agree to "usual stipulations" if you do not know what they include. There may be no need to state that the deposition shall proceed under the applicable rules or that all objections shall be preserved according to the applicable rules, because the applicable rules will apply. It may be useful to suggest some stipulated procedures, such as:

> In a non-party deposition, it is useful to determine who, if anyone, is representing the deponent. That attorney will be the one who can counsel and instruct the deponent during the deposition.

> In multi-party cases, it may be useful to suggest that an objection by one attorney will be considered an objection by all attorneys to avoid repetitive objections.

> If the deposition is proceeding differently than required by the rules, a stipulation to that affect should be confirmed on the record to avoid objections being raised later. If the deposition has not been properly started, correct any deficiencies unless it is to your advantage to either object to these deficiencies or not do anything to correct them.

> If you object on the grounds that the table is veneer and not solid wood, you may want to keep that objection to yourself.

Directions and Questions. It is common for the deposing attorney to explain to the deponent common deposition procedures to ensure the deposition will proceed efficiently, such as:

> *Mr. Alladin, I represent Princess Jasmine in this lawsuit. I am going to ask you a series of questions about this case, and the reporter will record your answers. If at any time you don't understand any question, please tell me and I will repeat or rephrase the question. Is this understood and acceptable to you? (The witness will invariably say yes.)*

> *Everything needs to be recorded accurately and completely. Please state your answers to the questions and do not merely*

nod your head or make a gesture. We all need to speak one at a time, so please wait until I complete my question before answering. Is this understood and acceptable to you? (The witness will invariably say yes.)

Would you please sit on the chair and not on your magic carpet? (The witness will invariably move.)

Additional explanations may be useful depending upon the approach you wish to take during the deposition:

You may want to make certain the deponent understands what is happening:

Do you now understand what a deposition is? (or, Has your attorney explained to you what a deposition is?) (If no, explain in more detail.)

You may want to emphasize the witness's obligation to tell the truth:

Your testimony will be under oath, as if you were in a court of law. You have sworn to tell the truth, and if you fail to do so, adverse consequences may result. Do you understand this?

You may want to explain to the witness what will happen if they give incorrect or inconsistent answers in the future:

Everything that is said here today will be recorded. At the trial, we will have the testimony available you give today. If I ask you the same questions then that I ask you today, and if your answers differ then from the answers you give today, you will be held accountable for the difference in your answers. Do you understand this?

You may want to create a cooperative atmosphere:

We are here to find out what you know to help us evaluate this case. If at any time you need a glass of water, please tell us. We will take a break within a reasonable time.

There ordinarily is no duty under an applicable rule to begin the deposition with these statements. It is usually done to make sure the witness understands what is about to happen and to avoid later misunderstandings. It is also done to create a constructive atmosphere for the deposition. You could begin by asking relevant questions, which could be easy or tough questions.

13.18   WHAT SHOULD MY DEMEANOR BE?

There are two aspects affecting your demeanor and conduct. The first is your obligation to conduct yourself during a deposition professionally as if you were at trial. The rules and court decisions prohibit you from conducting an examination by being unreasonable, by harassing the deponent or attorney, or by acting in bad faith. You need to—and should want to—act responsibly and civilly.

The second factor influencing your demeanor is your strategic and tactical approach to the deposition. Your approach will depend upon the type of witness you have. Will the witness be favorable or unfavorable? Cooperative or uncooperative? What is the most effective approach you can use? A friendly, empathetic approach? A firm, persistent approach? A cooperative, informal approach? An assertive, confrontational approach? What approach will best create a constructive atmosphere?

How you conduct yourself during this deposition may be as important as the questions asked. An approach that is perceived by the deponent to be reasonable and fair will generally produce a more cooperative story, and a more stern approach will produce a more restrictive story. A calm approach may be more effective with some deponents, and a more spirited approach may be more useful with others. Your tactical demeanor should be designed to meet the purposes of your taking the deposition.

13.19   WHAT SHOULD I ASK?

You are already prepared to ask questions. Review section 13.14.

You could decide to submit written deposition questions instead of taking an oral examination. See Federal Rule 31. This method is seldom used in practice. It can be a less costly way to obtain information from a witness who lives some distance from the lawsuit and who has useful, objective, and non-critical information. Written questions are submitted to the deponent by an officer, and the deponent answers them in writing. The attorneys need not be present during this process.

13.20   HOW DO I EFFECTIVELY ASK QUESTIONS?

Your goal is to achieve completion, clarity, and closure. You can do all this by asking:

Anything and everything. Ask what you want to know. Search for supportive and helpful information and also search for harmful and negative information. You need to learn about the weaknesses as well as the strengths of your case.

Who, what, when, where, and how. These questions will produce the story.

Why. Why? To learn about what happened.

Facts and opinions. Learn what happened and what the deponent believes or perceives what happened.

Feelings, emotions, attitudes, and thoughts. These questions often produce useful fact and opinion information.

The source of the information. Determine whether the information is based upon personal observation or knowledge, hearsay, inference, or assumption.

Comparison stories. Ask why the deponent may have a different story than another witness or a document.

Closing questions. Make certain you know everything the witness knows by periodically asking "Do you know anything more about . . ." or "Have you told us everything you know about . . . ."

Curious questions. You might be tempted to—but don't—ask why in the world they think their lawyer is better than you.

13.21   HOW DO I EFFECTIVELY PROBE?

Insist on responsive answers. Have your specific questions answered completely. Follow up with certain responses:

If they say "I don't know," ask why they don't know.

If they say "I don't know for sure," ask for their opinion or estimate.

If they say "I think so" or "I believe so," you may want to insist on a more specific answer or you may be satisfied with this response because it is sufficiently favorable.

If they say "I don't remember" or "I don't recall," attempt to refresh their recollection by asking what will help them remember or by asking leading questions.

Encourage deponents to talk and talk. Ask them to tell you more about what they know, unless they are rambling or providing irrelevant information.

Explain what you want and why. They may be able to provide more information if they understand what you want and why. Or, you may prefer not to disclose this to them.

Help witnesses recall. If they are uncertain, ask questions that place them at the event, hopefully prompting their memory. If they look confused, ask them what they do not understand. If they are tired, take a recess and provide them with some vitamins.

Search for details and more details. Deponents may answer with generalities or summaries. Pursue details. If they are describing an event, ask them questions about different times or different views of the event. If they are restating a conversation, ask who said what first, then who spoke what next, and who said what last. Determine whether an answer is a summary, an impression, a close approximation, an exact detail, or some other recollection.

Repeat questions. Repeat questions. Not with the same words, but with the same purpose, until they answer fully.

Ask about their hair color. Maybe it affects their memory.

13.22 HOW SHOULD I ASK QUESTIONS?

Use a structured approach. An effective technique may be to ask general, open ended questions, followed by clarification questions, concluding with very specific questions.

Change the format of your questioning approach.
Shift from an orderly approach to a seemingly more haphazard
approach. Skip around, and return to topics previously covered
to obtain more information.

Take notes. These notes will allow you to pursue topics
you needed to skip, reconfirm what the witness previously said,
or search for inconsistencies.

Pace the deposition. A reasonable pace may keep everyone focused and alert. A fast pace may provide less time for
reflection and listening. Too slow of pace may remind you of
some of your law school classes, but not this course.

Seek specific admissions. You may know what you want
the witness to know.

Lead the witness. You may want the witness to answer
with a specific response to support your theory of the case. For
example, if you want to establish that the deponent has a poor
grasp of the circumstances of an auto accident, you could ask
leading questions such as: "This accident happened very quickly. This was a frightening experience for you. You became
tense anticipating the crash. You were moving at the time of
the collision." If you want to establish that the deponent had a
good grasp of what happened, you could ask: "You have a vivid
memory of this event. You were especially alert because of the
potential danger. You had a clear view of the scene. You were
paying a lot of attention to what was happening."

Ask about other witnesses. Who else might know what
they know or what they don't know, besides the Shadow?

13.23 WHAT DO I DO ABOUT DOCUMENTS?

You can bring with documents the deponent knows or
should know about. You can review documents the party deponent brought to the deposition. Section 14.5 explains this procedure.

You may have to take the deposition of a non-party to obtain
documents. The only way to obtain documents from a third
person not a party to a case may be to schedule their deposition
and serve them with a subpoena duces tecum requiring them to
produce the documents at the deposition. See Federal Rule 45.

During the deposition, you can also:

Ask questions of the deponent about all or part of the document. Have the deponent read aloud or to themselves, or read to the deponent the relevant portion of a document on the record. Have the deponent authenticate or explain the document.

Ask the deponent how documents were disclosed and produced. Ask how deponents searched for documents in their possession, custody, or control.

Ask about documents not produced which should have or could have existed. Ask whether specific documents were created, maintained, misplaced, or lost, and how.

Ask about destroyed documents. Determine whether any documents were destroyed before or during the case.

Create an exhibit. Have deponents draw a diagram to help tell their story.

Review written stuff. Review pleadings, written discovery disclosures and responses, and other case documents with the deponent. The witness may be able to explain and elaborate pleading responses, answers to interrogatories, and other documentary information.

Seek an agreement to produce documents during the deposition. If you discover the existence of relevant documents during the deposition, you may ask the custodian party to allow you to inspect or copy them or to provide you with a copy of them without the need for a formal document production request. This stipulation should be reflected on the record with a description of the documents to be provided and a deadline for this disclosure. If you are the attorney asked to produce such documents, you should decline to do so until you have had a chance to review them to determine their relevancy and discoverability.

Search for documents used by the deponent to refresh recollection. You are usually allowed to obtain documents which the deponent read or reviewed before the deposition and which helped refresh their recollection for the deposition. Ask the deponent: "Did you read or review any documents before this deposition? Did they help refresh your memory?" If the answer to these two questions is yes, say to the opposing lawyer, "Counsel, please have these documents produced now or before the end of this deposition so I can review and determine whether I wish to have them introduced as exhibits." If counsel refuses, you may compromise by asking them to provide the documents at a later date when the deposition will be resumed. Or you may serve them with a formal request for production of documents and wait until they respond.

Try and get copies of the opposing lawyer's old blue book exams. Just for the fun of it.

13.24   HOW CAN I HANDLE EXHIBITS EFFECTIVELY?

Exhibits may be marked before or during the deposition by the court reporter with a designated letter or number. Having them marked ahead of time saves time. Having them marked during the deposition may be necessary to surprise the deponent:

> Please mark as Plaintiff's Exhibit 1 this three page will, dated October 1, 1978, signed by Howard Hughes and witnessed by St. Peter and Bugs Bunny.

You can and should ask the deponent questions you need to about the exhibit to authenticate or explain it. Ask two basic questions and then follow-up questions: Ask *"what is it"* and *"how do you know?"*

Q: I hand you Plaintiffs Exhibit number 2. Do you recognize it?

A: Yes.

Q: *What is it?*

A: This is a letter that I wrote.

Q: *How do you know* that is a letter you wrote?

A: It is on my stationery. It looks like the letter I wrote.

Q: Is this your X on the signature line?

A: Yes, I signed it with my distinctive X mark.

Your follow-up questions should be designed to make certain there is a sufficiently complete foundation for the authentication and identification of the exhibit.

With exhibits, you can also:

Ask about the content of the document before showing it to the witness. If you want to inquire about the deponent's understanding or recollection of a document, ask about it before showing it to the deponent.

Show the deponent the document first before asking any questions. If you prefer to have the deponent review the document before answering questions, do so. When you first show it, the deponent has a right to review it before being asked questions.

Provide a copy of the exhibit to opposing attorney. It is a professional courtesy and may be an efficient use of time to provide opposing counsel with a copy of the exhibit. It usually is more productive to have multiple copies of the exhibit available for the attorneys present while the deponent reviews the exhibit. A short exhibit may be able to be reviewed simultaneously by the deponent and attorney.

13.25 WHAT DO I DO WITH THE EXHIBIT?

You need not and should not offer the exhibit. There is no reason to offer an exhibit on the record at a deposition because the process is not a trial and there is no judge to receive the evidence. It becomes part of the deposition after it is marked, and it or a duplicate copy is usually attached as an exhibit to the transcript.

You should make sure the exhibit is preserved. A copy of the original exhibit used during the deposition is usually made available to the court reporter for inclusion as part of the transcript. See Federal Rule 30(b)(1). The original exhibits used during the deposition are returned to the party who provided them and must be retained by this party for future use. In some cases, it may be necessary to secure the originals in a neutral location. Administrators and court clerks usually do not accept these exhibits because they do not have sufficient storage space.

13.26 WHAT ABOUT CONFIDENTIAL INFORMATION?

You already know the law protects specific types of information from discovery, based on irrelevancy, work product, privileges, attorney mental impressions, and trade secrets. Some attorneys improperly claim general privacy or broad confidentiality protections afforded to information and documents. The law may or may not recognize these claims.

You may inquire into areas that the opposing lawyer claims are private, confidential, or non-discoverable. You can offer to stipulate on the deposition record that you and a designated client representative will be the only ones to hear or see this information. If this stipulation is refused, you can agree to stipulate on the record that the other side does not waive any objections or rights applicable under the law to the protected status of this information. If this fails, you should ask detailed questions about the basis of the claimed protection and the existence of the information or documents without inquiring into the content.

If you foresee these issues arising during a deposition, you can discuss them with the opposing attorney ahead of time (or during the deposition) to reach an agreement about the disclosure of this information. It is common for the attorneys to enter into confidentiality agreements or stipulated protective orders which allow the disclosure of protected information to specific individuals. If these discussions fail, you may seek an order from the court allowing the disclosure of this information under restricted conditions. You may ask the judge to review the information or materials *in camera* (that is, alone) to determine if there is a basis for the protection claimed.

13.27 HOW DO I DEPOSE AN EXPERT?

The previous suggestions about how and why to ask questions apply to all deponents, including lay and expert witnesses. In addition, there are some specific areas to explore with experts, including:

- Their qualifications.
- Their opinions.
- The basis of their opinions.
- The sources of information relied upon in forming their opinions.

- Their fees and whether they expect to testify for the party in the future.

- The number of times they have testified for plaintiffs and defendants in previous cases.

- Insufficient information, tests, or sources of information they do not know or did not perform.

- Possible causes or explanations contrary to their opinion.

- Their familiarity with treatises which contain contrary opinions.

- How and why they differ with opinions held by your experts.

- How they pronounce those words with all consonants.

13.28 WHAT SHOULDN'T I SAY OR DO DURING THE DEPOSITION?

Here is a list of "stupid deposition tricks":

Don't listen to the deponent's responses. If you don't pay close attention or ask obvious follow-up questions, you will miss critical information, although you certainly will speed up the deposition.

Don't observe the witness. Witnesses may react in the most telling ways to certain questions with facial expressions and body postures revealing their uncertainty or anxiety. If you don't watch the witness, you don't have to worry about what these reactions mean.

Fail to be curious. If you don't understand something or are unsure about a response, keep your puzzlement to yourself. You will have enough to do already, so don't bother asking even more questions.

Assume everything is in your best interests. Guess what happened rather than asking detailed questions to determine whether you are right or wrong.

Insist on generalizations and not specific responses. It takes an effort to ask "How do you know that?" and "What facts do you have to support that position?" Be content with incomplete information.

React visibly to damaging information. As your case disintegrates before your eyes, make sure the opposing lawyer and the deponent know how weak you believe your case to be.

Ask complex and unclear answers, chock full of legalese. If you ask these kinds of questions, they may think you are a law professor.

We, of course, were just joshing. If you do these things, you will contribute to your losing case percentage.

13.29 HOW SHOULD I REACT TO OBJECTIONS?

Your opponent has the right to make proper and limited objections during a deposition, even though no one is there or authorized to rule on the objections at that time. See Section 13.32.2. Ordinarily, your reaction is to insist on an answer to the question, which is your right. See Federal Rule 30(c). If your opponent does not specify grounds to support an objection or suggests an inappropriate ground, insist on a response. If there may be some merit to the objection, you may want to do something about your question or the anticipated response:

- If an objection to the form of the question is raised, you should decide whether your question is appropriate and insist on an answer or whether you should rephrase the question.

- If the objection is lack of foundation, you may want to establish more foundation by asking additional questions.

- If an objection is based on relevancy, you may insist on an answer if your question is relevant or cure the objection by rephrasing it or focusing on more relevant information.

- If an objection is based on any other ground, you can ignore the objection and insist on an answer from the deponent.

- If the attorney objects and properly instructs the deponent not to answer, you will find it impossible to extract an answer. Your recourse is to seek a court order compelling an answer. Section 13.32.3 explains the proper use of instructions not to answer.

Reacting to objections should not include arguing with the deponent or other attorney about the correctness or appropriateness of the objection. If an attorney insists on making frequent objections, there are several ways to control the situation:

You may suggest that the record reflect a continuing objection to all or certain of your questions to avoid the other attorney constantly interrupting you.

You may tactfully remind the other attorney that nearly all objections are preserved for trial, and there is no need for these objections.

You may advise the other attorney that such unnecessary objections unduly interfere with the deposition and that such conduct is improper.

You can seek a protective order or a sanction order against the attorney.

You can ask the attorney to stop watching reruns of the O.J. trial.

13.30 HOW DO I CONTROL INTERFERENCE DURING A DEPOSITION?

Rules of civil procedure and court decisions prohibit an attorney from unnecessarily interfering with the deposition, but these restrictions do not deter some attorneys from attempting to interfere. You may counter interfering tactics with the following approaches:

Insist the rules be followed. Remind the attorney of these rules and that their breach will not be tolerated. Hand the attorney a copy of Federal Rule 30 or its state court equivalent.

Insist that court decisions regulating deposition practice be followed. Advise the lawyer, or better yet, provide the lawyer with a copy of a judicial decision (be sure to bring one along) admonishing attorneys doing what is being done to you.

Record everything that occurs, especially non-verbal conduct by the opposing attorney, whether it involves passing a note to the witness, whispering in the deponent's ear, signaling the witness, conferring with the client, or other interfering conduct.

Refuse to take unnecessary breaks. Insist on continuing with the deposition and note on the record the frequency and duration of these breaks unilaterally taken by the other lawyer and deponent.

Insist that the deponent respond to your questions and advise the opposing counsel not to testify.

Admonish an attorney from unnecessarily conferring with the deponent. If the deponent is unrepresented, another lawyer at the deposition cannot advise them. If the deponent is represented, and if you are in a jurisdiction that prohibits a lawyer from counseling the client during a deposition, so advise the attorney.

Advise the opposing attorney you will telephone a judge to seek a ruling regarding the improper behavior. A judge may be available for a conference call.

Advise the opposing attorney you will adjourn the deposition if the misconduct continues and seek a protective order with sanctions against the attorney.

Reschedule the deposition. In unusual cases in which the opposing attorney is uncontrollable, conduct the remainder of the deposition in a court house or before a referee or magistrate judge who can control the situation.

Suggest a career change for opposing counsel. Suggest counsel become that mud wrestler we mentioned some chapters back.

13.31 HOW DO I CONCLUDE THE DEPOSITION?

Before concluding the deposition, you should review your prepared topics and questions to determine whether you asked everything you needed and whether the deponent provided you with any information you need to explore further. You may consider asking broad questions to make clear the witness has both understood everything and has told all. Questions such as "Have you understood all the questions you answered?" or "Did you answer all the questions truthfully and completely?" may produce something, or may produce only an affirmative response "to the best of my recollection." You may also want to advise deponents that they have an obligation to provide supplementary answers to the deposition questions if they recall any additional information after the deposition or if they need to update answers. And, if the deposition has been particularly long, you could start singing: "It's quarter to three. There's no one in the place except...."

After you are done asking your questions, the attorney for the deponent and other attorneys involved in the case have an opportunity to ask questions of the deponent. Typically, these attorneys ask a reasonable number of questions for rehabilitation purposes or to clarify or supplement areas you explored. After they are done, you have an opportunity to ask follow-up questions of the deponent if you deem it necessary. Additional considerations concerning the end of the deposition are explained in section 13.34.

E. THE DEPONENT

13.32 DEFENDING THE DEPONENT

Attorneys defending deponents have three primary responsibilities:

- Preparing the deponent.
- Making objections during the deposition.
- Protecting the deponent.

13.32.1 Preparing the Deponent

Your preparation of the deponent should include a thorough explanation of the general procedures of the deposition and the specific elements of the case. You can provide deponents with a set of written general deposition instructions to educate them, and you can also have them observe a video tape of a simulated deposition. Your specific preparation about a case should include the following elements:

Explain what the case is all about to the witness. You ought to make certain the witness understands not only what is happening but why it is happening.

Review all the facts and documents they may be asked about. Prepared deponents make more effective and credible witnesses.

Explain conflicting stories. Deponents need to understand that their story will differ from the stories of other parties or witnesses to the case and that this is to be expected and is normal.

Be the devil's advocate. Explain the type and scope of questions the deposing attorney will probably ask, and the approach the attorney may take with the deponent.

Rehearse the deponent. Ask the deponent questions, listen to the answers, and suggest accurate, alternative answers.

These preparation suggestions apply to deponents who are clients and can also be used with deponents who are not clients. You can meet and help non-client deponents prepare, but, because they are not your client, you can not provide them with legal advice or otherwise counsel them, and what you discuss with them will not be protected by the attorney/client privilege.

13.32.2 Making Objections During the Deposition

You have a right to make limited objections to questions asked of the deponent, including client and non-client deponents. See Federal Rule 30(c). You can say "Objection" followed by a one or two word or brief statement of the ground in support of the objection. Whether your objection is correct or not, the examining attorney still has a right to insist on an answer, unless you have a right to instruct the client deponent not to answer (soon to be explained). No judge or other person is present at the deposition to rule on the appropriateness of any objection or disagreement between the attorneys. Appropriate and inappropriate objections made during a deposition include the following (Federal Rule 32(d)):

Objections to errors or irregularities in the deposition notice or in the initial deposition procedures must be made on the record at the beginning of the deposition, otherwise they will be waived. Examples include a defective deposition notice and a failure to place the deponent under oath or affirmation.

Improper questions by the examining attorney that can be corrected at the deposition must be objected to in order to preserve the objection for trial. For example, objections to the form of the question (vague, ambiguous, complex, multiple, and argumentative questions) should be made. You may also object if a deponent's response is inappropriate and non-responsive or rambling.

Objections to the substance of the response need not and usually should not be made. These objections will not be waived and are reserved for trial. Objections such as irrelevant, improper opinion, and hearsay will be preserved even if not made during the deposition. The liberal scope of discovery allows a broad examination into these areas, unless, for example, obvious irrelevant information is sought.

Objections based on grounds of privilege or similar rules must or should be made to prevent an inquiry about the privileged matter. If information is privileged, it can be protected from disclosure during the deposition. If the examining attorney insists on an answer, an instruction not to answer can be interposed, otherwise the objection may be waived.

Many depositions are conducted without any or many objections being made, because there is no need for them. Some attorneys may attempt to make many objections, either because they misunderstand the rules or because they are trying to prevent the examining attorney from discovering weaknesses in the case. This conduct is improper. Illegitimate objections should never be made.

13.32.3   Protecting the Deponent

There are some things a defending attorney can legitimately do during a deposition to protect a deponent. An attorney can instruct a client deponent not to answer in limited circumstances. An instruction not to answer occurs when the attorney representing the deponent advises the deponent not to answer a question which is objectionable. In most jurisdictions, an attorney may only instruct a deponent not to answer in a few, limited situations: to preserve a privilege, to prevent the examining

---

attorney from proceeding in bad faith, to protect a deponent from harassment, or to enforce a protective order. See Federal Rule 30(d). If there is no legitimate reason supporting an instruction not to answer, the attorney has acted improperly and is subject to sanctions. An attorney not representing a deponent cannot instruct that deponent not to answer.

There is much that cannot be done. An attorney cannot interrupt proper questions, testify instead of the deponent, or demand frequent breaks to consult with a client. Some jurisdictions prohibit an attorney from counseling a client during the deposition. The following situations reflect what can and cannot be done:

If you do not hear a question, you can ask the court reporter to read the question back.

If you do not understand the question, you can object if the deponent does not understand either.

If the deponent becomes visibly fatigued, you can insist on a brief recess.

If the deponent has difficulty remembering, you cannot interrupt and volunteer the information. The examining attorney has a right to determine what the deponent knows and not what you know.

If the deponent has answered a question and begins to ramble, you can object on the ground that the deponent has answered a question and is being non-responsive.

If a deponent has difficulty providing an answer which is contained in a document, it is usually inappropriate for you to show the deponent the document to provide the answer. The examining attorney has a right to assess the memory of the witness without reference to a document.

If the deponent is shown a document by the examining attorney during the deposition, you and the deponent have a right to review the document before any further questions are asked.

If the deponent has incorrectly answered a question, you cannot interrupt and testify to a correct response. You may object on the ground the deponent did not understand the question if it appears so; you may be able to discuss the issue with the deponent during a break; and you may ask questions at the end of the deposition to correct or clarify the deponent's answers.

It is improper during the deposition to signal deponents with some gesture or facial expression, or whisper an answer in their ear, or otherwise interfere with the deposition.

If you and your client deponent wish to consult during the deposition, you may or may not be able to do so. Some jurisdictions prohibit an attorney from consulting with a client during a deposition, and a few prohibit consultation even during recesses of the deposition. These jurisdictions hope to encourage lawyers to prepare a deponent properly before a deposition and prevent undue influence during a deposition. Jurisdictions which permit consultation during a deposition generally permit only infrequent and short discussions to avoid unnecessary interference and overly long depositions.

An examining attorney facing situations of improper behavior can do what was suggested in Section 13.30, or become a transaction lawyer.

13.33   QUESTIONING THE DEPONENT

You can ask questions of the deponent after the examining attorney is done. There may have been responses that need correction or clarification, or there may be some relevant areas you want to cover. You may not want to or need to ask any questions. You may not want to give the examining attorney another opportunity to ask questions. If the deposition is being taken to preserve testimony because the deponent will not be available to testify at a later hearing or trial, you will want to ask questions and obtain information which supports your case.

F.   THE END

13.34   CONCLUDING THE DEPOSITION

After all the questioning has been completed, there are a number of concluding matters that may need to be addressed.

13.34.1 Review of the Deposition by the Deponent

The deponent has a right to review the deposition after it is completed. See Federal Rule 30. The deponent may read a transcript of the deposition or review the recording. Most jurisdictions require that the deponent review a transcript or recording within 30 days after receiving a copy or after being notified of its availability. An attorney representing a party other than the deponent may request that the deponent review the deposition. If the deponent fails to review the deposition within the time permitted, the deponent waives any right to later review the deposition.

It is usually a wise practice to have the deponent review the deposition. It is critical that testimony be complete, and a review of the deposition will assure this accuracy. The court reporter may have misunderstood the witness; there may have been some malfunction in the recording system causing an incomplete or inaccurate transcript; the deponent may have inadvertently misspoken and this will not be apparent until the deposition is reviewed; or, the deponent may want to change an answer.

A deponent has a right to make changes to answers. See Federal Rule 30, again. A deponent can make any change for any reason. The deponent may correct typographical errors, misunderstood questions, and wrong answers, but may not erase the entire transcript. The deponent must usually explain the reason for the change. The typical manner of making changes is by the witness completing a separate written statement identifying the changes and stating the reasons. The original deposition transcript or recording and any changes are available to be used at a later hearing or trial.

Tactical reasons militate against making changes all over the transcript. Reasonable inferences may be drawn from changes in the deponent's testimony. These inferences may not be favorable to the deponent because the changes may appear to be alterations of relevant responses or inconsistent testimony. Substantive changes in the record make a deposition incomplete and allow the examining attorney to reopen the deposition for further questioning.

There are reasons not to review a deposition. If the deponent is satisfied with the responses, there may be no need to take the time and incur the additional expenses. The attorney representing the deponent may not want the deposition to be reviewed, which may help the deponent avoid impeachment attempts at trial. The attorney taking the deposition may want the record to remain unchanged and not want the deponent to review the transcript.

13.34.2 Signing the Deposition

A deponent may have a right or obligation to sign a deposition transcript or recording. Some jurisdictions require deponents to do so, and others provide deponents with an opportunity to do so which they may decline. If changes are made to a deposition, the deponent will need to sign the changes. Deponents often do not sign because there is no advantage to do so. A disadvantage is that they can be more effectively impeached at trial. Whether a deposition is signed or unsigned does not effect its use for a motion, hearing, or trial.

13.34.3 Filing the Deposition

A deposition transcript or record after being completed by the officer taking the deposition is usually delivered to the attorney who noticed the deposition or is filed with the court in those few jurisdictions which require filing. Either the officer or noticing attorney must advise all parties of the completion and filing of the deposition. It is critical that a deposition be stored in a safe place for later use. It is common for other parties to request a copy of the transcript or recording from the officer for a fee or from the custodial attorney.

13.34.4 Stipulations

Attorneys at the deposition may stipulate on the record concerning the review, signing, and filing procedures. These agreements make clear what happens after the deposition is concluded. "Usual stipulations" suggested by an attorney should only be agreed to if everyone understands what is included in the stipulations. If in doubt, specific agreements should be stated on the record.

G. THE FUTURE

13.35 USE OF THE DEPOSITION

Deposition testimony may be used for any purpose permitted by the rules or law and is typically used (Federal Rule 32):

- In support of or in opposition to a motion for summary judgment.

- As evidence at a hearing or trial.

- As admissions. Statements made by a deponent party may be offered against that party as party admissions.

- As testimony. The deposition may be introduced as evidence in lieu of the live testimony of the deponent who is unavailable as a trial witness.

- For cross-examination purposes. The deponent may be impeached with prior inconsistent deposition testimony.

- To refresh the recollection of a witness. Witnesses who do not recall something may have their memories refreshed with the use of their deposition testimony.

- To determine whether the deponent read and understood the following chapter.

Chapter Fourteen
DISCOVERY METHODS: IS THAT ALL THERE IS?

I'm as helpful as you are.

All you are are written questions.

Interrogatories, please.

Pardon me. I can get documents.

But neither of you can examine people.

I can get to the heart of the matter.

Admit it, all of you. Only I can seek admissions.

Well, we can each do different things.

Let the reader decide which of us can help the most.

A. INTRODUCTION
14.1 MORE DISCOVERY METHODS

In addition to asking questions and seeking information at depositions, advocates can:

- Get documents.
- Get answers to interrogatories.
- Get admissions.
- Get exams (not yours).

How is the subject of this chapter.

B. GETTING DOCUMENTS
14.2 HOW DO I OBTAIN DOCUMENTS?

You can obtain documents that the other side has not voluntarily disclosed by asking for them or demanding them pursuant to a procedural rule.

You can ask for documents by saying please. You can describe the documents you want, and ask the other side to provide you with the originals for inspection or copying or for an identical copy of the original. It is usually best to make this request in writing through a letter or formal request, but you may also do so orally. If the other side concurs with your request, you have what you want. If they do not, you will have to demand the documents in accord with the applicable procedural rule. Federal Rule 26 and similar rules from other forums provide that any party may serve any other party with a demand to produce original documents for inspection or copying or tangible things and to permit entry onto land or other property.

14.2.1   Whom Can I Ask?

You can ask anyone who has what you want. If they are a party, you can usually submit a written demand. If they are a non-party, you usually have to serve a subpoena duces tecum and schedule a deposition for them to appear and produce the documents. See Section 14.11.

14.2.2   What Can I Demand from Parties?

You can request any document, tangible thing, or property in the possession, custody, or control of the party that is relevant as discoverable information. It makes sense to ask only for what the other party has which bears on the case. Possession and custody include both actual and constructive possession, and control means a party has a legal right to obtain the documents. The liberal scope of discovery typically provides for broad access to all sorts of documents, things, and property.

14.3   WHEN CAN I MAKE A DEMAND?

You can usually make a demand whenever you need the documents. If the applicable rules require voluntary disclosures, you usually have to wait until these disclosures have or have not been made before making a demand. Practically, you may have to wait until the litigation pleadings, arbitration claim and response, or administrative petition and answer have been exchanged. Tactically, you may want the documents early in the case in order to evaluate the case, decide how you want to proceed, and prepare for depositions or a hearing.

14.4 HOW DO I MAKE A DEMAND?

The written demand typically describes the documents to be produced and specifies the reasonable time, place, and manner for making the inspection or producing copies. A production of documents request under Federal Rule of Civil Procedure 34 provides:

> Plaintiff A.B. requests defendant C.D. to respond within 30 days to the following requests:
>
> 1. Defendant produce and permit plaintiff to inspect copies of the following documents [list the documents individually or by category].
>
> Defendant shall produce these documents at ___ o'clock ___m. at the office of [place] and plaintiff shall review and copy the documents.
>
> 2. Defendant produce and permit plaintiff to inspect and to copy, test, or sample each of the following objects: [list the objects individually or by category].
>
> Defendant shall produce these objects at [state time, place, and manner of making the inspection].
>
> 3. Defendant permit plaintiff to enter [describe property] and to inspect and to photograph, test, or sample [describe property and objects].
>
> Defendant shall permit this entry and inspection at [state time, place, and manner of entry and inspection].

14.4.1 How do the Documents Need to be Described?

In writing and usually with "reasonable particularity." This description should be sufficient to allow a person of ordinary intelligence to say "I know what they want," and to permit a judge or arbitrator to determine whether all the items have been produced.

14.4.2 How do I Draft These Descriptions?

You want to draft with specificity to make certain you obtain the documents you want and to avoid allowing the other side to withhold documents. You also want to draft with sufficient breadth to make certain that no existing documents escape your attention. Three drafting techniques that help produce these results are: use *definitions* of important words, draft *requests* seeking both specifically designated items and generally described items, and include *instructions* to the other side.

An example of a *definition* is:

The term *documents* means all writings of any kind, including the originals and all non-identical copies, including without limitation, correspondence, memoranda, notes, diaries, statistics, letters, telegrams, minutes, contracts, reports, studies, checks, statements, receipts, returns, summaries, pamphlets, books, interoffice and intra-office communications, notations of any sort of conversations, telephone calls, meetings or other communications, bulletins, printed matter, computer printouts, teletypes, telefax, invoices, worksheets, drafts, alterations, modifications, changes and amendments of any of the foregoing, graphic or oral records or representations of any kind (including, without limitation, photographs, charts, graphs, microfiche, microfilm, videotapes, recordings, motion pictures), and any electronic, mechanical, or electric records or representations of any kind (including, without limitation, tapes, cassettes, discs, recordings, and computer memories).

Whew!

An example of a *request* is:

Provide all documents concerning any contractual breach by defendant alleged in paragraph two of the complaint including but not limited to:

The original and all copies of each letter or written communication between the plaintiff and defendant between May 1, 1995 and August 1, 1995.

All writings submitted by the plaintiff to the Banking Commissioner which contain any reference to the defendant.

Examples of *instructions* are:

If you refuse to disclose some of the documents in existence, specifically identify these documents and state their location and explain your objections in detail.

If your response is that the documents are not in your possession or custody, describe in detail the unsuccessful efforts you made to locate the records.

If your response is that the documents are not in your control, identify who has control and the location of the documents.

14.5 HOW AND WHEN CAN I OBTAIN THE DOCUMENTS?

The demand states a time, place, and manner for production. The date is typically scheduled at least 30 days after service of the request. The hour is usually during business hours. The place is the office of the requesting attorney where copying equipment is available, or the location of the documents. The manner depends upon the kinds of items requested.

14.6 HOW MAY THE OTHER SIDE RESPOND?

The party receiving the demand may within the allowable time:

Abracadabra! Provide copies of the documents. It is common practice for a party to provide the requesting party with copies of the originals. This may be the most efficient and inexpensive method of responding, especially if the documents are not numerous. Usually the party producing the documents incurs the cost of reproducing them, or may insist that the demanding party pay reasonable copying costs. These matters are often discussed and mutually agreed upon by the attorneys.

Produce the requested items according to the suggested time, place, and manner. The party producing the items usually has to produce them as they are kept in the ordinary course of business or organize them and label them to correspond with the categories in the request. If a party requests many documents which would take a substantial amount of time to organize, the responding party may make them available for the requesting party to search through and copy.

Provide copies or disclose the requested documents at another time, place, and manner agreeable to the requesting attorney, or serve a written response upon the requesting party stating that the production will be permitted at another time, place, and manner which may be agreeable to the requesting party.

Seek a protective order to prevent or safeguard the disclosure of certain items. If a party believes the request to be improper or burdensome, or if the request seeks privileged or confidential information, it may be necessary to obtain an order from a judge or arbitrator restricting the request.

Serve a written response objecting to all or part of the request. The response may indicate which documents will be produced and which will not with the objections explaining the grounds for the refusal.

Ignore the request, although this is not authorized by the rules or supported by competent practice. So in other words, don't do it.

14.7 HOW DO I KNOW I GOT EVERYTHING?

Your inspection and approval of the requested items should include several considerations: Has everything you requested been turned over to you? Too little? Too much? Do the records indicate that other relevant documents exist? Have you dreamt these documents may exist?

You should maintain some means of listing and identifying the documents and things examined, which will help you organize the production and quell later questions about what was produced when. Copying the items is usually done at your own expense. You can arrange to use another's copying equipment and reimburse those costs. These details are usually worked out by the attorneys.

14.8 HOW DO I TEST AN ITEM?

You may have a right to test relevant items in certain cases. The decision to test turns on a number of considerations: Is the test likely to do more harm than good by destroying or materially altering evidence? Will the test produce supportive information, or may it help the other side? Will the results of the proposed tests be admissible at a hearing or trial? Are you likely to be tested next?

Whatever testing is done must be done with the full knowledge of the other side. Your request for testing should spell out in detail what and how you intend to test. It is wise to seek a written stipulation or order detailing the testing procedure. An expert will usually be involved in testing procedures.

Some testing may result in the destruction of all or part of an item. A specific court order prior to the conducting of these destructive tests is usually required. The court's discretion in deciding whether to issue an order allowing destructive testing is guided by two factors: the usefulness or need of the discovery to the party requesting it and the prejudice that will occur to the party opposed to destructive testing. The terms of a testing protective order frequently include: a testing plan, an opportunity prior to testing for all parties to examine and photograph the object to be tested, notice of the testing, the right of any party to be present at the testing with their experts, thorough recording of the test, the availability of test results and written reports for all parties, and the right of other parties to take additional samples for similar testing.

14.9　HOW DO I OBTAIN COMPUTERIZED INFORMATION?

Ask HAL. You can usually obtain the discovery of information stored on disks, CD–ROM, recording tapes, data cards, and other computer storage systems. The responding party typically must furnish this information in a manner understandable to the requesting party, and bears the cost of compiling the data and translating it into a readable printout or other machine readable format.

14.10　WHAT ARE AVAILABLE OBJECTIONS TO PRODUCTION DEMANDS?

A responding party may object to part or all of a request for production and may withhold these documents from discovery. All objections must be bona fide and be supported by sufficient reasons. The more common objections to document production requests include:

- Irrelevant beyond the scope of proper discovery.

- Not in the possession, custody, or control of the responding party.

- Privilege, trial preparation, or attorney mental impression materials.

- Materials from experts who will not testify at trial.

- Imposes an undue burden or expense.

- A vague, ambiguous, or overly broad request.

- Public records equally available to the requesting party.

- Etched in indecipherable Sanskrit in an underground cave in France which is yet to be discovered.

The responding party should consider whether there is any tactical advantage in disclosing documents or items that are supported by a proper ground for an objection. If the disclosure of the information supports the responding party's case or weakens the opponent's case, it is usually wise to disclose the information.

14.11 HOW DO I OBTAIN DOCUMENTS FROM NON-PARTIES?

To obtain documents from a non-party you usually serve them and other parties with a notice of the non-party's deposition accompanied by a subpoena duces tecum ordering the non-party to produce documents at the deposition. Some forums permit the service of a subpoena duces tecum without a scheduled deposition, hearing or trial. The scope of the obtainable information is the same as the scope of discovery from parties. See Federal Rule 45.

14.12 HOW DO I OBTAIN DOCUMENTS FROM THE GOVERNMENT?

If the government is a party, you can obtain information the same way you obtain information from any party. If the federal government is a non-party, you can obtain information through the Freedom of Information Act, (FOIA) 5 U.S.C. § 552. If it is a non-federal governmental unit, you may be able to obtain information pursuant to state statutes similar to the FOIA. The

FOIA allows the broad disclosure of documents held by the government and provides that the government agencies must release any records in the agency's possession to any person upon request. Access to the records is provided either by the publication in the federal register, access at the agency's headquarters, or by making copies available upon request. See, your tax dollars serve some useful purposes. Specific exceptions to disclosure include privileged, confidential, national security, and law enforcement documents.

C. GETTING INFORMATION

14.13 WHAT ARE INTERROGATORIES?

Interrogatories are written questions submitted to another party who has to respond with a written answer. Interrogatories can be an effective and efficient way to obtain objective, specific information from parties regarding their claims, defenses, existence of documents, expert information, and other relevant data. Interrogatories can also be ineffective and relatively useless if they seek general information or allow the other party to respond with self-serving responses. Interrogatories cannot be served on non-parties.

14.13.1 When Can I Submit Them?

When you need the information. You can serve interrogatories with litigation pleadings, or serve them later in a case to obtain information to help draft a document production request or to prepare for a deposition or hearing. The responding party usually has a minimum of 30 days to respond.

14.13.2 What Information Can I Seek?

You should seek specific types of information which cannot be obtained more effectively, efficiently, or economically through other discovery devices. Information based upon testimony or interpretive explanations and information depending upon the demeanor and credibility of a person is usually better sought through depositions. Information regarding the content of documents is better left to document production requests. Examples of useful information sought through interrogatories are:

The identity (name, address, and telephone number) of individuals likely to have discoverable relevant information and a summary of this information.

Specific information a party has to support an allegation in a specific claim or defense stated in a complaint or answer.

The existence, description, location, and condition of relevant documents, tangible things, data compilations, witness statements, property, and objects.

Specific information about damages sought, the computation of damages, and a description of any documents and material supporting the damage computations.

The existence and coverage of liability or other insurance, if not previously disclosed.

The identities of expert witnesses who will testify at trial, or who are employees of a party, or who have been retained or specially employed.

Specific information about expert trial witnesses including their opinions, bases of opinions, prepared reports, authored publications, paid compensation, qualifications, and other cases in which the expert has testified at a trial or deposition.

Business and corporate information concerning the principal place of business, date and state of incorporation, and states that license the business.

Summary financial information or summary technical or statistical information.

Opinions, conclusions, and contentions can be inquired about in addition to factual information.

14.14 HOW DO I DRAFT INTERROGATORIES?

There are three parts to the interrogatory request:

- Instructions
- Definitions
- Questions

14.14.1 Instructions

Instructions include a prefatory statement and a variety of instructions.

Preface: Plaintiff requests that the defendant answer the following interrogatories in writing and under oath pursuant to Rule 33 of the Rules of Civil Procedure and that answers be served on the plaintiff within thirty (30) days after service of these interrogatories.

Procedural instructions: In answering these interrogatories, furnish all information, however obtained, including hearsay, if it is available to you and information known by or in possession of yourself, your agents, and your attorneys, or appearing in your records.

Response instructions: If you cannot answer the following interrogatories in full after exercising due diligence to secure the information, answer to the extent possible, specifying your inability to answer the remainder, stating whatever information or knowledge you have concerning the unanswered portion, and detailing what you did in attempting to secure the unknown information.

Document production instructions: A question that seeks information contained in or information about or identification of a document may be answered by providing a copy of such document for inspection and copying or furnishing a copy of such document without a request for production.

Supplementary answer instructions: These interrogatories shall be deemed to be continuing until and during the course of trial. Information sought by these interrogatories that you obtain after you submit your answers must be disclosed to the plaintiff by supplementary answers.

Identification instruction: The person or persons who provide information and answers to the following interrogatories will each identify which answers have been provided and furnish their name, address, and title.

14.14.2 Definitions

Definitions may precede interrogatories defining certain words used in the questions to make certain everyone will use the same definition, to identify a word that is peculiar to the interrogatories, to shorten questions by avoiding the need to repeat the meaning of a term, and to ensure complete responses. Examples of definitions are:

Describe: This word means to specify in detail an answer to the question and not just to answer in a summary or outline fashion.

August 15 contract: This term refers to the contract signed by both the plaintiff and the defendant on August 15, 1995, attached as exhibit A to the complaint.

Identify: The word identify means to state the name, address, telephone number, employment, and title of all persons identified in a response.

14.14.3 Questions

Read the explanations in the following sections.

14.15 HOW DO I EFFECTIVELY DRAFT QUESTIONS?

Interrogatories should contain clear, precise, direct questions. They should not be vague nor broad. The questions should have the other attorney thinking: "Yes, I understand what they want to know." Such thinking comes easier for some lawyers than others. After you draft your interrogatories you can review their effectiveness by asking:

- Can the question be redrafted in a simpler, less complex manner?

- Will the answer to the interrogatory provide me with the information I want?

- Should some questions be eliminated or consolidated?

- Can the other side reasonably avoid answering all or part of a question?

An effective drafting technique is to use the "branching" approach. A broad question is asked and then followed by specific questions relating to one or more of the possible responses. For example:

State whether defendant is a corporation or a partnership. If a corporation, identify the members of the board of directors. If a partnership, identify all the partners.

14.16 HOW MANY QUESTIONS CAN I ASK?

Most jurisdictions limit the number of interrogatories. Federal rule 33(a) limits interrogatories to 25 in number including subparts. Many state courts limit the number of interrogatories to no more than 20 or 50 interrogatories. A question is counted as one interrogatory if it is one question or if it includes subdivisions that directly relate to the initial question. For example, one interrogatory will be:

State whether the plaintiff owns an automobile. If the answer is yes, describe the make and model, its current market value, the state in which it is licensed, and whether it has manual or power seats.

Drafting techniques that help reduce the number of interrogatories asked are:

Use discrete subparts, and avoid prefacing them with letters or numbers. Ask:

Reread the above automobile question.

Do not separate the sub-topics conspicuously, with conjunctive or disjunctive words or with unnecessary punctuation. Avoid using and, or, the, semicolons, and colons. Ask:

Please identify all schools that plaintiff has attended, beginning with nursery school.

Reduce a clause or lengthy phrase to one word or a concise phrase. Ask:

Describe in detail defendant's spaceship.

Include necessary specifications or exact details by using subtopics. Ask:

Please describe plaintiff's hair, including, but not limited to the color, style, number of gray hairs, approximate length of sideburns, color of the roots, and the curvature and degrees of the cowlick.

Ask simple and straight forward questions. Ask:

Identify all members of the faculty skittlepool team and name their positions.

Employ questions that seek only one possible response from a list of alternative suggested answers, unless you do not want to suggest the answer. Ask:

State whether the attorney for plaintiff prefers to be called by the name of lawyer, attorney, attorney at law, counselor, or hey you.

Use definitions with your interrogatories.

Reread Section 14.14.2.

There are many examples of effective interrogatories appearing in cases similar to yours and in form books. Forms should be reviewed to determine their usefulness, and edited to apply to your case.

14.17 HOW ARE INTERROGATORIES RESPONDED TO?

A responding party may:

- Answer the questions.

- Assert objections.

- Provide documents instead of written answers which contain the information sought.

- Seek an extension of time to answer.

- Move to a country that does not require responses.

14.17.1 How Are Questions Answered?

With the right answer. What is the right answer? A party must provide complete answers to interrogatories that are not objectionable.

14.17.2 What Is an Appropriate Answer?

Answers must be full and complete. All information known to the answering party must be disclosed, whether it is helpful, neutral, or harmful. Three factors influence the drafting of answers:

- Interpreting questions

- Gathering information

- Drafting answers

Interpreting questions. Questions must be interpreted reasonably. If a reasonable person can understand the question, the responding attorney must answer the question. Unreasonable extrapolations, quibbling, and stretched interpretations have no place in responding to an interrogatory.

Gathering the information. A party has a duty to conduct a reasonable investigation to obtain information for the response. Parties must reveal whatever information they or their employees, offices, or agents know personally, learn through hearsay, believe to be true, appear in their documents, or have in their possession or control. A party must make a conscientious effort to obtain all information that does not require undue labor or expense.

Drafting the answers. Interrogatory answers must be in writing and under oath and signed by the party providing the information, and usually the attorney. The rules of most jurisdictions require that the question be repeated in full before each answer.

The client needs to take an active role in reviewing the questions, gathering the information, and helping to prepare the answers. In most cases, it is the client and not the attorney who will know the answer. In some cases, the client will gather documents which will be reviewed by the attorney in drafting answers. It is important to involve clients directly because it is their case, because they have to sign the answers under oath, and because the answers may be used later in the trial for substantive and impeachment evidence.

The attorney can and should take an active role in preparing and drafting answers. The party can provide the information or create a first draft, and the attorney can shape the information into an appropriate response. Answers can be phrased in the best possible way to support the position of a party as long as they are full and complete responses. More information than asked for can be provided if you want the party to know specific information helpful to your case.

Answers cannot be evasive, incomplete, or deceptive. Situations may arise when a response must be qualified:

When a party is unable to answer a question because of a lack of information or some other reasons the party must indicate those reasons.

If a party does not know an answer at the time the response is due but later learns the information, the information can be provided in a supplementary answer.

A party may answer one interrogatory by referring to a previous response, as long as the previous response fully answers that interrogatory.

14.18 WHAT OBJECTIONS MAY BE MADE TO INTERROGATORIES?

Objections must be stated with specificity and must usually include all grounds to support the objection. If an interrogatory is only objectionable in part, the non-objectionable part of the interrogatory must be answered. Objections that may be applicable to interrogatories include:

- Irrelevant and beyond the scope of discoverable information.
- Privilege, trial preparation, or attorney mental impression information.
- Unduly burdensome and requiring extensive cost and time.
- Excessive number.
- Seeks legal conclusions.
- Seeks information only available during odd numbered leap years.

The party objecting to an interrogatory has the burden in any subsequent proceeding to establish the validity of the specific objection. It is not enough to believe there is an objection, there must be a legal basis for the position. Unfounded objections subject a party and the attorney to sanctions.

Questions that are objectionable on legitimate grounds should still be answered in some situations. If the answer will help a client's case, it should be provided. If an easy response will provide information that does not prejudice a client's case, the response should be given to avoid wasting time and money objecting and facing the prospects of enforcement. If a question can be modified to avoid an objectionable feature, it may be advisable to submit a responsive answer.

14.19 WHAT CAN I DO IF I DON'T GET WHAT I WANT?

You can contact the other attorney and negotiate a compromise solution. You may be able to redraft the interrogatory to make it acceptable. The other side may be willing to give some but not all information. This may satisfy you. If not, you can seek a court order enforcing your discovery request. Or you can pout.

D. GETTING ADMISSIONS

14.20 WHAT ARE REQUESTS FOR ADMISSIONS?

Request for admissions are written statements submitted by one party to another seeking admissions. See, you too could write this section. The purpose of these requests is to seek the agreement of the other side to a relevant fact, opinion, conclusion, authentication of a document, content of a document, or other useful information. This approach narrows undisputed issues and also obtains some discoverable information. Admission requests are usually submitted in the latter stages of a case at the end of discovery and can be helpful in determining what issues need to be decided and what evidence needs to be introduced in a hearing or trial.

14.21 HOW DO I DRAFT REQUESTS FOR ADMISSIONS?

Requests should be concise and understandable statements. If you understand this concise statement you can draft effectively. The format of a request looks like:

> Plaintiff AB requests defendant CD within 30 days of the service of this request to make the following admissions for the purposes of this action only and subject to all objections to admissibility which may be interposed at the trial:

Each of the following statements is true:

1. You said, "The sky is falling" when you saw the sky falling on February 2, 1996.

2. The color of the sky you saw falling was blue.

3. A one foot square piece of sky hit your school desk on February 2, 1996.

Each of the following documents, exhibited with this request, is genuine:

1. Exhibit 1 to this request is the written statement you signed with your claw on February 3, 1996.

Additional instructions and definitions of some of the words used in the statements may also be included.

14.22 WHAT ARE RESPONSES TO REQUESTS?

A party receiving a request for admission may:

Admit the statement. A party must respond to a request in a truthful, specific, and unconditional way. Honesty determines how to respond. A party admits something by responding yes or by some other specific affirmative response.

Deny the statement. A party can deny a statement if it is untrue. The responding party should ask: "Can I in good faith, honestly, and unconditionally deny all or part of this request?" To be effective, a denial must deny the truth of the matter.

Qualify the answer. If part of a statement is true and part untrue, the party can admit the true part and deny the untrue part. If a party cannot admit or deny a statement, the party must set forth in detail the reasons why an admission or denial cannot be made. A party may be uncertain or have some reasonable doubt about a response. If so, the party must explain why they cannot say yes or no answer to the statement. A party cannot attempt to be evasive or to avoid direct responses by using qualifying answers. A party can add more information in response than the request seeks. It is appropriate for an attorney to include information supportive of a case in a response.

Object to the request. A party has a right to object to inappropriate requests for admissions. The same types of objections applicable to interrogatories and requests for production apply to request for admissions and evidentiary objections. See Sections 14.10 and 14.18. The ground for the objection must be specifically stated.

Obtain an agreement or order. A party can obtain an agreement from the requesting party or a court order extending the time to respond. The applicable rules usually provide that an untimely response to the request for admission deems the statements to be admitted. The agreement of the other side or judge is critical to obtaining an effective extension of time.

Do nothing. This is a really bad choice because the statements will be admitted, as just explained. This tactic is only effective if the attorney then leaves the country, as previously suggested.

14.23　CAN I CHALLENGE A RESPONSE?

The rules typically allow a requesting party to challenge the sufficiency of any response through a motion and hearing. If the response is an appropriate objection or explanation, you will need to obtain a court order requiring the other side to respond fully. If the response is a non-response or an unacceptable response, the request may automatically become an admission after the time runs to respond. In some jurisdictions, you still may need to seek a ruling from the judge declaring this statement to be an admission.

14.24　CAN A RESPONSE BE CHANGED?

A party may be able to withdraw an admission and substitute an amended response. This may be permitted when the other party will not be substantially prejudiced by such a reversal. If the admission was a genuine mistake and should not have been made, a withdrawal will likely be allowed. If the request for the withdrawal occurs on the eve of trial and should have been discovered earlier, the request will usually be denied.

14.25　WHAT IS THE EFFECT OF AN ADMISSION?

Admissions are conclusive proof of the matter asserted for purposes of a pending action. The admission has the same effect as a pleading admission or a stipulation of facts. The fact finder must accept the admissions as true and cannot disbelieve them. The party that made the admissions cannot contradict or rebut the admissions at trial. Admissions are automatically admissible at the trial. A party need only offer them as evidence.

E. GETTING AN EXAMINATION

14.26 WHY WOULD I WANT TO REQUEST AN EXAMINATION?

You may want to have an adverse party examined by a medical doctor or psychiatrist because the party's condition is in issue and in controversy. Federal Rule 35 and similar state rules apply broadly to any case in which there is a controversy about the physical, mental, or blood condition of the person to be examined. Examinations are common in personal injury cases, and may also be involved in parentage, citizenship, incompetence, and undue influence cases.

14.26.1 What Is a "Controversy?"

Adverse parties must have placed their physical, mental, or blood condition in controversy and good cause must exist in support of an examination. Parties who are to be involuntarily examined by a doctor should only have to do so if they voluntarily place their condition in issue in a case. An opposing party has the right to have an examination conducted if other parties seek a remedy for their condition. The most common example is a plaintiff who seeks damages for physical injuries or emotional distress. Non-parties cannot be examined involuntarily. Fortunately or unfortunately, the rule does not permit an examination of the lawyers, regardless of their mental condition.

14.26.2 What Examination Documents are Needed?

Examinations are usually conducted pursuant to a stipulation between the parties. Parties can mutually agree to the terms of the examination. If there is a disagreement, the party seeking the examination will need to serve and file a notice of motion, motion, affidavit, proposed order, and legal memo and schedule a hearing before the judge. The stipulation or order for examination typically covers the following provisions of the examination: time, location, manner of examination, person conducting the examination, scope of the examination, who may be present during the examination, and any conditions restricting or relating to the procedures.

14.27 WHAT HAPPENS AT THE EXAMINATION?

The examination typically takes place at the office of the doctor conducting the examination. Obviously, the person to be examined is there, and sometimes the person's attorney. The examination is limited to the specific issues relevant in the case.

14.28 WHAT HAPPENS AFTER THE EXAMINATION?

The examining doctor ordinarily prepares a report of the examination. This document is a detailed statement of the doctor's examination, specific findings, and overall conclusions. A copy of the report is ordinarily forwarded to the party examined and to other parties. It would be rather unusual, and even eccentric, to conclude the examination with a blue book exam, . . . as it would this book.

EPILOGUE

And now the end is near ... of this book, but it is only the beginning of your work as a lawyer. One of our primary goals expressed in Chapter One was to provide you with the information and opportunity to become a competent and confident professional. We hope that our explanation of lawyering theories, skills, strategies, approaches, and tactics has provided you with the foundation to be the best practitioner you can be. We hope that your review of the available videotapes has helped you understand how these skills are conducted effectively. We hope that your tolerance of our attempts at humor has made you a more understanding person.

Becoming an excellent lawyer is work that never ends. You will need to—and want to—constantly analyze and critique what you do and what other lawyers do to in an effort to improve continually. This is a reasonable goal for a professional, and more importantly, this is what our clients and the community expect. We can eloquently explain why we should maintain high standards for our work. But our clients'—and the public's— expectations should be enough to motivate us to do our best. We practice law to *serve* them and their interests.

This book covers much of the work of the lawyer, but not all. A companion book covers the work of the advocate. *Advocacy by Haydock and Sonsteng* (West, 1994) provides you with the theories and skills to prepare and present a case effectively before judicial, arbitral, and administrative forums. You need to learn how to be a competent, confident advocate when your clients want or need to have their case resolved by a judge, jury, or arbitrator. This five book series explains case planning, opening and summation, direct and cross-examinations, exhibits, evidentiary objections, and jury trials. These books are as educational and entertaining as this book, and make wonderful holiday gifts, along with this masterpiece.

We conclude this book with our sincere wishes that you will delight in being a lawyer. For those of you who practice, we hope you will experience the joys, challenges, frustrations, and feelings of accomplishment that await you. For the rest of you, we hope you will apply your lawyering skills to be a better professional. To all of you, we wish the very best.

*

Index

References are to Sections

ADMINISTRATIVE PROCEEDINGS
Claims, 11,7
Hearings, 11,7
How to initiate an administrative case, 11.7

ADMISSIONS
Challenging a response, 14.23
Changing a response, 14.24
Definition of, 14.20
Drafting, 14.21
Effect of, 14.25
Objections to requests, 14.22
Responses to requests, 14.22

ADVISING CLIENTS
Assessment of issues, 4.2
  Assessment skills, 4.2.2
  Importance of assessment, 4.2.1
Legal advice definition, 4.1

AGREEMENTS
Agreement, disclosure and discovery by, 12.8
Agreements to produce documents, 13.23
Business agreements, see Business Agreements
Mediation settlement agreements, 9.8.1
Written agreements, 8.9.3
  Drafting, 8.9.4
  Type of, 8.9.5

ALTERNATIVE DISPUTE RESOLUTION
  See Dispute Resolution Methods
Mandated, 6.15

ANSWERS
Components of answer,
  Admissions, 11.10.1
  Affirmative Defenses, 11.10.2
  Counterclaims, 11.10.3
  Cross-claims, 11.10.5
  Defensive motions, 11.10.4
  Denials, 11.10.1

ANSWERS—Cont'd
Components of answer—Cont'd
  Third party claims, 11.10.5
Response to claims, 11.10

ARBITRATION PROCEEDINGS
Arbitration, 6.9.4
Hearings, 6.9.4
How to bring an arbitration claim, 11.6

ATTORNEY-CLIENT PRIVILEGE
  See Privileges

ATTORNEY JOKES
There are none.

BUSINESS AGREEMENTS
Express agreement and authorizations, 3.13.3
Importance of, 3.13
How to discuss, 3.13.1
  Fees and costs discussion, 3.13.2
Responsibility issues, 3.12
Written business agreements, 2.6.7
Written representation agreement, 3.13.4

CLIENT DEVELOPMENT
Attracting and retaining clients, 2.5
  Advertising, 2.5.2
  Referrals, 2.5.1

CLIENT RELATIONSHIPS
  Generally, 1.3.1
Building trust, 3.2
  Elusiveness of, 3.2.2
  Importance of, 3.2.1
Communication, see Communication with Clients
Expectations of clients, 1.7
Extent of client relationships, 1.8

COMMUNICATION WITH CLIENTS
Appropriate comfort, 3.3.2
Competent communication, 3.3
Confidential matters, 3.3.3
Listening, 3.3.1, 4.3

COMMUNICATION WITH CLIENTS —Cont'd

Meetings with clients
  Advice from experienced lawyers, 4.15
  Agendas, 4.16
  Fact investigation, 4.14.2
  Information needed from clients, 4.13
  Legal investigation, 4.14.1
  Lists, 4.16
  Logistics of, 3.15
  Preparation for, 3.14, 4.14
  Structure of, 3.16, 4.17
  Thinking and planning, 4.14
Presenting options, 4.6
  Cost considerations, 4.6.4
  Downside of options, 4.6.3
  How the option fits the goals, 4.6.2
  Process description, 4.6.1
  Time considerations, 4.6.4
Predictions
  Describing success, 4.7.1
  Flexibility, need for, 4.8.1
  Language of prediction, 4.8
  Prediction factors, 4.7
  Reasonably definite information giving, 4.8.2
Talking to clients, 4.4
Techniques for obtaining information, see Obtaining Information
Updating on negotiations, 8.4

COMMUNICATION WITH OTHER SIDE

Communication during mediation, 9.6.2
Information exchange plan,
  Information you want other side to have, 8.1
  Legal effect of disclosures, 8.2
  Protecting information from disclosure, 8.3, 8.3.1
Mediator communications, 9.7.2
Negotiation,
  Contacting opposing attorney, 7.14
  Obtaining information from other side during, 8.3.2

COMPLAINTS

Components of, 11.5
  Caption, 11.5.1
  Contents, 11.5.2
  Request for Relief, 11.5.3
  Signature, 11.5.4
Importance of, 11.8

COMPLAINTS—Cont'd

Sample complaint, 11.5.2

COUNSELING CLIENTS

See Advising Clients

DECISION MAKING

Assessment of issues, 4.2
  Assessment skills, 4.2.2
  Importance of assessment, 4.2.1
Checklist for negotiation, 7.7
Client decisions, 4.10
Evaluation
  Lawsuits, 7.9
  Lawyer interests and values, 7.10
  Other side, 7.11
  Transactions, 7.8
Factors which influence, 1.3.4
  Feeling good, 1.3.4
  Financial considerations, 1.3.4
  Needs and interests, 1.3.4
  Values, 1.3.4
Helping clients reach a conclusion, 4.11
  Goal and option matching, 4.11.1
  Reframe the choice, 4.11.3
  Winnow the list, 4.11.2
Lawyer decisions, 4.10
Lawyer's role in, 4.9
Reserving options, 4.12
Transactional goals, 5.7
  Clarifying immediate goals, 5.7.1
  Client's role, 5.8
  Promoting long-range goals, 5.7.2
  Understanding client goals and preferences, 5.9

DEFENDANTS

Choosing a proper defendant or respondent, 6.7

DEPOSITIONS

Attorney demeanor, 13.18
Choosing deponents, 13.2
Concluding matters to be addressed, 13.34
  Filing deposition, 13.34.3
  Review by deponent, 13.34.1
  Signing by deponent, 13.34.2
  Stipulations, 13.34.4
Conclusion of, 13.31
  How to conclude, 13.31
Confidential information, 13.26
Cost estimate, 13.13
Deponent,
  Defending, 13.32
  Preparing, 13.32.1
  Protecting, 13.32.3

DEPOSITIONS—Cont'd
Deponent—Cont'd
  Questioning by non-examining attorney, 13.33
Documents,
  Agreements to produce, 13.23
  Creation of exhibits, 13.23
  Questions about, 13.23
  Requests, 13.7
  Review of, 13.23
Exhibits,
  Authentication, 13.24
  Creation of, 13.23
  Handling of, 13.24
  Offering, no need, 13.25
  Preservation of, 13.25
Expert depositions, 13.27
  Areas to explore, 13.27
Failure to appear, sanctions for, 13.10
Frequency of, 13.4
  Instructions not to answer, 13.32.3
  Limitations on, 13.32.3
Interference, controlling, 13.30
Length of, 13.6
Limitations on, 13.4, 13.6
Location of, 13.5
Logistics of,
  Directions and explanations to deponent, 13.17
  Preliminary information, 13.16
  Procedure explanation, 13.17
  Room arrangement, 13.15
Notice of, 13.7
  Sample notice, 13.7
Objections,
  Appropriate objections, 13.32.2
  Handling, 13.29
  Making, 13.32.2
Persons present at, 13.9
Preparation for, 13.14
Questions,
  Asking effective questions, 13.20
  Probing, 13.21
  Techniques, 13.22
  Written, 13.19
Reasons to conduct, 13.1
Recording, 13.11
Scheduling, 13.8
Stupid Deposition Tricks, 13.28
Timing of, 13.3
Transcript, need for, 13.12
Uses of deposition, 13.35

DISCLOSURE AND DISCOVERY
Agreement, disclosure and discovery by, 12.8
Court orders, 12.9, 12.10

DISCLOSURE AND DISCOVERY
—Cont'd
Court orders—Cont'd
  Enforcement orders, 12.10.2
  Protective orders, 12.10.1
  Sanctions, 12.10.2
Expert information, 12.5
  Employee experts, 12.5.2
  Inexpensive experts, 12.5.4
  Informally consulted experts, 12.5.3
  Hearing experts, 12.5.1
  Retained experts, 12.5.2
  Trial experts, 12.5.1
Meet and confer requirement, 12.9
Methods of discovery, 12.2, 14.1
  Admissions, requests for, see Admissions
  Availability in various proceedings, 12.2.1
  Document productions, see Documents and Things
  Examinations, requests for, see Examinations
  Interrogatory answers, requests for, see Interrogatories
Planning of disclosure and discovery, 12.7
  Sample plan, 12.7
Purposes of, 12.1
Relevancy standards in discovery, 12.3
  Administrative proceedings standard, 12.3.3
  Arbitration standard, 12.3.2
  Litigation standard, 12.3.1
Report to court, 12.9
Restrictions on discovery, 12.4
  Attorney mental processes, 12.4.3
  Privileges, 12.4.1
  Work product, 12.4.2
Rule 26(f) discovery plan, 12.9
Scope of discovery, 12.3
Stipulations, 12.8
Supplemental disclosure and discovery, 12.6
Timing of,
  Disclosure during proceedings, 12.1.2
  Early disclosure, 12.1.1

DISPUTE RESOLUTION METHODS
Case evaluation, 6.11
  Early neutral evaluation, 6.11.3
  Mini-trials, 6.11.1
  Summary jury trials, 6.11.2
Forums for dispute resolution, 6.9
  Administrative hearings, 6.9.4
  Arbitration, 6.9.3

DISPUTE RESOLUTION METHODS
—Cont'd
Forums for dispute resolution—Cont'd
    Creation of own dispute resolution
        process, 6.12
    Fortune teller, 6.13
    Litigation, 6.9.2
    Mandated alternative dispute reso-
        lution, 6.15
    Mediation, 6.10, *see* Mediation
Goals of, 6.14
Negotiation between parties, 6.8

DISPUTE RESOLUTION PLANNING
Assessing the dispute, 6.2
Claim assessment, 6.3
    Types of claims, 6.3.2
    Whether to pursue a claim, 6.3.1
Goals, 6.14
Planning, 6.1

Documents and Things
Computerized information, obtaining,
    14.9
Government documents, obtaining,
    14.12
How to obtain, 14.2
Manner of production, 14.5
Non-party documents, obtaining, 14.1
Objections to production demands,
    14.10
Place of production, 14.5
Request for,
    Description of documents, 14.4.1
    Drafting descriptions, 14.4.2, 14.4
    Sample request, 14.4
Response by producing party, 14.6
Scope of production,
    Inspecting for completeness, 14.7
Testing an item, 14.8
Timing of demand, 14.3
Timing of production, 14.5
What things can be demanded, 14.2.2
Whom to ask, 14.2.1

ETHICAL ISSUES
Advising witnesses, 10.10.2
Client direction, 3.11.2
Confidential matters, 3.3.3
Disclosures of,
    Cases, 7.20.2
    Data, 7.20.1
    Evidence, 7.20.1
    Fact, 7.20.1
    Law, 7.20.2
    Precedent, 7.20.2
Ethical norms, 7.19.1

ETHICAL ISSUES—Cont'd
Ethical rules, 7.19
Opinions, 7.20.3
Positions, 7.20.3
Referral fees, 2.5.1
Remaining ethical, 7.21
Supervision of staff, 2.9
Tactics, 7.20.3
Truthfulness, 7.20
Written business agreements, 2.6.7

EXAMINATIONS
Controversy, condition in, 14.26.1
Documents needed, 14.26.2
Procedure during, 14.27
Reasons to request, 14.26
Report after examination, 14.28

EXHIBITS
Deposition,
    Authentication, 13.24
    Creation of deposition exhibits,
        13.23
    Handling of, 13.24
    Offering, no need, 13.25
    Preservation of, 13.25

Expert Witnesses
Expert depositions, 13.27
    Areas to explore, 13.27
Expert information, 12.5
    Employee experts, 12.5.2
    Inexpensive experts, 12.5.4
    Informally consulted experts, 12.5.3
    Hearing experts, 12.5.1
    Retained experts, 12.5.2
    Trial experts, 12.5.1

FEES CHARGED
Billing mechanics, 2.6.6
Costs, 2.6.4
Discussion of, 3.13.2
Estimation of cost, 4.6.4
Types of fees, 2.6
    Contingent fees, 2.6.2
    Flat fees, 2.6.3
    Hourly billing, 2.6.1
    Retainers, 2.6.5
Written business agreements, *see* Busi-
    ness Agreements

GOALS
As a lawyer, 1.12

HOLIDAY GIFTS
Buy this book.

HUMOR
See Varying Efforts Throughout Text.

IMAGE OF ATTORNEYS
Clients' views of lawyers in transactions, 5.10

INTERROGATORIES
Definition of, 14.13
Information, what can be sought, 14.13.2
Number of, 14.16
 Techniques to reduce number, 14.16
Objections to, 14.18
Options, when don't receive adequate answers, 14.19
Parts of, 14.14
 Definitions, 14.14.2
 Instructions, 14.14.1
 Questions, 14.14.3
Questions,
 Drafting of, 14.15
Responding to, 14.17
 Appropriate answers, 14.17.2
 Client's role in drafting answers, 14.17.2
 How to, 14.17.1
Timing of requests for, 14.13.1

Interviewing Clients,
See Obtaining Information and Communication with Clients

INTERVIEWS
Advising witnesses, 10.10.2
Approaches,10.10
Recording the interview, 10.11
 File memo, 10.11.1
 Recording the statement, 10.12
 Witness statement, 10.11.2
 Writing a screenplay, 10.13
Techniques, 10.10.1

INVESTIGATION
Determining importance of information, 10.9
 How, 10.9.1
 When, 10.9.2
 Where, 10.9.3
 Who, 10.9.4
Discussions with other lawyers, 4.15
Documents, 10.6
 Format, 10.6.3
 Sources, 10.6.2
 Types of, 10.6.1
Fact investigation, 4.14.2
Interviews, *see* Interviews

INVESTIGATION—Cont'd
Legal investigation, 4.14.1
Methods for obtaining information, 10.8
 Asking, 10.8.1
 Demanding, 10.8.3
 Looking, 10.8.2
Scope of information, 10.1
Things, definition of, 10.7
Witnesses, 10.2
 Adverse witnesses, 10.2.3
 Advising witnesses, 10.10.2
 Difficult witnesses, 10.4
 Experts, 10.2.4
 Friendly witnesses, 10.2.1
 Neutral witnesses, 10.2.2
 Obtaining cooperation, 10.3
 Payments to, 10.5

JURISDICTION
Selecting a jurisdiction, 11.2
Types, 11.1
 Personal, 11.1.1
 Subject Matter, 11.1.2

LAW FIRMS
Organization of law firms, 2.4
 Limited liability companies, 2.4
 Limited liability partnerships, 2.4
 Partnerships, 2.4
 Professional corporations, 2.4
 Sole proprietorships, 2.4

LITIGATION
Claims, 11.4
How to bring a litigation claim, 11.4
Notice pleading, 11.4
Proceedings, 6.9.2

MALPRACTICE
Laws regarding, 1.5.3
Protection against, 2.7
 Insurance, 2.7.2
 Risk management, 2.7.1

MANAGEMENT OF A LAW PRACTICE
Equipment needed, 2.8
Operating a law practice, 2.8
Staff employment and management, 2.9
Taxes, 2.10

MEDIATION
Communication with other side, 9.6.2
Conclusion of, 9.8
Disclosure of information considerations, 9.6.1
Mediation session, 9.6

MEDIATION—Cont'd
Mediation session—Cont'd
Preliminary procedures, 9.6
Mediator preparation, 9.5.2
Mediator tactics and techniques, 9.7
Advanced mediation approaches, 9.7.5
Alternative resolution proposals, 9.7.3
Assessment of case, 9.7.1
Communication with parties, 9.7.2
Conclude mediation, 9.7.4
Continue mediation, 9.7.4
Participants, 9.2
Preparation for, 9.5
Assessment factors, 9.5.1
Reasons against, 9.4
Reasons for, 9.3
Settlement agreement, 9.8.1
Termination of, 9.8
When to mediate, 9.1

MOTIONS
Asserting the right motion, 11.11
Documents required, 11.11.5
Reasons not to bring motion, 11.11.4
Resources on motion practice, 11.11.6
Types of,
Amend, motion to, 11.11.3
Compel, motion to, 11.11.3
Default judgment, motion to set aside, 11.11.3
Dismiss, motion to, 11.11.1
Include or exclude issues, motion to, 11.11.3
Injunctive relief, motion for, 11.11.3
Rule 12 motion, 11.11.1
Sanctions, motion for, 11.11.3
Summary judgment, motion for, 11.11.2
Supplement, motion to, 11.11.3
Vacate judgment, motion to, 11.11.3

NEGOTIATION PLANNING
Approaches, 7.4
Authority to negotiate, 7.3
Presence of client, 7.16
Checklist for, 7.7
Choosing the negotiator(s), 7.16
Ethical concerns in, see Ethical Issues
Evaluation,
Lawsuits, 7.9
Lawyer interests and values, 7.10
Other side, 7.11
Transactions, 7.8

NEGOTIATION PLANNING—Cont'd
Goals, 7.2
Client goals, 7.2.1
Differing perceptions, 7.2.3
Other side's goals, 7.2.2
Influences on, 7.6
Experience, 7.6.3
Power, 7.6.1
Trust, 7.6.2
Information exchange plan,
Information you want other side to have, 8.1
Legal effect of disclosures, 8.2
Protecting information from disclosure, 8.3, 8.3.1
Interest based model, 7.5
Disadvantages of, 7.5
Positional bargaining model, 7.5
Disadvantages of, 7.5
Preparing for, 7.13
Agenda, 7.13.2
Location of, 7.15
Negotiation notebook, 7.13.1
Settlement considerations,
Assessment of tax considerations, 8.6.7
Structured litigation settlements, 8.6.8
Stages of planning, 7.1
Theory of deal or case, 7.12
Time factors, 7.17, 7.18

NEGOTIATION PROCESS
Accountability, maintaining, 8.3.3
Adjusting positions, 8.5.6
Assessing responses, 8.3.4
Beginning a negotiation, 8.5.1
Component issues, 8.5.4
Concluding, 8.9
Final positions, determining, 8.9.1
Reconvening after a final position, 8.9.2
Contacting opposing attorney, 7.14
Cooperation, gaining, 8.7.3
Creative solution examples, 8.8
Consumer Camper Case, 8.8.1
Selling the Farm Case, 8.8.5
Seven Percent Solution Case, 8.8.4
Ski Accident Case, 8.8.3
Surviving Spouse Case, 8.8.2
Deadlocks, unlocking, 8.7.5
Diversions, 8.7.4
Responding to, 8.7.4
Explaining positions, 8.6.5
Objective reasons, 8.6.6
First proposals, advantages and disadvantages, 8.5.2

INDEX

References are to Sections

NEGOTIATION PROCESS—Cont'd
Gambits, 8.7.4
    Responding to, 8.7.4
Not reaching an agreement, 7.2.4
Obtaining information from other side, 8.3.2
Overview of process, 8.10
Persuasive statements, 8.6
    Alternative positions proposal, 8.6.4
    Complementary interests, 8.6.1
    Real interests of party, 8.6.2
    Valuable concessions exchange, 8.6.3
Positions expression, 8.5.3
Resolving problems, 8.7.2
Responding to proposals, 8.5.5
Sub-issues, 8.5.4
Success determination, 8.9.6
Take-it-or-leave-it approach, 8.7.6
Threats,
    Making, 8.7
    Responding to, 8.7.1
Walking out, 8.7.7
Wish making, 8.5
Written agreement, 8.9.3
    Drafting, 8.9.4
    Type of, 8.9.5

NON-LITIGATION PRACTICE,
See Transactional Practice

OBTAINING INFORMATION
Agenda differences, 3.8.5
Difficulties in, 3.8
Eliciting direction from the client
    Definition of, 3.10
    Immediate goals, 3.10
    Importance of, 3.9
    Limits on client direction, 3.11.2
    Over-arching goals, 3.10.2
    Process preferences, 3.10.3
    Techniques for, 3.11.1
Information needed from clients, 3.4
    Background information, 3.4.2
    Context, 3.4.3
    Importance of information, 3.4.4
    Legal data, 3.4.1
    Narrative data, 3.4.1
Narrative, building a, 3.6
    Directive prompts, 3.6.4
    Neutral prompts, 3.6.3
    Opening Snapshot, 3.6.1
    Recapping, 3.6.6
    The videotape, 3.6.2
    Time posting, 3.6.5
    Obtaining information from the other side, 8.3.2

OBTAINING INFORMATION—Cont'd
Probing for additional information
    Flashback, 3.7.1
    Slow-motion, 3.7.2
Refreshing memory, 3.8
    Other sources, 3.8.3
    Setting the scene, 3.8.1
    Triggering detail, 3.8.2
Sensitive subjects, 3.8.4
Snap judgments, 3.8.6
Techniques, 3.5

PLEADINGS
Amended pleadings, 11.10.5
Answers, *see* Answers
Complaints, *see* Complaints
Drafting techniques, 11.9
Importance of, 11.8
Related procedures, 11.10.5
    Intervention, 11.10.5
    Joinder, 11.10.5
    Separation, 11.10.5
    Severance, 11.10.5
Replies, 11.10.5

PREPARATION
Planning process, 1.11

PRIVILEGES
Attorney-client privilege definition, 1.5.1
    Waiver, 1.5.1
Common privileges, 12.4.1
Restrictions on discovery, 12.4

PROFESSIONAL RESPONSIBILITY
Rules, 1.5.2

REGULATION OF ATTORNEYS
Attorney-client privilege, 1.5.1
Malpractice laws, 1.5.3
Professional responsibility rules, 1.5.2

RELATIONSHIPS WITH OTHERS
Balancing life, 1.4
Clients, *see* Client Relationships
Colleagues, 1.3.7
Decision makers, 1.3.4
Other attorneys, 1.3.2
Other parties, 1.3.2
When seeking help or information, 1.3.3
Within the legal profession, 1.3.5
Yourself, 1.3.8

REMEDIES
Enforceability of judgments, 6.9.1
Liable parties, 6.7
Limitations on, 6.5

REMEDIES—Cont'd
Structured litigation settlements, 8.6.8
Types of,
    Attorneys fees, 6.4.4
    Cost recovery, 6.4.4
    Declaratory relief, 6.4.3
    Equitable relief, 6.4.2
    Injunctive relief, 6.4.2
    Monetary compensation, 6.4.1
Who can seek relief, 6.6

REPLIES
When to respond with a reply pleading,
    11.10.5

REPRESENTING CLIENTS
    Generally, 1.5
Hallmark of lawyering, 1.5
Threads to weave together, 1.2
    Application of law to facts, 1.2.1
    Facts, 1.2.1
    Law, 1.2.1
    Theory and skills, 1.2.1

ROLES
Business person, 2.1
    Business side of law practice, 2.2
    Practice within a business entity,
        2.3
Client views of, 1.7
Counselor, 1.6.2
Creator, 1.6.3
Non-practitioner, 1.3.6
    Business executive, 1.3.6
    Lobbyist, 1.3.6
    Public employee, 1.3.6
    Public service worker, 1.3.6
Practitioner, 1.3.6
Problem-solver, 1.6.3
Technician, 1.6.1
Thinking lawyer, 1.10
    Creativity, 1.10.1
    Productivity, 1.10.2

ROLES—Cont'd
Thinking lawyer—Cont'd
    Thinking like a lawyer, 1.10

SOURCES OF LAW
    Generally, 1.9
Factors that influence law, 1.9
    Economics, 1.9
    Jurisprudential thinking, 1.9
    Political trends, 1.9
    Psychological influences, 1.9
    Public policy, 1.9
    Sociological trends, 1.9

STUPID DEPOSITION TRICKS
Tricks, 13.28

TRANSACTIONAL PRACTICE
Client role, 5.8
Clients' views of lawyers in transac-
    tions, 5.10
Creating and defining relationships,
    5.2.2
Differences with litigation, 5.3
    Lack of formal procedure rules, 5.5
    Timing of attorney-client relation-
        ship, 5.4
    Voluntariness of transactions, 5.6
Goals, 5.7
    Clarifying immediate goals, 5.7.1
    Promoting long-range goals, 5.7.2
    Understanding client goals and
        preferences, 5.9
Non-litigation matters, 5.1
Transactions with other parties, 5.2.3
Translating the law for clients, 5.2.1

VENUE
Determining venue, 11.3

WORK PRODUCT
Work product protection, 12.4.2
    Attorney mental processes, 12.4.3

WHEW!
Whew, 14.14.2

†